American Public Policy

A Citizen's Guide

American Public Policy

A Citizen's Guide

Kenneth M. Dolbeare
The Evergreen State College

McGraw-Hill Book Company

New York St. Louis San Francisco Auckland Bogotá Hamburg
Johannesburg London Madrid Mexico Montreal New Delhi
Panama Paris São Paulo Singapore Sydney Tokyo Toronto

This book was set in Times Roman by Black Dot, Inc.
The editors were Eric M. Munson and Barry Benjamin;
the production supervisor was Dominick Petrellese.
The cover was designed by Robin Hessel.
R. R. Donnelley & Sons Company was printer and binder.

AMERICAN PUBLIC POLICY
A Citizen's Guide

2 3 4 5 6 7 8 9 0 D O D O 8 9 8 7 6 5 4 3 2

ISBN 0-07-017405-9

Library of Congress Cataloging in Publication Data

Dolbeare, Kenneth M.
    American public policy.

    Bibliography: p.
    Includes index.
    1. United States—Economic policy—1971
2. Energy policy—United States. 3. Medical policy
—United States. 4. Income maintenance programs—
United States. I. Title.
HC106.7.D63   361.6'1'0973   81-11801
ISBN 0-07-017405-9   AACR2

Contents

PART **1** POLICY MAKING: STRUCTURE AND PROCESS

PART **2** PUBLIC POLICY: PRACTICES, PROBLEMS, AND ALTERNATIVES

PART **3** CONCLUSIONS

List of Tables

Preface

This book is intended for the person who wonders *what* the United States government is doing, particularly in the four vital areas of managing the economy, energy, health care, and income support; *why* it does such things; and *how* (or whether) it can solve current problems in each area. The book emphasizes what government does and might do, rather than the process by which the decisions get made in Washington. This is because it is not the process but the *results* of policy making—jobs or the lack of jobs, new or reduced taxes, regulations, rights, and opportunities—that citizens have to live with in their everyday lives. Moreover, the choices that are made about what government shall do in any given area are choices involving values and preferences—not just technical data and experts' recommendations—so that citizens have very good reason and every right to be concerned about what their government does. Public policy affects, and should be subject to the preferences of, all American citizens.

For all these reasons, there is little or no attention paid to models of the policy-making process or sophisticated techniques of policy analysis. The bulk of the book is addressed to the four key problem areas and the policies, problems, and alternative solutions involved in each. The early chapters, however, provide some background materials on the cultural, economic, and historical sources of public policy, and on the nature of the American policy-making process. They also raise some questions that should help to guide analysis in the four policy areas and make them more meaningful. In the final chapter, I offer some tentative answers to those questions, draw out some further implications, and point out opportunities for more advanced study in the public policy field. In other words, this is an introductory book, addressed to the citizen's needs and interests, in the real world and in a variety of college courses. A major purpose is to inspire further, more rigorous inquiry in this area.

A number of readers of early drafts have helped to improve the book. In addition to the publishers' reviewers—namely, Kristi Anderson and Lawrence Baum, Ohio State University; George Edwards, Texas A & M University; Robert Eyestone, University of Minnesota; Ed Greenberg, University of Colorado; Charles O. Jones, University of Virginia; Mike King, Penn State University; Daniel Metlay, Indiana University; Stephen Pendleton, State University College at Buffalo; Mark Rushevsky, University of Florida; and Bruce Williams, Penn State University—I am grateful for the assistance and encouragement of my colleagues John Brigham, Sylvia Forman, and Irving Howards. Research assistance by Jerry Fresia, Diane Lukac, and Joe Peschek was invaluable. So much is owed to Linda Medcalf that I will not try to itemize my obligations.

Kenneth M. Dolbeare

American
Public Policy
A Citizen's Guide

Chapter 1

Introduction: Understanding Public Policy

Public policies make us richer or poorer, proud or angry, live or dead. "Public policy" is what a government *does*. Past practices are joined with current perceptions and preferences in a purposeful effort to shape the future. Sometimes public officials choose *not* to act. That choice also becomes public policy. Whether the choice is to act in a particular way or not to act at all, it is almost always made in a context of assumptions about *non*governmental institutions and practices. Over time, these also become part of public policy, For example, health and medical policies assume that private insurance companies should play a major role in financing people's hospital and surgical bills. By extension, those corporations and their practices effectively become part of public policy.

Why and how should a citizen try to understand American public policy? This chapter first identifies three major purposes and then describes the approach the book takes toward achieving them. Our approach compares similar policies in other industrial democracies as a means of gaining perspective on American practices. It focuses, however, on the historical development, present character, and current dilemmas of United States national public policy in four crucial problem areas: managing the economy, energy, health, and income support.

1

THREE PURPOSES OF PUBLIC POLICY INQUIRY

To Understand What Government Does, and Why, and How It Shapes Our Lives   By means of thousands of statutes and decisions, hundreds of thousands of regulations and appropriations, and literally millions of day-to-day actions by employees and agents, national government policies shape our lives. Some of these policies have obvious and intimate impact. Examples include the revival of the military draft, court rulings about rights to abortion, and regulations about the availability of food stamps or educational assistance or welfare. Others seem to be more abstract and removed, but often generate the same personal impact. A decision to raise interest rates, or to decontrol domestic oil, or not to fund health services may appear remote. But it may soon translate into the loss of a job, or sharp increases in gasoline or heating oil prices, or a disastrous hospital bill.

Government policies thus affect us the proverbial "every day in every way." However, they do not affect all people in similar ways. Because people are situated so differently in terms of wealth, status, power, and needs, they could not be affected similarly by most policies even if that were intended. But in most cases, the very purpose of public policies is to implement choices made about how problems should be dealt with or how benefits and burdens should be distributed within the society. Deliberate discrimination between categories or groups of people, corporations, or other objects of policies is essential to many such purposes. Most statutes, regulations, and appropriations, therefore, contain criteria for application or eligibility; those who *must* or *may* do or not do, pay or receive, etc., are carefully specified. To understand how government shapes people's lives, we shall analyze policies both in terms of what they *say* (the categories established and the purposes they express) and their *effects* (what they have actually meant to the people and corporations that are their objects). In defining what government did and what difference it made, we should also be alert to the *patterns* of consequences, the recurring ways in which some people are relatively advantaged and some relatively disadvantaged by policies. This will enable us to understand the broader meanings of public policies for the shaping of people's lives.

Once we know what public policies are in a given area, we shall ask *why* they have that particular character. The explanation may lie outside of government, in the basic cultural values we hold or the nature of our economic and social systems. Or it may be found in the structures and processes of the government's policy-making system. Although a complete explanation will involve both sets of factors, and may not be fully achieved in any substantive policy area, some start on such understanding is necessary in order to be able to evaluate alternative policies that are proposed.

To Understand the Alternative Policies That Are Possible Responses to Current Problems, and to Choose Between Them   Not all social problems *have* solutions, or the costs may be too high, or other priorities or obstacles may prevent solutions. Crime or physical decay in the nation's largest cities, for example, may appear to be insurmountable without massive changes in national priorities, governmental organization, and cultural values themselves. But there remains a vast range of alternative means of coping with these and other problems, from deliberate or benign neglect to minimal treatment to drastic preventive measures. Each choice implies a dramatic difference in the quality of life for millions of people, often engendering bitter controversy and conflict. Understanding the alternatives, their costs, and their probable consequences precedes informed choice.

Perhaps most important is the premise underlying this second purpose: the selection of one policy alternative rather than another is *not* primarily an objective or "scientific" matter. Despite oft-voiced claims, there is no way that the most highly trained and experienced expert in a field can make a decision purely "on the merits" of an issue. To be sure, important components of policy choice are assembling facts and using reason and logic—to all of which this book seeks to contribute. But the essence of the choice comes down to competing values and priorities, or to contrasting beliefs and assumptions, some of which are about the unknown or unknowable. Given such a nature, it is the inherent democratic right of *citizens*, not technical experts, to make such choices. Moreover, in so doing, citizens develop their critical and reasoning faculties, as well as other aspects of human potential, as they work together to see the public interest realized. Such old-fashioned images of the democratic citizen explain the subtitle of this book.

To Use the Policy Products of Our Political System (a) as a Window Through Which to See Our Social Order and Values More Clearly; and (b) as a Means of Evaluating the Problem-solving Capabilities of Both Political System and Social Order   Just because government policies play so large a part in shaping our lives, distributing benefits and burdens, etc., they also reveal much about our society, politics, and culture. Our tax policy, for example, is a measure of the things we value and the power of various industries. The pattern of exemptions and deductions gives distinct preferment to homeowners over tenants, farming and small business over salaried work, and so forth. Large businesses are able to take advantage of a variety of ways to reduce their taxes, such as depreciation allowances, offsets for losses and for taxes or royalties paid to other countries, credits for participation in various government programs, and the like. For example, some of the nation's largest corporations (e.g., Ford Motor Company, Western Electric, Bethlehem Steel, Lockheed Aircraft) paid no taxes at all in 1975. The contrasting rates at which various industries enjoy depletion allowances (deductions for the exhaustion of mineral or other natural resources mined or otherwise produced) serve as a visible scale of their respective political influence in Washington. In short, to look through the window provided by the Internal Revenue Code is to see the belief system and power distribution of American society laid bare.

Once such beliefs and power distribution emerge, moreover, the range of the possible for future public policy begins to be more understandable. The future does *not* have to be merely a projection of the past. Beliefs and power distribution can change along with changing problems, conditions, and priorities attached to them. But a first step in assessing what can be done about a problem today or tomorrow is to understand what (probably continuing) forces shaped public policy in that area yesterday and the day before. Other necessary steps, of course, are a clear analysis of developing problems and conditions and the examination of alternative possible solutions. By combining all of these—or, perhaps, by contrasting them—we shall be able to draw some conclusions about the capacity of our political system and social order to cope with the problems we face.

THE USES OF COMPARISON

Other industrialized democracies, such as those of Western Europe, Canada, and Japan, have much in common with the United States. All have predominantly capitalist economies, though with varying degrees of public ownership and government direction, and all are committed to some form of welfare state provision of multiple social services. All face similar problems, particularly those of inflation, unemployment, low economic growth, high energy costs and possible shortages, etc., amid growing recognition of their mutual interdependence.

But they have also responded quite differently than the United States to many of these shared problems. The United States is in several respects quite distinctive in its public policy actions, both historically and currently. These differences provide us with a deepened perspective on our policies, showing that they are not inevitable and suggesting questions about why our policies have the particular form that they do.

For example, the United States has always trailed the European countries in instituting social insurance programs (government-sponsored programs in which people make regular contributions to obtain protection against future disabilities). The delay has run from an average of two or three decades to as much as eighty-two years, as is shown by the following contrasts in dates that major programs were begun:

	Invalid, old age, and survivors	Sickness or maternity	Unemploy- ment
Germany	1889	1883	1927
France	1905	1928	1905
Britain	1908	1911	1911
United States	1935	1965	1935

Interestingly, several programs were begun under quite conservative governments, such as Germany in the 1880s. The longer democratic tradition of the United States did not result in the provision of these social services *earlier*, but *later*, than in the relatively more authoritarian European nations. The only major service area in which the United States consistently led was public education. In elementary, secondary, and higher education, opportunities and requirements in the United States preceded those in European countries. The others have still not caught up, even after great expansion in the 1960s.

The United States also spends proportionally much less than the European countries on social insurance programs. In recent years, the American government's investment in all social insurance programs combined has averaged between 7 percent and 8 percent of our total Gross National Product (GNP, the total of all goods and services produced). This is less than half of the *average* of *all* the European countries, which are led by Germany's nearly 20 percent figure over this period.

The other side of lower spending levels is lower tax revenues and rates. When tax revenues are expressed as percentages of GNP, the United States government averages slightly over 20 percent—down from the mid-20s during the late 1960s and early 1970s. But the European countries are all in the mid-30-percent range, with Sweden's government absorbing more than 40 percent of the country's GNP. When it is remembered that military expenditures represent a considerably higher proportion of United States public spending than in the European countries, the difference in tax revenues raised for social programs is even greater. Government simply plays a lesser role in American society than it does elsewhere. This fact is reflected again in tax *rates*: Americans pay lower rates of income tax at all income levels than do any Europeans except the French, who employ other forms of taxation to raise public revenue.

Perhaps consistently, complaints about high taxation and skepticism about the propriety and desirability of government services have always been loudest in the United States. But the recent wave of taxpayer resistance, tax-limiting referenda in the states, and budget reduction at the national level has had a parallel in Europe. In several countries, taxpayer resistance has appeared and welfare services have been challenged, almost for the first time. Shared economic pressures have apparently led to similar reactions, despite the contrasts in levels of services and taxation.

It is this latter feature, of course, that raises interesting questions for analysis. Clearly, a trade-off (a choice between conflicting alternatives) exists between public investment in social services for all (and relatively high taxes) and retention of money in private hands to buy such services or for other uses (and relatively low taxes). We have not looked at the character or quality of any of these services, but it appears that the European countries are committed to the first of these options and the United States to the second. What explains this pattern of choices? The United States was always more democratic than the others, at least in the sense of public opportunities to take part in the electoral process. Did Americans not want such services to be socially provided, or did their political system somehow thwart their desires? As we shall see in the next chapters, observers have suggested that both of these interpretations are partially true. But other factors have also played a part. For the present, the point is to see how comparison deepens our understanding of our own policies.

THE PLAN OF THE BOOK

The focus of this book is on the *substance* of public policy. We look at what government does today, and what it is being urged to do tomorrow, in regard to some pressing national problems. The problem areas selected include the two most vital domestic public policy areas that are currently on the political agenda—managing the economy and energy—and the two leading social service areas—health care and income support. We shall explore each of these problems to the point where we can understand what is at stake in the choices that must be made between specific alternative policies.

Part Two of the book—almost three-quarters of its entire length—contains eight chapters, two on each of the four policy areas just identified, in which present policies are described and analyzed in the following manner. The first chapter in each pair provides an overview of the policy area, a description of current policies, and an account of the historical developments that have led to these policies. The second chapter analyzes current problems in the area and explores the major alternative policies that have been proposed. The special section comparing United States policies with those of other industrial democracies is located at the end of the first chapter (energy, health care) or the beginning of the second (managing the economy, income support) wherever it appears to shed the most light on American practice.

But the three purposes set forth earlier are not fully served by these substantive analyses alone, although they could not be served at all *without* such analyses. Our first goal was not only to understand what government policies are in the various areas, but how they came to be that way. To an extent, the latter question is answered by the sections in the first chapter on each policy area on the nature and origins of current policies. To a somewhat greater extent, however, this is an analytic task that the reader must undertake independently. Part One of the book contains two chapters that provide some background for this purpose. The first presents some factors external to government itself that are often thought to play important roles in shaping public policies. The second looks at some general characteristics of government structure and the policy-making process that also affect policies produced. Together, these two chapters should provide the tools to answer the question of why government policies are what they are in each of the four problem areas. In the last chapter of the book, Part Three, we shall try to bring some of these explanations to a summary focus.

In that same concluding chapter, we shall also try to complete the work of fulfilling our other two purposes. Our second purpose involved choosing between alternatives in each area. But that is only part of the problem, for choices of alternatives must be made in all areas at the same time. Each choice carries implications and effects for the other choices, and resources of time, energy, and money are probably not adequate to do all that is desired. How policies relate to each other, and what trade-offs are involved in allocating scarce resources, are subjects to be considered in this last chapter.

We shall also draw some necessarily speculative conclusions about the problem-solving capabilities of our political system—as promised in our third goal. This is the final cumulative effort toward which all our previous analyses and interpretation should be steadily leading. Although our four policy areas are far from a comprehensive picture, their importance will give us an opportunity both to see the essence of our social order and values and to speculate about whether today's problems are soluble in this context—and, if so, how. We shall ask whether the better, and/or tolerable, alternative solutions to the problems are *politically* and *economically* possible in the United States in the near future. For example, do we as a people have the political will to do what is necessary or desirable to solve our problems? Do our political institutions and processes provide ways to accomplish such ends? Do we have the economic resources, social flexibility, cultural adaptiveness, etc., to do what is needed? What are the obstacles and limits in each case? No final answers will be reached, but at least some beginnings can be made.

Part One

Policy Making: Structure and Process

To understand why policies have the form they do, we must have some idea of the factors that converge to produce them and how they relate to each other. In other words, what factors, in what relationship, *explain* the distinctive characteristics of United States policies? How important is our ideology, such as our beliefs in individual responsibility and the primacy of the economic free market? How important is the sheer size of the United States and its division of legal powers between the states and the national government? How controlling are the structure and imperatives of our economic system? What part is played by the particular institutional characteristics, participants, and style of our policy-making process?

Our premises are that public policies do not arise in a vacuum but in a wide and deep historical context. Problems have causes, some of which are grounded in the most fundamental levels of our society—in the character of our economic and social systems, in our underlying cultural values, and even in the way we think. All of these factors operate interdependently and coherently to shape day-to-day policies and practices. To understand public policies, we must see them together and as the result of all the things that have contributed to their creation. Policies are not isolated events in an incoherent world. Some of the factors making up the causal context of American public policies can be hypothesized from other policy studies and built into a tentative framework for analysis.

Chapter 2 takes up some of the broad shaping forces that set the context for government policy making, including cultural values, economic and social structures, and the nature of current problems. Chapter 3 examines the legal structure of American government and the policy-making process within it. At the end of Chapter 3, we present a brief case study involving the policy problem of staffing the military (conscription versus the voluntary army) in order to show how the two sets of factors converge to shape public policies. With this framework as background, the sources or causes of public policies in our four problem areas should become more readily visible.

Chapter 2

Factors Shaping Public Policy in the United States

This chapter will draw upon the views of various scholars to set up three major categories of factors *external* to the public decision-making system itself that appear to have shaped policy choices in the past.[1] These are: (1) American cultural values and ideology; (2) economic and social structures and conditions; and (3) the nature of the world and national problems that are on the political agenda. Whether, and if so how much, each has actually affected policies produced is a question we can take up only in the final chapter. In each case, we shall see at least that firm limits seem to be placed on the range of choice that is open. New departures in public policy, then, may depend on changes in these shaping factors.

AMERICAN VALUES AND IDEOLOGY

Values are the concepts or objects that a particular society defines as "right" or "good." Societies may well differ in the definitions and priorities they attach to specific values. Valuations and definitions develop over time and are transmitted to new generations as part of their received culture.

However, each society tends to think of its distinctive version as natural or universal.

Ideology is a set of beliefs about how the social order does and should work. Usually the beliefs supplement and reinforce each other to make up a coherent package, a belief system. This system functions to connect the basic underlying values to everyday events. It helps to assure people that the social order is working toward the implementation of the valued concepts and objects.[2]

In the United States, certain values, beliefs, and ideology are apparently widely shared, at least in general terms. But there are significant differences over how some values should be defined, which values take priority, whether or not they are actually being implemented, and for whom. We shall first summarize the characteristic American values and beliefs. Then we look at some of the tensions between definitions and priorities that are of particular relevance to understanding public policy in the United States.

Characteristic American Values and Beliefs

Probably the most important American value is *individualism*. A number of unique and separate individuals together form a society. But the primary goal of personal *and* social life is always the satisfaction of the individual's wants and needs. Thus the individual must be the basic unit when thinking about problems of social ordering. In pursuit of personal goals, each person is held to possess certain "natural" rights—life, liberty, and property. However, since human nature is assumed to be acquisitive, aggressive, and often irrational, naturally harmonious social ordering of unique and complex individuals pursuing their own ends becomes problematic.

Government exists in response to the basic tension created by competitive individuals living in society. Its major function is to keep the struggle within bounds. Objective, legal enforcement of each person's natural rights allows free pursuit of individual ends without social chaos. However, other than the maintenance of order, government should not interfere with the individual. Indeed, there is a danger that government will be used by some to gain unfair advantage in the competitive struggle. Therefore, government itself should be formally limited in powers and set up in such a way that its component parts check and balance (keep an eye on) each other.[3]

Three important and related beliefs flow from the value attached to individualism and its concept of human nature. One is that each individual carries personal responsibility for his or her relative success or failure in life. Because each individual is thought to have roughly equal opportunities, later attainments or lack of them must be due to the talents, efforts, and determination that each actually applied to the struggle.[4]

This leads to another important belief, that of the "work ethic." People develop themselves and rise in wealth, status, and power only through hard work. Disparities in wealth, status, and power are primarily the product of differences in the amount and quality of work effort and willingness to sacrifice. All should *want* to work hard as a means of self-development and social mobility. Conversely, those who have not been successful must *not* have worked hard. Therefore, they are less deserving of respect.

A third related belief "blames the victim."[5] When an individual cannot provide for his or her own needs and requires some kind of assistance, it indicates a personal failure, either of character or of work effort. In any event, a request for help signals a defect that requires correcting and/or clouds any claim for assistance. Often resented by others, such persons can be made to feel guilty about needing help, regardless of the actual causes of their problems.

A second basic value is that of *property*.[6] From the earliest settlements, Americans regarded property as the basis of responsibility and independence. Whether land or other tangible assets, property provides the focus of the competitive struggle. Its possession, or lack thereof, measures a person's talents, character, and efforts. Protection of property, and of the freedom of its use, thus becomes one of the "givens" of the American social order. Of course acquisition or use of property can be limited by government. However, such infringements always require justification and are subject to legal challenge as violations of individual rights.

A third basic value is that of *the economic free market*. The market provides the mechanism through which buyers' demands are met by suppliers in such a manner that economic resources are used most efficiently, needs are maximally satisfied, and the greatest progress with the lowest level of coercion is achieved. It assumes that: (1) suppliers will be induced by competition to try to meet buyers' demands with the highest-quality product at the lowest possible cost; (2) that buyers will know about the availability, quality, and cost of the products they seek and act rationally in filling their needs; and (3) that the mechanism will continue to harmonize demand and supply in a self-regulating manner such that output and employment will be maximized and prosperity maintained. Outside control by governmental interference or monopolistic organization by participants hinders this process. The market must be "free" to work properly.

These three values make up the underlying premises of American thinking about public policy. Other values, such as freedom and equality, are also important. But they are more controversial in definition and application, depending in part on the position one takes with respect to the three core values. Those connections will be considered shortly.

Some further beliefs surround this set of basic values. One is the belief in mobility, in both the social and the geographic sense.[7] Geographic mobility is important because it helps to provide economic opportunity and to serve as a means of equalizing opportunities for all. Belief in social mobility is vital because it allows the portrayal of the clear inequalities in individual wealth, status, and power as a measure of talent, character, and effort. Belief in social mobility helps to deny or obscure the existence of a social-class system where life chances are controlled by birth into one or another fixed level of the social pyramid.

Other integral beliefs include racism—the conviction that nonwhite races are somehow genetically inferior to whites and need not be treated equivalently.[8] Americans inherited racism from the Western European tradition but substantially developed it in the course of rationalizing the acquisition and development of a rich continent. Paralleling racism is sexism, the belief in the superior powers and entitlements of men over women. Women's roles have historically been defined in subservient ways in accordance with male needs amidst changing social and economic circumstances. Less fundamental but still shaping is the belief sometimes called "ageism," in which both the oldest and the youngest sectors of the population suffer discrimination. Each of these beliefs has had broad public policy significance in the past. Each remains a focus of public policy today, both as a substantial residue and because of efforts to right past wrongs.

Conflicts in American Values and Beliefs

Not all Americans share the same definitions of these values, place the same emphasis on them, or even subscribe to all of the related beliefs. People differ according to their life experience, self-interest, hopes, and fears. Building on the base of the widely shared if somewhat generalized values and beliefs just described, we can identify some major points of disagreement among people today. Such disagreements often take on a consistent form (one set of definitions or priorities opposed to another set) and ripen into continuing conflict. We shall move from specific disagreements to comparison of two polar-opposite sets of conflicting positions that shape the context of present public policy. Table 2-1 summarizes these relationships.

One disagreement arises over the extent to which the individual should carry personal responsibility for being able to attend to all of his or her needs in today's complex society. Nobody argues that there is never any social responsibility for the plight of others. Even in the harshest days of early industrialization, there were some forms of public assistance for some people.[9] Rather, the issue has to do with the *balance* between individual and social responsibility. A related issue involves how much one

Table 2-1   The Value Bases of Major Issues

Issue	Polar Positions on the Continuum of Conflict	
(1) Who carries responsibility for people in need?	Responsibility should be social, that of the community as a whole	Responsibility should be personal, to each his just deserts
(2) How large a role for the economic free market?	The market must be supplemented; government must do what it cannot or will not do	The market should be determinative; its allocations are necessary and noncoercive
(3) Values emphasized	Equality	Freedom
(3A) Definitions of values	Equality as equality of condition; freedom as multiplicity of opportunities provided	Equality as equality of opportunity; freedom as absence of government restraint
(4) Principles of distribution	Equity, justice, needs	Efficiency, availability of resources

believes people will take advantage of public assistance by cheating, reducing their own effort, and so forth. This question plays a continuing shaping role in social services, for example in debates over the levels of Social Security payments or the scope of national health insurance. But it also can be found in the energy field in issues such as whether to ration gasoline by price or by some other equitable principle, or whether to aid payment of poor people's heating oil bills. In the economy-managing field, it rises as the debate over extending unemployment compensation or combating inflation by promoting unemployment. Essentially, the question is *how much* individuals should be required to assume personal responsibility for being poor or sick or unemployed, and *how much* the society as a whole should accept as a shared responsibility appropriate for government action.

Another disagreement exists over the present status and proper role of the economic free market.[10] Some believe the market no longer works. The elimination of competition by the size of contemporary corporations and their domination over industries, markets, and prices, or the control of consumers by advertising, renders it obsolete. Others argue that, even if it worked, the market is animated by profit considerations. Therefore, it simply *cannot* provide such social goods as pollution-free air and water, or safer working conditions, or high-quality health care for the poor. These positions can accept efforts to minimize the role of the market and increase the scope of government management and regulation, as well as direct services. The economic free market remains the basic allocator of goods and services, with government supplementing as needed. Further down this road are those who could even accept large-scale planning over investment and production.

In opposition, others deny any failures of the market, or the relative desirability of social goods, or the efficacy of government as an alternative provider. Government interference should only be for the purpose of maintaining proper conditions for the economic free market. Smaller, less centralized, and competitive private enterprises are most capable. Inefficiency, waste, and bureaucracy are the price of government interference if it does become necessary. In general, private profitability ranks highest, both for its own sake and as the inducement to greater effort on the part of people generally. Again, the issue is not either-or, but rather how much freedom and how much control.

A third disagreement arises over value priorities and definitions. *Freedom* and *equality* are the best examples. To Americans, freedom means the absence of restraint, especially the freedom to acquire property and use it as one wishes without limitations, governmental or otherwise. With this understanding of freedom comes a definition of equality as solely equality of rights and opportunity. Each individual possesses the right to take part in the competitive struggle to achieve wealth, status, and power goals. The definitions complement one another. Each person is assumed to be free and equal, regardless of material possessions—free in the sense that the same limitations necessary for order apply to all, and equal in the sense that each possesses the same rights and same opportunities, and stands in the same relationship to government, as all others.

Of course, the reality of the situation is that people enjoy very unequal resources of wealth, status, and power from the start, and these often provide advantages in the competitive struggle. They also very often translate into greater disparities over time—or at least reproduce the same pattern of inequality of resources. In practical terms, then, even equality of rights and opportunity is difficult to achieve, especially since freedom values prevent interference with others' lives or possessions. Efforts to compensate for initial disadvantages or discrimination, to make equality of rights and opportunity a reality, constantly run afoul of others' freedom. Furthermore, they seldom even result in changes in the basic patterns of inequality of wealth, status, and power.

For purposes of illustration, try to imagine the equality valued to be defined as a rough parity of all in wealth, status, and power. To accept such a definition of equality, even as an ultimate goal, requires also a redefinition of freedom. In this context, freedom would have to be something like the capacity to realize one's full potential as a person, measured by personal satisfactions and happiness, rather than material possessions.

Governments would have to ensure that no one's material needs went unmet and that equal sharing in all the advantages and opportunities prevailed.

The point is that value definitions and priorities are connected to and complement one another. Freedom in the American sense fits best with equality of rights and opportunity and ranks much higher in our value scale. But freedom's precedence is threatened the more that people are dissatisfied with the results of policies conceived under the principle of equality of opportunity. If the definition of equality begins to expand toward rough parity (or "equality of condition"), it must command a higher ranking than freedom, and/or freedom must be redefined to fit with equality of condition.

Other values or principles of distribution line up in opposition to each other as the two sets of conflicting positions begin to take shape. For example, associated with acceptance of social responsibility and reduced reliance on the economic free market are the distributive principles of equity, justice, and the needs people have. Associated with individual responsibility and a maximal role for the market are concerns for efficiency and the limited availability of resources. Table 2-1 shows the polar positions in several areas. Of course, any specific disagreement actually involves a continuum of views in which balances are struck between the polar positions. Most public policies reflect the particular balance produced by contending forces of the time. The polar positions on the left and right columns of Table 2-1, moreover, when combined vertically, make up coherent packages of values and beliefs. The two sets of opposing viewpoints clash over and over again in policy choices. Both critiques of existing policy and suggestions for alternatives emerge out of their continuing conflict as they effectively set the range of the possible for American policy.

One major exception exists to the point that policy choices are shaped by the tension between opposing sets of values and beliefs. The anomaly occurs when people whose views lie to the right of center actually *act* consistently with left-of-center principles. For example, they may *support* broader distribution of services or greater restraint on business, as if they *believed* in social responsibility, reducing the role of the market, and greater equality. But their real reasons may be *tactical,* a willingness to grant concessions, in the face of strong popular demand or unrest, in order to preserve the basic structures of the socioeconomic system.[11] We shall want to be alert to this possibility throughout our analysis because it might help to explain relatively sudden policy initiatives or departures after periods of inaction.

American values and beliefs play a powerful part in shaping *both* people's understanding of "the facts" of any problem situation *and* their choices of policy alternatives.[12] The idealized "rational" decision-making process in which objective facts speak for themselves and determine the choices "on the merits" is simply unknown to most public policy questions.[13] Facts are almost always selected by people with a point of view. Even the understanding of what a fact is and how to identify it is shaped by values and beliefs.[14]

Further, not everything can be known about the present, much less the future. There is simply no way to accurately predict—particularly to predict the future behavior of thinking people. Though social scientists can produce a great volume of such facts, analysis, and prediction, the role of values and beliefs in the presentation and understanding of the facts of a problem area can never be eliminated. The decision-making process has been shaped from the very beginning by people's values and beliefs.

But at the stage of choosing among alternatives, values and beliefs become the most determinative. Trade-offs are almost always necessary; i.e., one policy can be adopted only if another policy or goal is modified or abandoned ("you can't eat your cake and have it too"). Policies and goals must be ranked in some priority order. And such ranking can be done only in terms of one's preferences. The details of a policy require repeated choices over who is to get what, again calling for value choices.

The *way* in which value choices predominate in the making of public policy, however, is not simple or straightforward. Sometimes such choices are masked in a body of apparently scientific facts and technical analysis, or in the overwhelming persuasiveness of past precedent. More often, value choices articulate with the givens of economic and social structure and/or the characteristics of the political system. Values and beliefs merge with institutional factors so that they are less visible. The question of whether or not to nationalize the oil companies, for example, may not be raised because it is unthinkable given present values and beliefs. But the sheer size and power of such companies, their close ties with global finance, their many friends with great power in state and national offices, also play inseparable roles such that the answer appears inevitable. More likely, the question simply becomes a nonquestion. We now turn to the part played by economic and social structures.

ECONOMIC AND SOCIAL STRUCTURES

Of necessity, this will be a very brief review of only the most salient structural characteristics of the American economy and its associated social system. By "structures," we mean the basic organizational principles and major institutions that give these areas of social life their distinctive forms and character. In the economy, that means private ownership of very large corporations and banks which function primarily to make profits. In the society, that means a closely related distribution of wealth, status, and power. A few possess the most, while the rest have relatively little. Important institutions include unions, professions, churches, etc. These structural characteristics serve as "givens," or landmarks, around which public policies are designed and implemented.

The Structure of the American Economy

We first identify three major characteristics of the contemporary American economy and then look at their implications for public policy. Perhaps the most striking fact is the sheer size of the economy's major units. Although there are many more smaller firms, great industrial corporations, insurance companies, banks, utilities, etc., give the economy its basic dynamics and directions. The longest-lived and best-known comparative analysis of the size and characteristics of American corporations, *Fortune* magazine's "Fortune 500," annually lists the sales, employment, and other features of manufacturing and mining (including oil production) corporations. Since publication began in 1955, thirty-five years of dramatic growth and change are readily summarizable.

In 1955, the top 500 industrial corporations accounted for about 40 percent of all industrial sales and 25 percent of all profits.[15] Since then, their sales have grown at an annual average rate of almost 10 percent. By the late 1970s, their sales amounted to about two-thirds of all industrial sales and three-quarters of all profits—despite the fact that there are literally hundreds of thousands of other industrial companies. Exxon and General Motors, alone, now have nearly $150 *billion* in annual sales, more than the entire 500 list in 1955. During those twenty-five years, Fortune 500 companies have acquired about 4,500 other companies by merger or purchase, expanding in sales and assets in this way as well. The *proportion* of the industrial workforce employed by the top 500 has increased from about 40 percent in 1955 to nearly 75 percent, despite the fact that *total* employment by the 500 barely increased at all.

The size of the major corporations in today's new economy may be grasped from the comparisons in Table 2-2. Here sales and number of employees of the ten largest corporations are compared with their closest equivalents among states and cities of the United States. The table will repay close study. For example, the sales volume of Exxon, the leading corporation, is more than three times the revenue receipts of California or New York, the leading states. Six companies' sales receipts exceed those of California or New York, and most states trail well behind the top thirty or so corporations. General Motors employs almost three times as many people as California or New York, and General Electric and IBM are ahead of both of those states in personnel and payrolls. Again, many states and large cities trail the major corporations in number of employees. The

**Table 2-2   Leading Corporations Compared to
Selected States and Cities**

	Sales or revenues (in $ billions)	Number of employees (in thousands)
Exxon	79.1	169
General Motors	66.3	853
Mobil	44.7	213.5
Ford Motor Co.	43.5	494.5
Texaco	38.3	65.8
Standard Oil (Cal.)	29.3	39.7
California	26.1	298
Gulf Oil	23.9	57.6
IBM	22.8	337.1
New York	22.7	203
General Electric	22.4	405
Standard Oil (Ind.)	18.6	52.3
New York City	15.9	318
Illinois	9.9	141
Oregon	2.6	54
Los Angeles	1.9	44
Kansas	1.8	50
Chicago	1.5	48
Delaware	0.7	17
Houston	0.5	14
Seattle	0.4	9

Sources: Corporate data from *Fortune* magazine, May 1980; state and city
data from *Statistical Abstract of the United States, 1979.*

implications of all these data are that the largest corporations represent aggregations of economic and social power that stand second only to the United States government in the American political economy.

The second major characteristic of the corporate economy is the extent of concentration. This can take many forms, but two important ones are: (1) the way that a relatively few companies dominate key industries; and (2) the way that banks control many companies. Four or fewer large firms account for more than 80 percent of all sales in several areas, including automobiles, aircraft, computers, heavy electrical equipment, metal containers, steel, rubber, and many food products.[16] Competition is thus likely to be minimized. Since 1928, the seven major oil companies have provided a model of how tacit cooperation can avoid the dangers to assets and profitability that follow from vigorous competition.[17] With reduced competition, prices are likely to be less responsive to changes in demand or usage patterns.

Banks can control nonfinancial corporations by exercising the voting powers of stock they hold. Such holdings include those held in trust as well as those managed for pension funds or institutional or individual investors. Banks also influence corporate management through placement of bank representatives on boards of directors or through arranging large loans. They currently hold more than 30 percent of all corporate stock, and the ten largest banks hold more than a third of all such trust assets. A study of the 200 largest nonfinancial corporations in 1969, based on United States government data, showed that 39 percent were under the control of groups of the leading banks, themselves tightly interlocked. The group headed by Chase Manhattan Bank, for example, controlled twenty-nine companies (oil, airlines, railroads), while another fifteen (computers, office machines) were controlled by the group headed by Morgan Guaranty Trust.[18] The major banks are thus able to wield influence over corporate behavior well in excess of their own financial leverage. If there is a central nervous system to the current economy, it lies within the financial community; the major banks, plus insurance companies and pension funds and investment brokerage houses.

The third distinguishing feature of today's corporate economy is its international character. Since the 1950s, American companies have increased their direct foreign investment at the rate of about 10 percent per year. Now hundreds of billions of dollars are invested overseas. The "multinational" corporation, with plants or mines and/or marketing facilities all over the world, is now an unremarkable fact of life. International trade has also increased rapidly; imports and exports were valued at $270 billion in 1979.[19] The export trade accounts for one out of every eight manufacturing jobs in the United States, and the production of one out of every three acres of farm land. All international activities combined provide $1 out of every $3 of United States corporate profits.[20]

What do these three leading characteristics imply for American public policy? The question is not whether any of these trends is good or bad, but what they mean for the nature and priorities of public policy.

By its sheer size and concentration, the corporate-banking sector of the economy acquires significant power, imposes imperatives, and serves as the wellspring of government resources for coping with other problems. The power flows from the inevitable impact that investment and production decisions by such aggregations of assets have on prices, employment, and the quality of life in general (pollution, discrimination, alienation, etc.). It also stems from corporate efforts to mobilize and apply their influence through staffing the executive branch, lobbying, financing electoral campaigns, and developing popular support.

The imperatives that the corporate-banking sector impose on the public policy agenda include stabilizing, rationalizing, and rendering predictable an increasingly complex and internationally interdependent economic system. The other side of size and predominance in the economy is risk and dependence on government support. Giant corporations must avoid competitive threats to their vast assets; they must make profit to exist; and in most instances, they must grow to both pay debts *and* make profit. To do so they must be able to plan ahead and count on continuing consumer demand at home and/or markets abroad. The only vehicle for assuring a stable and profitable national market and protection abroad is the United States government. Nor can government officials, elected or appointed and of either major political party, afford to face the prospect of unemployment or depression if the needs of the corporate-banking sector are not served.

Moreover, the health of this economy—its productivity, sales achievements at home and abroad, and profitability—is determinative not only of the desired high employment–low inflation ratio, but of the government's capacity to cope with domestic problems and undertake significant social programs. The needs of the corporate economy must have priority, if only to maintain a threatened standard of living. When a prosperous economy makes tax revenues available, a variety of new or expanded social programs become possible. Human services are absolutely dependent upon a steadily rising economy, as the contrast between the Great Society of 1964–1970 and its aftermath clearly demonstrates. The character and needs of the corporate economy profoundly shape and provide priorities for the agenda for public policy.

In so noting, however, we should not ignore the part played by the hundreds of thousands of other business firms that complete the economy. For them, the competitive market, and the threat of elimination by big business or by government regulation, are everyday realities.[21] They live the traditional individualism, property orientation, and free market convictions of the American value system. They keep the belief system alive, and they and their supporters enforce it with all the influence (and votes) they can bring to bear. The corporate economy can be divided against itself, or opposed by the smaller but more numerous firms of the competitive sector. No simple set of formative pressures on public policy emerge from the economy. But there are some clear needs and no American government can fail to give them precedence.

The American Social Structure

The distribution of wealth, status, and power in most societies is unequal. A relatively few people have large shares of each, and most people have little. Stable patterns emerge such that it makes sense to think of such societies as stratified social pyramids. Large numbers of people at the lowest levels form the base; steadily decreasing numbers are at each upward level until finally a very few occupy the top. The United States is distinctive only in a general reluctance to recognize how sharp and permanent such inequalities are. The American social pyramid, shaped primarily by wealth and income distribution, is as sharply skewed toward the bottom as that of any industrialized country of Western Europe. If wealth distribution were the measure, and our pyramid's base were scaled to match the size of this page, 80 percent of Americans would be within several inches of the page but the top would be more than 40 feet high![22] We shall characterize wealth and income patterns briefly and then consider some of their implications.

Wealth consists of income-producing assets (stocks, bonds, real estate) and personal assets (houses, cars, checking accounts). Since income-producing assets carry the opportunity to generate more wealth and income, they are the most significant. The first two columns of Table 2-3 show the distribution of all wealth and of one form of income-producing wealth, the ownership of corporate stock.[23] The top 1 percent of wealth-holders, for example, holds 33 percent of all wealth and 62 percent of all corporate stock.[24] These are permanent patterns as well: at no time since World War II has the share of all wealth held by the top 1 percent been less than 25 percent.[25] The ownership of wealth is so fully concentrated at the top that the lower 95 percent of the population has less than half of all wealth. But even wealth concentration is less than that of corporate stock ownership, where the lower 95 percent owns only 14 percent.

Income is somewhat more evenly distributed—but only somewhat. The third column of Table 2-3 shows the shares of income earned by the top 5 percent and each fifth of the population in 1978. Here again the patterns are permanent: at no time since World War II has the lowest fifth earned as much as 6 percent of all income, nor has the highest fifth earned

Table 2-3   Wealth and Income Distribution in the United States

Proportions of total population	Wealth	Corporate stock ownership	Family before-tax income	Net income after taxes and other adjustments
Top 1%	33	62	NA	9.3
Top 5%	53	86	17.3	22.0
Top 20%	77	97	45.2	48.0
Second 20%			24.8	23.0
Middle 20%	}23	}3	16.4	16.5
Next 20%			9.7	9.5
Lowest 20%	–	–	3.8	3.0

Sources: Columns 1 and 2: E. C. Budd, *Inequality and Poverty* (Englewood Cliffs, N.J.: Prentice-Hall, 1967), p. xxii. Column 3: U.S. Bureau of the Census, *Current Population Reports*, ser. P-60, 1978. Column 4: Author's estimate, based on consensus of authoritative estimates.

less than 40 percent. In other words, the highest 20 percent regularly earns more than the bottom 60 percent, even though there are three times as many people in the lower category. And the top 5 percent *average* over the years more than three times the earnings of the bottom 20 percent. Even these disparities are considerably understated. For example, capital gains (increase in values of property held) are not included in the Census Bureau definitions, nor are (naturally) unreported or underreported income. Both of these sources of inaccuracy apply chiefly to the kinds of income earned by wealthier people, as do tax "loopholes." The last column shows what the actual income pattern might look like after all such corrections were made.

This gap between rich and poor closely follows the pattern of ownership of the corporate economy, levels of education, and occupations. These factors mutually reinforce each other, remaining relatively permanent over time. For example, the opportunity for advanced education and higher occupational status is directly related to parental income categories.[26] Factors of race and sex are also visible in the pattern of income distribution in the United States. At the start of the 1970s, for example, employed blacks earned about 70 percent of what full-time white workers earned, and women about 60 percent of what men earned. These ratios rose for a few years, but first women's and then blacks' wages began to decline. By 1980, the gap was almost as wide as in 1970.[27]

The pattern of wealth and income distribution at the bottom of the social pyramid also shows the effects of discrimination along race, sex, and age lines. Wealthholding is either negligible or negative (net indebtedness) at this level. Income is marginal, and many live in official or unofficial poverty. The characteristics of the 25 million people in this lowest income category are shown in Table 2-4. This table rests on the official Social Security Administration definition of the "poverty line," a figure continually adjusted for geographic location, family size, and the cost of living. The totals employed are so low, however (e.g., $1.15 per person per day for food), that the number of people included within the definition is probably much lower than it should be. One study, using the Bureau of Labor Statistics' "subsistence budget" (a figure calculated in terms of living needs for a family of four), argues persuasively for a total more than double that of the official "poverty population."[28] In any event, the table clearly shows the disproportionate representation of blacks and Hispanics at this level, and the particularly acute situation for children. Male- and female-headed families also contrast sharply (despite inclusion of all welfare and other assistance payments), reflecting education, job, and wage discrimination.

The presence of such sharp and relatively permanent disparities suggests the existence of a social-class system in which life chances

Table 2-4   Poverty-Level Population, 1977

	Percent below poverty level					
	All races	White	Black	Spanish-origin	Families with male head	Families with female head
Total	12	9	31	22	7	33
Persons under 14 years	17	12	43	28	NA	NA
Persons over 65 years	14	12	36	22	NR	NR

Note: This table employs the (understated) Social Security Administration definition of poverty (see text). It does, however, include all transfer payments as income, so that these proportions of each group remain in official poverty *after* all welfare and other assistance.
Source: Statistical Abstract of the United States, 1979, tables 760 and 761.

distinctly differ according to level. Social status accrues to those with the recognizable attainments of wealth, income, education, and occupation. But, in turn, all of these primarily depend on prior attainments in the same areas by family members. In time, their mutually reinforcing effects can hardly help but generate distinctive values, beliefs, and views about how government policies should be designed.

Moreover, social-class position translates into social, economic, and political power. This process can be illustrated quickly from the leading study of top decision makers in the major corporations, mass media, law firms, foundations, universities, civic and cultural organizations, and in the national government.[29] The study identified slightly more than 5,400 key positions. It then traced the social and economic origins and status of those positions' occupants. Figure 2-1 is reproduced from this study and shows the relationship between social class and decision-making power. Thirty percent of the power positions in the major institutions of our society were held by persons from the upper 1 percent of the social pyramid. Only 3 percent were held by persons from the 78% of the population described as middle and lower class.

Another way in which high social status translates into social, economic, and political power is through the organization of key professionals (doctors, lawyers, scientists, engineers, business executives) into active associations. Such associations often acquire official governmental power to control admission into their ranks, assert the right to speak on behalf not only of other professionals but also of their clients, and lobby governments vigorously in regard to matters of both immediate and general concern. As professionals, they have both status and credibility. Because both have

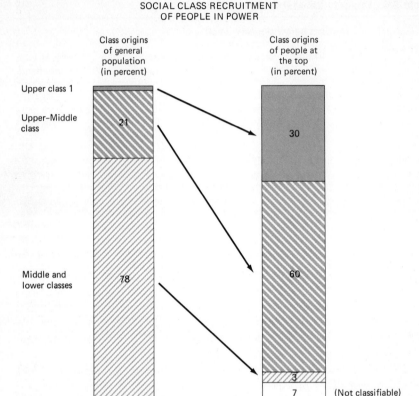

Figure 2-1 The relationship between social class and decision-making power in the United States. *(Source: Thomas R. Dye,* Who's Running America? The Carter Years, *2d ed., Englewood Cliffs, N.J.)*

been gained under conditions of the world as it is today, they are not likely to seek dramatic change in it.

What do these findings imply for public policy? They suggest at least that the upper levels of the social pyramid are capable of exerting economic and political power. Presumably they will do so primarily in furtherance of their own interests as they understand them. Policies that would seriously reduce their positions of affluence and influence are likely to be unwelcome, or at least must appeal strongly to altruistic or moral sensibilities. People in the upper strata might divide against each other, of course, or seek consciously to serve the needs of lower-class people. But even in such instances, the balance would ordinarily seem to be tilted in behalf of maintaining the status quo in all fundamental respects.

THE NATURE OF CONTEMPORARY PROBLEMS

The third set of external factors that shape public policy is the particular character of the problems (international and national, economic and social, military and political) that are on the political agenda at any given time. These problems are more variable over time than either values and ideology or economic and social structures. Each policy-making era thus faces a distinctive mix of problems that commands its attention and shapes its priorities. American policies of the post-Vietnam period (roughly, 1972 to the present) have been and are being profoundly affected by the particular world and United States conditions and problems of those years—and by the priority attached to their solutions. Some are general and continuing, others specific and acute. Together, they add up to a body of economic and political troubles that is unprecedented since the Great Depression of the 1930s. The priorities they command create an atmosphere of crisis and a mood of urgency that affect all forms of policy making. We shall touch briefly on the range and diversity of these problems here, and analyze some of them in greater detail in subsequent policy chapters.

The most pressing problems are those that have to do with national survival and well-being. When war seems an immediate prospect, or the basic economic and social order is otherwise threatened, all other issues are relegated to a second-priority level.

The general level of prosperity in the economy always has high priority, because the agenda of government is totally dependent on it. An expanding economy with stable prices means profits for business and jobs and income for people, more tax revenues for government, and an opportunity to improve the general quality of life.

But when prices are rising sharply, and the economy is stagnating and/or jobs are declining, the situation is entirely different. Everything government buys or does costs more, and there are many more and higher demands on it for assistance (such as extended unemployment insurance, greater welfare costs, etc.). When inflation and unemployment continue for some time, even securely funded programs of high priority may be threatened. An example is the Social Security System, whose benefits for retired workers are based on contributions from people employed today. According to the Congressional Joint Budget Committee in 1980, sustained inflation and unemployment threaten the retirement program with bankruptcy in the mid-1980s.[30]

The state of tensions in the world and the condition of the economy are thus of paramount importance for all other policy areas. In the early 1980s, first the Carter administration and then the Reagan administration began to see the military threat posed by the Soviet Union as an urgent matter. Commitments were made to increase military budgets substantially for a period of years, in order to bring American capabilities to levels considered necessary to serve United States interests around the world. A record budget of $160 billion was appropriated in 1981, and then supplemented later in the year; each subsequent year, a new record of military appropriations was set. This dominant priority fundamentally determined how much money, time, and energy could be committed to other problem areas.

Moreover, the military commitment was made at a time when the condition of the economy was particularly weak. *Inflation* was raising prices by 10 percent or more per year, and nobody seemed confident of the cause *or* the remedy. Whatever was attempted in the way of a cure seemed more likely to make some other condition worse than to finally control inflation. Only recessions (periods in which the economy does not grow for two consecutive quarters of a year) succeeded in reducing the rate of inflation. Even then, inflation started up again, and from successively higher levels, immediately after each of the recessions of the 1970s.

Unemployment stood at around 7 percent of the labor force, about twice the postwar "normal" rate. Unemployed workers not only put additional burdens on unemployment insurance programs and welfare programs, but also effectively reduce the consumer demand necessary to maintain profitability and employment throughout the economy *and* pose a threat of social unrest at some stage. *Economic growth* was low or actually negative (*less* goods and services produced today than in comparable past periods). Therefore, an expanding population was less likely to be able to find jobs, businesses were hard pressed to pay their debts and still have some margin of profit left over, and government revenues were reduced.

These three factors are mutually reinforcing weaknesses: increasing jobs requires an expanding economy, which requires savings and new investment, but inflation undermines savings, deters investment, and inhibits expansion. In addition, the remedies conventionally applied by governments are mutually contradictory: controlling inflation usually requires slowing growth and inducing unemployment, and curing unemployment requires stimulation of the economy and resultant inflation. The policy dilemma thus posed is acute, and apparently requires choosing which of the weaknesses are most important, concentrating on efforts (none of them at all assured of success) to solve them, and enduring their undesirable consequences. Both Democratic and Republican administrations in the early 1980s chose inflation as the greater evil and sought to control it even if unemployment and recession were increased or sustained.

But these were not the only problems that shaped the political agenda of the early 1980s. *Resource depletion* had severe and reverberating economic and political consequences. Particularly in the case of fossil fuels (oil, gas, coal), finite supplies would clearly not be able to fulfill steadily growing demands for more than a few decades. Some countries were heavily dependent on supplies from other countries. When the latter organized to control prices and the amounts produced (such as the Organization of Petroleum Exporting Countries—OPEC), they were able to create devastating economic impact and generate new political leverage. Many other energy-related problems, such as the inability of undeveloped Third World countries to pay both their new oil bills and their debts to industrial world banks, also followed from the fact of scarce supplies. Other raw materials, too, were in increasingly short supply and/or were rapidly becoming more expensive as producer countries sought to conserve and derive full value from their diminishing resources.

Environmental conditions had in many cases deteriorated to the point of posing serious hazards to health and life itself. Pollution of water threatened food supplies, and air pollution was clearly linked to cancer and other diseases. Discoveries of toxic waste dumping in the past at thousands of sites led to recognition of new dangers to food sources and health all across the country. Much environmental destruction was brought about by ignorance, but a good share of it was caused by the systematic efforts of businesses to minimize their costs. Almost all efforts at preventing further environmental damage ran counter to the profit-seeking needs of major industries and seemed to put a serious obstacle in the way of economic growth. The government (the taxpayers) thus had to share in the costs of essential pollution prevention and assume the full burden of trying to clean up past damage. But the dilemma—profitability versus environmental quality—continued in a variety of forms, constantly requiring controversial new trade-offs and accommodations.

Social conditions too numerous to itemize fully place additional strain on the political agenda at a time when it is already overflowing. One dimension of our social anxieties has been characterized as "future shock,"[31] the tensions produced by cumulating changes in our lives. Other sources of tension are obvious all around us. The economic and social status of racial minorities not only relfects a permanent inequality that denies American ideals but also poses a threat of future explosion. Crime rates are rising steadily, at a time when the United States already has a proportion of its population in prisons that is comparable only to South Africa among nations of the world. Divorce rates are also rising steadily, and many people seem to feel that family relationships are disintegrating. Bitter conflicts exist over such issues as abortion rights for women and integration of public schools. Millions of people mobilize their political efforts around these and other issues to the exclusion of larger questions, making solutions of the latter still more difficult.

As if these specific problems were not enough, some continuing and general ones also have important effects. One of these is the *integrated nature* of many of today's problems. They are congruent, and just do not come in separate compartments in which they can be dealt with one at a time. Economic problems such as inflation, unemployment, and low growth are linked to each other and to international trade and monetary problems, energy and other resource shortages, and environmental degradation. In these circumstances, attempts to improve one condition almost inevitably worsen others. And all programs are dependent on the stage of the business cycle for their priority and funding levels, if not for their very existence. Policy makers must keep the economic engine going at maximum speed just to be able to reduce obligations and find the resources to try to cope with problems.

Problems also have *deep roots* in economic and social structures of the society. Poverty, for example, is grounded in decades of the development of our present industrial order, in which geographic, ethnic, and racial minorities have been systematically underemployed or utilized in the most limiting ways. It appears and reappears in a variety of forms (low education, poor health, lack of job skills, unemployment, family breakup, etc.), none of which can be finally dealt with by itself. At the same time, needs and demands on the part of poor people in the United States and throughout the world make food, health, welfare, and other basic human services compelling problems for even a highly productive economy. And this congruence of deeply rooted economic and social problems occurs at a time when perceived military threats, not to mention the proliferation of nuclear weapons to an increasing number of countries, are making the world a very dangerous place.

Finally, we should note the part played by *the past* in shaping the agenda of our present. Not only are many of today's problems the results of past policies and practices (resource depletion, environmental decay, racial and sexual disparities, etc.), but we tend to understand and act upon them in terms of the past. This is partly because cultural images from the past dominate our minds, and partly because past policies represent commitments and have created industries and investments that cannot now be reversed. Coping with the energy crisis, for example, starts by taking for granted the oil companies and the pricing system of the economic market, moves on to massive crash programs to develop alternative supplies (often involving those same companies), and includes images of past mobilization, sacrifice, and achievement ("the moral equivalent of war").

Problems are partly objective and real, and partly what we think they are on the basis of past experience, present hopes and fears, and the forecasts of "experts." The latter may know something about present conditions, but cannot predict the future—and certainly not the future behavior of thinking, feeling human beings. Therefore there are always some dimensions of a problem that are vague or unknown, waiting to be filled in by past precedents or by projections of our present ideology.

A somewhat similar process is involved in the way that priorities are assigned among problems. There is nothing automatic about the priority assigned to a given problem. Instead, it is a matter of choice and preference, often appearing to be automatic or necessary because of the way such questions were handled in the past. Perceptions of a buildup in Soviet military power, for example, regularly trigger American policy makers' highest priorities for funding new weapons development. Few questions are asked about giving military spending precedence over other needs, or about possible alternatives to costly competition for military supremacy.

These illustrations only begin to suggest the character and interrelationship of our current problems. Much more detailed analysis will follow in each of our substantive policy areas. But this survey should suffice to justify the earlier characterization of the present period as the most severe set of economic—and (partly therefore) social and political—problems since the Great Depression of the 1930s. And crisis-level problems cannot fail to play a major role in shaping the public policy agenda of our times.

SUMMARY

We have analyzed three types of forces external to the political decision-making system that many observers see as shaping American public policies. Among *values and beliefs*, we identified individualism, property, and the role of the economic free market as dominant values. Surrounding beliefs included personal responsibility for success or failure, the work ethic, "blaming the victim," social mobility, racism, sexism, and "ageism." Conflicts between definitions of the key values provide much of the tension in American politics and were summarized by the contrasting versions of the values of freedom and equality that are held by the two poles of opinion. *Economic structure* was seen to be dominated by giant corporations and banks, whose needs help to shape the policy agenda. *Social structure* was seen to be in the nature of an elongated social pyramid, with wealth highly concentrated in the upper reaches. People at the top are able to make or influence decisions in a large share of our major social and political institutions. Finally, *today's problems* were viewed as closely connected with each other and adding up to an unprecedented public policy agenda.

Each of these three categories of external shaping forces, as it is filtered through the policy-making system and makes its imprint on public policy, may play more or less of a part in different policy areas. One of our goals in each substantive policy area will be to try to see just how much effect each set of forces actually has, and in the final chapter we shall try to reach some conclusions on this question. But we shall also want to see how much effect on policies is generated by characteristics of the policy-making system itself. That system is the subject to which we now turn.

NOTES

1 This four-part characterization expands upon the structure–ideology– social conditions analysis contained in Arnold Heidenheimer et al., *Comparative Public Policy: The Politics of Social Choice in Europe and America* (New York: St. Martin's, 1975), pp. 258–259.

2 For a full discussion, see Kenneth M. Dolbeare and Patricia Dolbeare, *American Ideologies*, 3d ed. (Chicago: Rand McNally, 1976).

3 Much more might be said about this central American value, and has been. The best historical developments are Louis Hartz, *The Liberal Tradition in America* (New York: Harcourt, Brace, 1955) and Herbert Croly, *The Promise of American Life* (New York: Macmillan, 1909).

4 An empirical study of what the assumption of personal responsibility means to people is Richard Sennett and Jonathan Cobb, *The Hidden Injuries of Class* (New York: Random House, 1973).

5 William P. Ryan, *Blaming the Victim*, rev. ed. (New York: Vintage Books, 1976).

6 Hartz, op. cit.

7 David M. Potter, *People of Plenty* (Chicago: Phoenix Books, 1954).

8 Thomas F. Gossett, *Race: The History of an Idea in America* (New York: Schocken Books, 1963).

9 For the clearest statement of the polar position, which still acknowledged the need for *some* assistance, see William Graham Sumner, *What Social Classes Owe to Each Other* (New Haven: Yale, 1884.)

10 A good discussion of contrasting views may be found in Michael Best and William Connolly, *The Politicized Economy* (Lexington, Mass.: Heath, 1976).

11 James Weinstein argues that this is a leading characteristic of the American public policy process. See his *The Corporate Ideal in the Liberal State* (Boston: Beacon Press, 1963).

12 For an argument that ideology is *the* explanation for the distinctiveness of American policy, see Anthony King, "Ideas, Institutions, and the Policies of Governments: A Comparative Analysis," *British Journal of Political Science*, vol. 3, no. 4, October 1973.

13 Martin Rein, *Social Science and Public Policy* (Baltimore: Penguin, 1976). See also Duncan MacRae and James A. Wilde, *Policy Analysis for Public Decisions* (North Scituate, Mass.: Duxbury Press, 1979).

14 For an excellent full discussion of this important point, see Brian Fay, *Social Theory and Political Practice* (Boston: George Allen & Unwin, 1975).

15 Data in this paragraph are drawn from *Fortune*, May 5, 1980, pp. 88–93 and 274–275.

16 William D. Shepherd, *Market Power and Economic Welfare* (New York: Random House, 1970), pp. 152–154.

17 For a complete description of how *seven* formerly highly competitive companies operated to mutual advantage, see Robert Engler, *The Brotherhood of Oil* (Chicago: University of Chicago Press, 1977).

18 The foregoing data and analysis rest upon David M. Kotz, "Finance Capital and Corporate Control," in Richard Edwards et al., *The Capitalist System*, 2d ed. (Englewood Cliffs, N.J.: Prentice-Hall, 1978).

19 *New York Times*, June 17, 1980, p. D11.

20 Ibid.

21 For a full comparison of the corporate-banking sector and the competitive sector, see James O'Connor, *The Fiscal Crisis of the State* (New York: St. Martin's, 1973).

22 Derived from Stephen Rose and Dennis Livingston, "Social Stratification in the United States" (Baltimore: Social Graphics, 1979).

23 There are a number of problems pertaining to the reliability of data on wealth distribution in the United States. Reporting is infrequent and often deliberately inaccurate, for example, and a variety of measures are used by different analysts. But all studies employing United States government data agree within a very few percentage points, and concur that these are essentially permanent patterns. The leading studies are cited here, regardless of whether their data are from the early 1960s or the 1970s.

24 The results of the study cited in the table are confirmed by a very careful study conducted for the Federal Reserve Board, in which 1.2 percent of all households held 34.6 percent of the total wealth and 53.5 percent of all income-producing wealth. See Dorothy Projector and Gertrude Weiss, *Survey of Financial Characteristics of Consumers* (Washington, D.C.: Federal Reserve Board, 1966).

25 J. D. Smith and S. D. Franklin, "The Concentration of Personal Wealth, 1922–1969," *American Economic Review*, p. 166, May 1974.

26 Samuel Bowles, "Schooling and the Reproduction of Inequality," in Richard Edwards et al., *The Capitalist System* (Englewood Cliffs, N.J.: Prentice-Hall, 1978), p. 323.

27 U.S. Department of Labor, *Monthly Labor Review,* August 1980, p. 72.

28 Frank Ackerman and Andrew Zimbalist, "Capitalism and Inequality in the United States," in Edwards, op. cit., p. 302.

29 Thomas R. Dye, *Who's Running America?*, 2d ed. (Englewood Cliffs, N.J.: Prentice-Hall, 1979).

30 For a full analysis of this report and the threats posed to the financial integrity of the Social Security System, see Chapter 11.

31 Alvin Toffler, *Future Shock* (New York: Random House, 1970).

Chapter 3

The Political Process and Public Policy

To what extent do the characteristics of its political system have an independent effect on the policies of a country? We believe that in the United States the effects may be at times as important as the external factors just examined in Chapter 2. Our political system is not just a mechanical translator; it stamps its own distinctive imprint on the policies that emerge from it. Such effects are *systemic* in character. That is, they stem from basic characteristics of the legal distribution of powers, the nature of institutions, and resultant political style. Although particular decisions or other actions of individual policy makers or administrators can be very significant on occasion, the general shape of the political system's impact on public policy owes more to fundamental features of the underlying system.

We shall take up first three broad categories of these systemic features: (1) fragmentation of power at the national level; (2) decentralization of power in the federal system; and (3) the weakness of the political party system. We then examine some general characteristics of our policy-making system which have relevance for all the policy areas we later analyze. Finally, we shall illustrate how both external forces and internal system characteristics combine to shape public policy, *and* show how to look for such factors in the subsequent policy-area chapters, by means of a brief case study of the policy problem of staffing the armed services.

THE STRUCTURE

Fragmentation of Power at the National Level

The powers of the United States government are distributed among separate institutions, each of which responds to a somewhat different constituency (see Fig. 3-1). Moreover, each possesses a distinctive operating style and a variety of incentives for maximizing and defending its power and prestige. The greatest visibility inheres in the Presidency. But, except for emergencies in which the military must be ordered into action, the President has little independent policy-making power and must persuade or bargain to obtain necessary cooperation from the House of Representatives, the Senate, sometimes the Supreme Court, and often legally independent agencies of the national government (such as the Federal Reserve Board). The President even must struggle to gain implementing cooperation from top military leaders and executive department heads, who can readily appeal to the Congress or the public in opposition. And the millions of middle-management federal employees protected by civil service provide further roadblocks. As the only nationally elected public official, the President's greatest claim to leadership rests in the role of spokesperson for the national interest. However, few specific tools are available to translate this claim into action, and often their use simply provokes new opposition.

By contrast, the House of Representatives is districted so that each member represents a geographic unit averaging 500,000 people. Diversity and local parochialism are deliberately encouraged. The bargaining-logrolling process of decision making in the House often allows expression of such distinctive views in public policy. Moreover, the House works mainly through its committee system, within which individual members can rise to positions of great influence over particular policy areas. Members gain visibility, prestige, and reelection by serving the House and their districts. They have little incentive to follow the President's lead where it does not run parallel to those primary goals.

The Senate is districted by states. Each senator responds to the needs and traditions of an equally idiosyncratic body of people, ranging from less than half that of a House district to twenty times as large. The committee system, traditions of mutual courtesy and deference, greater institutional powers, and far fewer members combine to give more senators significant personal power. And there is as little incentive to cooperate with the

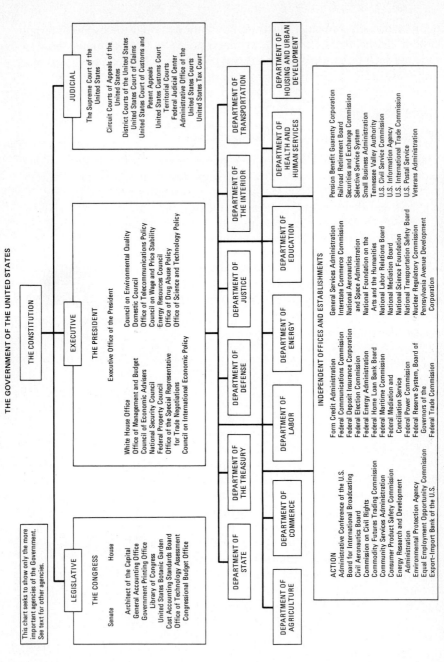

Figure 3-1 Structure of the United States government. (*Source: U.S. Government Manual, 1980.*)

President as there is in the House. Indeed, distinctive performance of some kind in the Senate often provides the visibility and credibility necessary for consideration as a possible future presidential candidate.

If the Senate and House have only modest incentive to cooperate with the President, they have even less to cooperate with each other. The pattern of constituency or personal preferences often widely differs in the two houses; agreement is sometimes impossible. But legislation and appropriations require the concurrence of both houses on every detail. Perhaps ironically, one of the ways effective pressure can be brought to bear to achieve agreement from enough members of each house is the mounting of a vigorous campaign by a lobbying group with sufficient financial resources. The other side of this point is, of course, that the division of responsibility between many committees opens up a large number of opportunities for such special interests to block proposed legislation.

Another fragment of national governmental power is held by the Supreme Court, which plays a larger governing role in the United States than its equivalent in any other country. Although nominated by the President (and confirmed by the Senate), Supreme Court justices acknowledge no constituency except their version of what the law (public policy) should be. Their powers to interpret statutes, void or endorse them, and approve or overrule state courts give the justices a continuing part in making and implementing policy.

Still other shares of national power divide among formally independent agencies. Created by the Congress and given specific responsibilities (such as managing the nation's financial system, as in the case of the Federal Reserve Board), independent agencies are deliberately insulated from executive or legislative control. They are able to act with independent legal powers, in the areas assigned them, just as if they were the Congress and President combined.

Decentralization of Power in the Federal System

The United States is a very large country with great physical and social differences between widely separated regions. It would be very difficult to govern such a nation from a single central source. With certain exceptions, central control has not really been attempted. Partly because the original states were sovereign bodies before the creation of the United States government, the states have always held a substantial share of the legal powers of government. Some part of that power has been granted to towns, counties, cities, school districts, and, more recently, a variety of special districts and functional agencies. The American governmental picture is thus one of national and state governments operating in the same geographic area on the same people at the same time. Each of these governments is supreme with regard to its own designated subjects of responsibility, and neither can control the other. Some subjects are shared responsibilities, in which the states are free to act as they wish as long as they do not conflict with national policies.

The principal areas of state responsibility are in regard to the health, safety, and welfare of the people within its jurisdiction. This includes the important function of education, as well as the administration of justice. Over time, great differences have developed in the ways that various states provide public services. Levels of welfare assistance, for example, might be four times as high in some states as in others, and entirely different criteria might be applied for eligibility for certain kinds of assistance, such as abortions for poor people. The United States government is virtually powerless to act directly in such areas, except where United States constitutional rights are held to be violated.

One major way, however, exists for the national government to powerfully influence state practices. The national government has much greater financial capacity than the states. This fact carries important implications for the federal policy process. States may hesitate to impose taxes in fear that businesses or people may move to other states or from concern that taxpayers' "revolts" against sales or property taxes (the primary source of state and local revenues) can find immediate targets. The national government faces much lower prospects of losing business or people to other countries; its income taxes are less visible; and there are fewer ways for taxpayer resistance to find expression (no initiative or referendum provisions, for example). Moreover, the national government's financial needs can always be met by the simple expedient of going further into debt and/or printing more money.

This greater financial capacity has been used in a number of ways to compensate for the national government's legal and practical inability to act directly or to order state and local governments to follow certain policies. One method is to impose a tax of some magnitude on employers and workers, *unless* their particular state government has a similar tax for the same purpose. The unemployment compensation system and Social Security were created in this way. Another is to make money available for functions the states are already performing, such as welfare assistance, provided that the states meet prescribed standards in disbursing it. Still another is to make appropriations available on a matching basis if the states will undertake new services considered desirable by the national government. For example, full national support might be offered for the first year of a program, with gradually phased reduction to 30 percent national and 70 percent state funding over a period of years.

The states and local governments are thus deeply involved in the implementation of many national policies. The results are a wider array of services and some greater standardization in their administration but continuing diversity of policy effects across the country. Recognition of state and local government power and intent to use it in diverse ways is a necessary part of the design of most national policies. Even where the national government has power and seeks to act directly, the power and preferences of local governments must be taken into account or the program will never succeed.

Power is also effectively decentralized by means of the special role of courts and lawyers in the American system. Issues are never finally settled by legislative compromise and enactment of statutes, or by executive implementation of programs. The prospect that individuals or corporations will take matters affecting them into court is always present. Courts routinely modify or void, in whole or in part, national or state policies. Disputes between individuals, or between individuals and governments over alleged denials of constitutional rights, may result in new court-generated policies that governments at all levels must follow, whatever the cost. The struggle between federal courts and local governments over the issue of busing for purposes of integration, or between state courts and state legislatures over funding for attorneys for criminal defendants, provide recent examples.

One result of this scattering of power among various levels of government is that no single authority is in charge or accountable. The consequences of almost every domestic policy are contingent upon the character of cooperation by independent or semiindependent levels of the implementing process. A certain unpredictability, and a significant capacity to initiate new policies, are present at all levels. Our policy system cannot be characterized by its neatness, coherence, and uniformity.

The Weakness of the Political Parties

The American political party system has never been a highly centralized one in which a national consensus on issues or programs could be enforced on officeholders at various governmental levels. Instead, the two major parties have been coalitions of state and local units, held together by the opportunity for mutual gain at the expense of the other party. A sense of shared risks and prospects provided some basis for cooperation among members of each party in Congress and the executive branch. In modest ways, party loyalties helped to make up for the fragmentation of power nationally and the decentralization of power among the units of the federal system.

But the present-day parties are weaker and less meaningful as organizations than at any time since the Civil War. A presidential candidate acquires a party's nomination by contending as an individual in a series of primaries. The candidate, if elected, owes little to the party as such, and yet claims the right to be its spokesperson. Members of the Congress, having done the same on a smaller scale, owe little to the party and (usually) nothing to the presidential candidate. Voters are so adept at splitting their tickets that there is little shared risk among presidential, senatorial, and House candidates. Indeed, local candidates may well gain support by opposing the views of the presidential candidate of their own party. Over this entire process stand the mass media, whose communication of an "image" of a candidate may be far more decisive than any other factor. Stands on issues, party identification, and even the real character of the candidate become far less important than what the candidate-as-presented-by-the-media appears to be like.

The political parties (with very few local exceptions) are no longer continuing social organizations with independent ideologies and programs and the capability of invoking loyal or cooperative action on the part of officeholders and members. They are increasingly labels available for the taking and convenient symbols for seeking the electoral support of those with long memories. Increasing proportions of voters apparently feel that *neither* party can or will deliver on its promises, or that there is no essential difference between them. The proportion of eligible voters who actually voted for President in 1980, for example, was only 52 percent, continuing a steady decline that began in 1960 and representing the lowest voter turnout since 1948.

But the deep roots of the two-party system, and the protections it is given by national and state electoral laws and practices, means that the only way voters can reject an incumbent President is to elect the candidate of the other party. The latter therefore may gain office in part because of reasons quite unrelated to the policy programs advocated during the campaign. Again using the election of 1980 as an example, a postelection poll showed that, of the 28 percent of the eligible voters who voted for President Reagan, nearly half gave as their primary reason disapproval of President Carter's performance. Only 16 percent of the total eligible electorate voted for Reagan primarily because they approved of his policy positions.[1] This contrasts rather sharply with the media characterization of the election as a "conservative mandate."

For all these reasons, the political parties are not effective means of translating voter policy preferences into government action. In some respects the parties seem to have abdicated policy and program functions they may have once performed. In others, conditions have changed so drastically (the rise of the electronic media, primary laws) that there seems little prospect that they could come to play a stronger role.

What do these characteristics imply for the American political system? Some have argued that this is an ideal system for *building* a consensus, but not for *moving* it into action or into a new form.[2] It might be more accurate to say that this system assures that whatever important domestic action is ultimately taken drops to the lowest common denominator. It must be something that practically everybody can agree upon. Moreover, it is a system that offers multiple opportunities for special-interest groups, particularly business and organized professionals, to exercise effective vetoes. American public policy is likely to proceed by fits and starts. Long initial delays are followed by a short period of sweeping and disruptive catching-up and a longer period of mixed consolidation and reaction.

The significance of these system and style characteristics may be underlined by comparison with the general pattern of institutional arrangements in the European countries and Canada. Most employ the "parliamentary" system, in which the leader of the majority political party in the legislature is elected to head the executive branch. He or she then selects other leading members of the elected legislature to head the various cabinet departments. The day-to-day work of the administrative branch, and a good part of its policy making (just below the major questions), rests in the hands of a career civil service. The political parties are centrally organized and "disciplined." This means: (1) their central organs are committed to the platforms framed by prior conventions; and (2) their local nominations are bestowed only upon people who agree to abide by those commitments. Local governments possess nowhere near the independence of the American states, functioning more like lower administrative units of the national government.

In these systems, power is considerably more centralized. The executive and the legislature are completely integrated. The executive is accountable to the legislature in the sense of being continually subject to a vote of "no confidence," which would result in a national election. The political parties are the principal vehicles of cooperation; they are "responsible" for the conduct of the government. All members stand or fall together. Although local preferences can be implemented, for the most part legal powers flow from the national source, and the career civil service sincerely seeks to follow national guidelines. Courts do not have independent authority in most cases. The legislature itself serves as the highest court. Much greater coherence of policy and implementation results, with more complete adherence to national standards.

POLICY-MAKING PROCESSES

How does policy get made within our fragmented, decentralized system? In many respects, there is a distinct policy-making system for each problem area: a particular set of executive departments, congressional committees, independent agencies, interest groups, etc., carries legal responsibility and a share of practical power to decide on policies in that area. For example, two of our policy areas (managing the economy and energy) involve both international *and* national affairs. This means that they are more exclusively the preserve of the national government, and within it presidential initiative is relatively more important. International conditions and the actions of other countries are significant factors, and the President's powers over the day-to-day conduct of foreign policy are basic to policy formation. The various regional and country experts in the State Department, United States ambassadors and their staffs abroad, the CIA and military intelligence agencies, the international monetary section of the Treasury Department, and the National Security Council are key sources of information and interpretation. A good portion of the details of the domestic political agenda is thus shaped by the incumbents of those offices. But because decisions are of such great consequence to all sectors of the business world, consumers, investors, local governments, etc., there are powerful pressures mobilized through the Congress and directly upon the President and such executive departments as Energy, Commerce, and Treasury.

The other two policy areas, however (health care and income support), involve primarily assistance to Americans with regard to major problems of everyday life. The international side of the policy-making system is little involved, and the federal government itself is placed in a supplementary role to the long-established powers and practices of the states and local governments. This is because the states, and not the federal government, have the general power to legislate for the health, safety, and welfare of citizens. With the exception of the Social Security System, veterans' services, and the food stamp program, there are no major federal services or benefits rendered directly to citizens in these key areas.

Instead, the federal government appropriates money for the states and local governments to spend. Of course, first the Congress and then the "guideline" and regulation writers in various little-known bureaus of the Department of Health and Human Services (HHS) specify in ever-increasing detail how the recipients must use that money. Another set of HHS employees monitors compliance with such criteria, notifying states and local governments when their practices endanger their continued funding.

The President proposes policy initiatives and funding levels to the Congress, and is remotely involved in the implementation process. But his role is not at all comparable to that in the first two areas. The Congress and HHS tend to dominate, and there is a special function for the courts in resolving disputes over individuals' claims and the propriety and administraiton of various regulations.

The idiosyncratic nature of the policy-making system applicable to each problem area means that each must be analyzed together with the substance of the policies involved. For example, energy policy making during the Carter administration was significantly affected by the fact that the House of Representatives had a single committee with jurisdiction over all aspects of energy policy, appointed specially by a Speaker anxious to cooperate with the President on this subject. The Senate, in contrast, broke the Carter proposals into five separate components and sent them to five separate standing committees—each of which had distinct and conflicting views about the proper form that energy policy should take. In each of the chapters on substantive policy that follow, we shall emphasize the particular characteristics of policy making that affect policies produced.

But some features of the American policy-making process are common to almost all policy areas. These general characteristics include (1) the fact-gathering and issue-shaping parts played by foundations, presidential commissions, private "think tanks," and government researchers— sometimes years before a policy issue actually reaches the practical political agenda; (2) the role of interest groups and lobbyists; (3) the ways that public pressure can be mobilized and/or manipulated, and public opinion formed, particularly through the mass media; (4) the legislative process itself, including presidential and party leadership and the workings of congressional committees; and (5) the politics of implementation and administration by executive departments and agencies, and oversight by Congress and the Presidency. Each of these general features of the policy-making process provides an avenue by which power and preferences can make their mark on policy. Each merits brief elaboration, with specific applications reserved for the chapters on substantive policy to follow.

The way that an issue or problem is presented, and the facts understood at the time of a decision, can play a major role in shaping policy choices. If solar energy usage can be made to appear an exotic or impractical project for which the technology is not yet perfected, funding priorities are much more likely to emphasize crash programs to develop synthetic fuels. Consequently, there is sharp competition among a variety of participants to establish the "factual" understanding of a problem and the alternative means of coping with it. There is no neutral body to sift through all the analyses and allegations and provide an authoritative interpretation for policy makers. Instead, they must choose their facts and alternatives from among the often numerous studies produced by organizations and people with varying credibility and hidden purposes.

The major foundations, such as the Ford Foundation, are likely to conduct comprehensive analyses of problems not yet on the political agenda, so that their reports may play a part in shaping general understanding of the basic nature of the issue as it becomes increasingly visible. The private research institutes, or "think tanks," normally conduct studies of current problems under contract with government agencies, but sometimes with their own funding. Each major institute acquires over time a distinct perspective and often expresses its political preferences in its work: the Brookings Institution is known for its thorough research for generally liberal causes, for example, while the newer American Enterprise Institute for Public Policy Research provides background and arguments for conservatives.

Presidential commissions are often formed when a problem is particularly pressing, and a hurriedly collected staff reviews existing reports and conducts limited studies so that the commission members can make timely recommendations and start a consensus-building process leading to new policies. Congressional committee staff and executive department or agency researchers often conduct major studies of current problems in their respective areas, more or less reflecting in their conclusions the perspectives of their employers.

Another source of information for policy makers is that provided by various special-interest groups and lobbyists. In this case, however, factual interpretations and suggested alternatives are clearly marked by their authors' preferences and often accompanied by significant political pressure. Nevertheless, credible and important studies are produced by such interest groups as the Committee for Economic Development (business) or the AFL-CIO (labor). Interest groups have steadily increased; very few issues (and no major ones) are decided without pressure being mounted by several such groups. Self-described "public interest" groups are a recent addition to the trade associations, professional associations, labor unions, etc., that take stands on a wide range of policies. Perhaps most influential among lobbyists are the Washington law firms, headed by former (and future) government officials with deep experience in various policy areas. Some of the best lobbyists are representatives of government agencies themselves, or of their suppliers; the military services and defense contractors have been particularly effective in shaping policy.

The general public participates less regularly in specific policy choices, but can play a major role on occasion. Grass-roots letter-writing campaigns are sometimes generated by industries or other groups likely to be adversely affected by policies under consideration, and the President may develop pressure on the Congress by appealing to the people. Public understanding of issues, as well as of the part played by various policy makers, is, of course, highly dependent on mass media presentations. The leading newspaper and radio-TV network reporters and columnists decide who or what is important and how it shall be presented to the public. The media are themselves big business, and their owners and editors are not reluctant to assert their own judgments of newsworthiness and their own political perspectives in the process of selecting and presenting the facts about issues and events.

Enacting legislation is a long and complicated process in which the persuasion, inducements, and coercive capability of the President and the party leadership are pitted against the parochialism and diverse preferences of members of Congress. A politically sensitive President may be able to gain support for his program, but it is almost always a full-time job requiring a clear sense of priorities and a willingness to compromise or abandon less important goals.

The legislative process in Congress is particularly vulnerable to special-interest pressures and to the capacity of a few representatives or senators to block action entirely unless their demands are met. This is primarily the result of the committee system. Both houses operate principally through *standing* (permanent) committees and subcommittees with jurisdiction over specific policy areas (see Table 3-1). While legislation may be amended during floor consideration by the full house, the major shaping decisions are made by the members who happen to be a majority of the applicable committee. In some cases, that majority may in turn be guided by the expertise of a chairman, or a two- or three-member subcommittee. For example, the evolving nature of the Social Security

Table 3-1 Committees of Congress

House	Senate
Agriculture	Agriculture, Nutrition, and Forestry
Appropriations	Appropriations
Armed Services	Armed Services
Banking, Finance, and Urban Affairs	Banking, Housing and Urban Affairs
Budget	Budget
District of Columbia	Commerce, Science, and Transportation
Education and Labor	Energy and Natural Resources
Energy and Commerce	Environment and Public Works
Foreign Affairs	Finance
Government Operations	Foreign Relations
House Administration	Governmental Affairs
Interior and Insular Affairs	Judiciary
Judiciary	Labor and Human Resources
Merchant Marine and Fisheries	Rules and Administration
Post Office and Civil Service	Veterans' Affairs
Public Works and Transportation	Aging (special)*
Rules	Ethics (select)*
Science and Technology	Intelligence (select)*
Small Business	Indian Affairs (select)*
Standards of Official Conduct	Small Business (select)*
Veterans' Affairs	
Ways and Means	

*Senate select and special committees are ad hoc appointments for particular purposes, but have long lives.

System was for many years due almost entirely to decisions made by Representative Wilbur Mills, chairman of the House Ways and Means Committee, whose experience and power were such as to gain the support of his committee and the full House for whatever modifications he proposed. In turn, Mills relied upon the System's chief actuarial accountant for statistical projections. Because the House carries constitutional power to initiate tax bills (the federal government's power to maintain the Social Security System rests constitutionally on its power of taxation), the Senate normally went along with whatever changes the House proposed. Thus, one representative practically single-handedly shaped the nation's retirement system affecting tens of millions of Americans.[3]

The policy decisions of standing committees affect legislation in their houses only, and even then floor amendments may change the shape of a bill before it is passed. Where the House and Senate pass different versions of a bill, as is often the case, a *conference* committee is appointed to try to iron out the differences. Normally such committees are composed of leading members of the relevant standing committees, but the selection of just who are to represent each house is a matter of great significance to the final form of the legislation. Assuming both houses accept the conference committee's compromises and pass the bill, and the President does not veto it, the "authorization" stage of policy making is complete.

Sometimes this is all that is needed for a new policy to become effective. For example, a change in the tax or criminal law could become operative with no further action by the Congress. But most new policies are not "self-executing" in this way. Instead, they require the creation of a new agency or department, the employment of inspectors or investigators to monitor compliance with new regulations, or new money to distribute to the states or the people in accordance with the authorizing legislation.

In such cases, a second, or "appropriations," stage of the policy-making process is required. The President submits a request in the proposed budget for a certain amount of money to carry out the tasks involved, and the *Appropriations* Committees of the two houses, again operating through two- to five-member subcommittees, make the initial determinations about just how much money should be appropriated to implement the legislation previously passed. Clearly, the distinctive preferences and priorities of such committee members might result in small or no appropriations to carry out the program so enthusiastically authorized before. At the very least, a second decision-making struggle is likely to be involved, with potential change in the ultimate practical form of the new policy. Floor amendments, conference committee conflicts, and the possibility of a presidential veto are also part of this appropriations process.

Finally, we should recognize that a good share of the actual policy making in any given area takes place *after* the Congress has completed all its actions. In most cases, the Congress has stated its goals and the manner by which they are to be achieved only in the most general terms. Sometimes this is quite deliberate, a form of compromise in which specificity is avoided in order to gain the majority needed for passage of the legislation. In any event, the executive departments or agencies involved are forced to make many quite fundamental policy decisions as they write regulations or issue instructions to their field personnel. Sometimes departments or agencies are more than glad to put their own preferences into effect under the guise of the congressional purpose. In the eyes of some representatives and senators, both the Occupational Safety and Health Administration and the Environmental Protection Agency have been overzealous in construing the congressional intent to promote safety at work and maintain clean air and water (see Fig. 3-2).

The day-to-day practices of enforcement or implementing personnel also require on-the-spot policy making, as do formal hearings within the agency regarding possible violations. At every stage, interested industries or other groups are actively seeking to persuade administrators to interpret the intent of Congress in accordance with their preferences. The politics of implementation can be as bitterly fought as any other part of the policy-making process, and perhaps more determinative of the actual meaning of a new public policy. Before the process can really be completed, however, any number of trips to court may be required.

Nor is the Congress willing to sit idly by and watch the agencies and the interest groups rewrite its legislation. Congress takes part in the implementation process by various forms of oversight. The policy-area committees and the appropriations committees regularly inquire into the manner in which administrators are carrying out legislation. The General Accounting Office of the Congress traces the uses of federal funds and raises questions about their congruence with congressional intent. The Congressional Budget Office conducts studies of developing problems that often implicate past practices. In both of the latter cases, congressional monitoring extends primarily to the uses of moneys appropriated. Given the difficulty that Congress has in overseeing the day-to-day operations of the far-flung federal bureaucracy and the fact that all appropriations must come from the Congress, the money power becomes the principal tool for controlling the executive branch. Those agencies or departments that repeatedly flaunt the will of Congress, or at least of its key members, can be punished by withholding appropriations in the future.

The President is also a participant in the politics of implementation. No President can take for granted that the career civil service personnel of the executive branch, many of whom started years ago and now have risen to managerial positions, will automatically share his preferences and seek to carry them out. Instead, detailed monitoring and redirection is carried

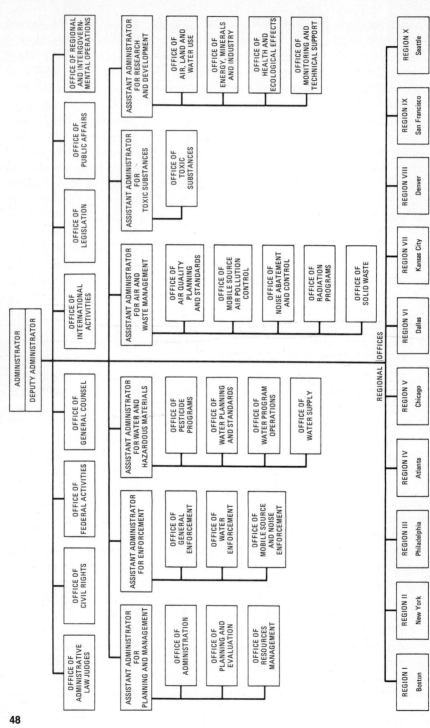

ENVIRONMENTAL PROTECTION AGENCY

Figure 3-2 The scope of a small federal government agency. (*Source: U.S. Government Manual, 1980.*)

out by the Executive Office of the President and particularly the Office of Management and Budget (OMB). The Environmental Protection Agency, for example, was instructed by the Carter White House to avoid stringent regulations lest they contribute to inflation. The Department of Justice is regularly queried about its enforcement of the antitrust laws or pending investigations that might prove politically embarrassing.

What does all this complexity and uncertainty mean for public policy? The merits of issues are obviously buried under a heavy layer of ideology, interest, institutional complications, various conflicting priorities, and continuing struggle for political power. They are not lost or irrelevant, but they surely do not control the outcome of the policy-making process. Power is parceled out to many participants in this policy-making process, each with distinctive goals, and each seeks to gain as much as possible out of the end product. Value-based choices of priorities have to be made, and then one strong policy preference traded away in order that a still-higher-ranked goal can be achieved (see Table 3-2).

In such circumstances, we simply cannot think of this process as a clean or "rational" one in which the merits of issues are the primary determinants of public policy. No abstract model really captures the way in which policy is made, except at a level that is too general to be helpful in understanding specific policy areas. About the best that can be said is that

Table 3-2 Changing Priorities, 1981–1984

	Carter Budget Proposals, 1981	Reagan Budget Proposals, 1984
Social benefits (Social Security, Medicare, public assistance, food stamps, veterans, civil service retirement, unemployment, education, etc.)	37%	41%
Military	24%	32%
Interest on debt	10%	9%
All other (Cost of government, aid to states and cities, aid to transportation, foreign aid, energy, pollution, public works, etc.)	29%	18%

we have a distinctive national style—once an issue has reached the national political agenda—of bargaining, compromising, anticipating others' power and preferences, and accepting partial achievements, that never really ceases shaping and reshaping public policies. All of this takes place, of course, within the boundaries and with the imperatives set by the values and beliefs, economic and social structures, and problem characteristics that were analyzed earlier.

SHAPING FACTORS AND SYSTEM CHARACTERISTICS COMBINED: THE CASE OF STAFFING THE ARMED SERVICES

The first major question set out in Chapter 1 asked why our public policies have the character that they do. In other words, why do we have this particular policy in regard to energy or health care or income support? The last two chapters have set forth some basic (external) shaping factors and some (internal) characteristics of the structure and process of our policy-making system that are often thought to explain the nature of our public policies. The weight to be given to any of these possible causes can be determined only after our four substantive policy areas have been explored, of course, but it seems safe to say that we may find some combination of external shaping factors and internal system characteristics involved in each. The purpose of the brief case study that follows is to show (a) how these two kinds of explanatory causes are combined and expressed in both the process of policy making and the substance of policy, and (b) how to look for similar effects and make judgments about which are more important explanations for the character of our public policies in the four substantive areas taken up in Part Two.

The policy problem of staffing the military services has been chosen because it is both a current and a continuing one that illustrates the part played by all the possible explanatory factors. The issue, of course, is how to get appropriate (motivated, trainable) people into the military in sufficient numbers to carry out its tasks. We shall look first at the external shaping factors, then at internal system characteristics, and finally at present and prospective policies.[4]

Shaping Factors

The values of individualism and freedom have always led Americans to oppose conscription except in times when war appeared to be forced upon us and opposition yielded to nationalism and patriotism. When wartime conscription has been implemented, there has always been a strong concern for equality of obligation to serve. At other times, the military has been forced to rely upon those persons whom it could attract by patriotic appeals, fringe benefits (including health, retirement, and other benefits), job security, travel opportunities, or (most recently) wages approaching those of the free market.

The relevance of these values can be seen from the historical record of military manpower policy. During the Civil War, conscription in the North permitted those who could pay $300 to escape service, and therefore focused on the lower classes and immigrants. In some areas it was implemented by the military through house-to-house registration. The result was a series of riots, one of which, in New York City, claimed hundreds of lives. During World War I, the lessons of the Civil War led to the creation of an ostensibly civilian agency with decentralized state-level administration and local-area boards to determine who should be drafted into the armed forces. The higher levels were staffed primarily with retired, reserve, or National Guard officers, and the local boards with patriotic volunteers, so that the needs of the military were well served. Opposition to the fact of conscription itself was reduced somewhat, however, and the appearance of equity maintained. Although there was principled opposition to the war and therefore to conscription, and to conscription's constitutionality as a form of slavery or enforced servitude, neither seriously interfered with fulfillment of the military's manpower needs.

World War II and to a considerable extent the Korean War were periods when a national consensus strongly supported the war effort and hence conscription. By the time of the Vietnam War, however, many things were different. The war was not only not strongly supported by a national consensus, but there was also a vigorous antiwar movement grounded in the very population that was subject to the draft. Perhaps even more important, there were much larger numbers of men of draft age, far more than the military services needed to fight the war. In order to focus the prospect of induction on *some* men (thereby inducing many of them to enlist, which is one of the major functions of the draft), many *others* had to be deferred from service. This was done through generous grants of deferments for employment in occupations considered vital to war production or the local economy, for physical or mental impairments, and for undergraduate or graduate education. The result was that several types of inequity in obligation to serve developed and further undermined support for conscription: men from families that could not afford to send them to college, particularly including minorities, were much more likely to be drafted into the Army. Wide variations occurred in the deferment criteria and practices of the more than 4,000 local boards, so that similarly situated men were treated very differently in different parts of the country. And some men went for years with the threat of induction hanging over them, with employers unwilling to hire or train them and themselves unable to plan careers or personal lives. This inequality of obligation to serve finally led to selection of men by annual lottery, and when military needs began to be lower the draft was abandoned entirely in favor of a "voluntary" military with much higher wages.

Opposition to conscription on the grounds of individualism and freedom remains strong today, and only a clear showing of necessity is likely to overcome its effects. Equality of obligation to serve when conscription *is* instituted also remains a strong value, but it is now complicated by the question of whether equality requires the extension of the obligation to women. The latter prospect awakens other strongly held values about family life, the proper role of women, and relations between the sexes.

The importance of economic and social structures in shaping military personnel procurement policy has already been suggested. Some people of draft age *are* vital to war production or local economies and probably should be deferred from military service. But many employers are likely to see their investment in training an employee as making that person vital to their business, and much pressure is brought to bear on draft officials to obtain deferments. All those who do not serve are, of course, free to take advantage of the many profit-making opportunities that develop during times of war or mobilization for war.

It is the basic social structure, and particularly the distribution of wealth and income within it, that makes the lower classes specially vulnerable to the draft. They are less likely to go to college or get the highly skilled and therefore deferrable jobs. Only their greater physical and mental disabilities prevented the incidence of service by lower-class men from being dramatically higher than that of middle-class men during the Vietnam War. Moreover, lower-class people are less politically active than others, so that their opposition to conscription is not much felt politically. This makes up for the fact that the draft has no strong constituency (except for veterans' and other military-support organizations) anywhere in the population. It can be tolerated by the middle and upper classes, apparently, as long as it is the children of the lower classes who are actually serving.

This pattern of induced education and vital-job-seeking by the middle classes and acceptance of military service by the lower classes was celebrated by the Selective Service System during the Vietnam War under the label of "channeling." The System claimed credit for maximizing the efficient use of human resources in the nation. Not until the issue of equity was forcefully raised did it retreat from citing this long-established practice as one of its major achievements.

The final set of shaping factors flows from the nature of the problems that the nation faces. As a leading world power, the United States clearly must maintain some level of military capability. Precisely how much and what form it should take are matters of controversy. But President Carter began to see the need for expanding military capabilities as early as 1978, and President Reagan is committed to still greater expansion. A voluntary army is expensive, and it has a number of other drawbacks as well. The question of how to staff the armed services is thus necessarily back on the political agenda, and probably back to stay. President Carter signaled this by requiring registration of 19- and 20-year old men in 1980.

The Policy-making System

In the fragmented American system, the initiative for policies involved in staffing the military services must come from the President as Commander in Chief. Congress can be expected to resist any effort to reinstitute conscription except in a recognized national emergency. But the committee system in both houses means that there also will be strong support for a draft if the Joint Chiefs of Staff strongly endorse it. The Armed Services Committees in both houses normally support military requests, and several members are already on record to the effect that the voluntary army approach is not working. They are concerned about the relatively low levels of education of the people attracted in recent years, their morale and readiness, and the problem of turnover. It is also much harder to maintain a large and ready reserve component when a relatively few persons serve in the active forces in this manner.

Once the constitutional question was resolved in World War I, the courts' involvement in this policy area was limited to working out the rights of and criteria for determining conscientious objectors to military service. But the question of women's obligation to serve will restore the courts to a major role if the draft is reinstituted in any way. No matter how the President and Congress resolve the issue, the American distribution of policy-making power to (ultimately) the Supreme Court will mean it will become engaged long before the matter is finally settled.

The decentralized character of the American system and its implications are also evident in this policy area. The Selective Service System, essentially the same national–state–local board system from World War I through the Vietnam period, effectively encouraged enlistments and produced inductees with relatively low visibility. The Director of the Selective Service System throughout this period, General Lewis Hershey, enjoyed support in the Congress second only to the then-legendary J. Edgar Hoover of the FBI. His assessments of what was practical or desirable were nearly always accepted. Loyalty from the System's paid staff and local board volunteers was equally strong, and the System seemed to be a part of the nation's ongoing life. But the price of first state-level and then board-level discretion within the system, and hence high variability particularly in the manpower-surplus years of the Vietnam War, was resentment at nonuniformity and inequity. Decentralization may be a familiar means of promoting acquiescence, but it can impose high costs.

Policy makers today would not necessarily have to follow past practices, but the burden of history is always felt. If new departures are to be taken, they must be justified in some way. Once the Joint Chiefs and the President have reached some judgment—in all probability, either to increase wages (particularly for the key noncommissioned officers of all services) or to restore some form of the draft—a major public effort would probably be necessary to build congressional support. This could well be paralleled by new warnings of the dangers of Soviet aggression and the need for preparedness. A blue-ribbon study group or a presidential commission might be created to certify the necessity if any major change in present practice were to be made. This was done in 1966–1967 by President Johnson, when mounting complaints forced consideration of changes in the System. At that time, he appointed the National Advisory Commission on Selective Service, which soon recommended the lottery system—a change that took some time to accomplish.

The Armed Services committees in both houses could be counted on as friendly forums, and the members of the military appropriations subcommittees probably would be equally supportive. Interest groups with major interest in the subject would certainly include all the veterans organizations, the retired officers associations, and the educational establishment. If the proposal were to reinstitute the draft, the now-dormant Selective Service System's planning staff would undoubtedly play a role in shaping the new policy and the manner of its implementation.

Problems, Policies, and Prospects

The basic problem is one of foreign policy: how much and what kind of military capability the United States needs is a product of what the government wants to do and/or thinks it must prepare for. But this translates quickly into the question of *how many* and *what kinds* of people are needed in the various military services, and *for how long*. There are both a basic policy dilemma and a more technical equation involved in working on this problem. The dilemma lies in the well-recognized opposition to conscription, shared by President Reagan himself, that is posed against the desire to hold down expenditures while increasing the size, technical capabilities, and stability of the armed forces. A voluntary army, enjoying near-market wages, is expensive even at modest force levels. But as these force levels are expanded, and particularly when people of greater skills or education are sought and it is desired to avoid speedy turnover (and costly training), the total wages mount up dramatically. If keeping national government expenditures to a minimum is also important, it may be necessary to employ conscription as a means of getting low-cost high-quality personnel into military service.

The equation involves the number of persons required to staff the armed forces, the wage levels to be paid and benefits to be offered, the national unemployment rate, and the extent of risk of a shooting war. At rising force levels, the draft becomes more of a necessity because costs would be prohibitive and not enough people would want to serve anyhow. If unemployment is high, wages and benefits can be relatively lower; when unemployment is low, wages and benefits must rise sharply. But if unemployment is concentrated among the less-skilled and the military needs skilled and/or better-educated and therefore more trainable people, wages and benefits have to be set at a level to attract such people. If low turnover is desired in order to maintain stability and develop experience, a higher benefit package has to be designed accordingly. Finally, if there is real risk of a shooting war, the costs of attracting enough people into service would rise so high that conscription would be an almost automatic necessity. These parameters and relationships define the problem in such a way as to suggest that serious consideration must be given to some form of conscription whenever modest force levels (say 3 million persons) are decided upon and total costs are a real matter of concern. Only quite high unemployment at all levels of the population would preserve the viability of the voluntary army under such conditions.

If the draft *were* to be revived, the lottery system would probably have to be employed. There are many more people in the eligible age categories than are needed in the military, and some way must be found to focus enlistment pressure on some of them. In the Vietnam era, such focusing meant that a relative few had to be inducted each year to produce a good-sized military force. But deferments by local boards produce nonuniformity and provoke opposition. The lottery is conducted nationally and is based on date of birth, so that all have an equal chance of being first or last in order of priority for induction. Arbitrary as it sounds, if fairness and uniformity are desired, the lottery is probably the only way.

One route out of some parts of the dilemma would be to institute some form of universal national service, in which all persons except those specifically exempted for certain limited reasons would perform some kind of national service for a period of two years somewhere between the ages of (say) 18 and 26. Wages would be low, and participants assigned to public works, social service, conservation, and other developmental tasks around the country. Those who wanted somewhat higher wages and subsequent benefits would be encouraged to enlist in the military for a longer period instead. The constitutional and practical problems in conscripting women would be avoided, and enough inducement provided to staff the military without resorting to conscription. Net costs to the government and to the private economy might actually be lower, as much work would be accomplished at low wages and other wage levels would thereby be kept lower, and savings would be realized in military salaries, unemployment compensation, and a variety of other government programs.

The alternatives, permutations, and combinations of possible policies are almost endless: that is part of the fascination of studying public policy. But they all tell us something—about our values and what we accept as given about economic and social structures, about our problems, and about our policy-making system.

Conclusions

What forces have and will shape the substance of policies for staffing the military? Dominant American values, the nature of the problem, and the references of major powerholders within our distinctive policy-making system all play important parts. Together, they shape the range and conditions of the possible. Nothing is predetermined, although several factors may converge in a single direction. There remains a certain amount of discretion over whether, when, and in what form a policy like the reinstitution of the draft might be sought. The President, the Joint Chiefs of Staff, and key members of Congress hold most of this discretionary power, but in a manner subject to changing world conditions and American public opinion.

The question of what explains the character of our public policies may have to be answered in such imprecise ways: basic directions are set by the external shaping forces, but important details are determined within the policy-making system. In some of the four areas that are analyzed in Part Two, the relative weights of certain shaping factors and particular system characteristics may emerge much more clearly. It is worth stressing again, however, that this question is only part of the purpose of this inquiry. The other two leading questions, developed at greater length in the next pages, are addressed to the relationship between the problems we face and the policies we have—and what that relationship tells us about the system we have.

NOTES

1 *New York Times,* November 7, 1980, p. 1 (reporting the New York Times–CBS poll of more than 12,000 voters).

2 Arnold Heidenheimer et al., *Comparative Public Policy: The Politics of Social Choice in Europe and America* (New York: St. Martin's, 1975), p. 262.

3 For a full account, see Martha Derthick, *Policymaking for Social Security* (Washington, D.C.: Brookings, 1979).

4 This case study rests on the author's original research. For background and details, see James W. Davis and Kenneth M. Dolbeare, *Little Groups of Neighbors: The Selective Service System* (Chicago: Markham, 1968; reprinted Westport, Conn.: Greenwood Press, 1980) and National Advisory Commission on Selective Service, *In Pursuit of Equity: Who Shall Serve When Not All Serve?* (Washington, D.C.: Government Printing Office, 1967).

Part Two

Public Policy: Practices, Problems, and Alternatives

The eight chapters in this part represent the bulk of our analysis in this book. Each of the four policy areas is addressed in two chapters following essentially the same standard format. The first chapter of each pair opens with an overview of the problem area, emphasizing those key concepts and/or characteristics of the policy-making process that are crucial to understanding of policies in that area. Two subsequent sections describe what current policies are and how they evolved.

The second chapter of each pair begins with a comparision with the policies of other industrialized democracies. In each case, we shall use those comparisons most revealing of characteristics of American policies, rather than always comparing to the same set of countries. Our goal is an understanding of American policies and alternatives, not a general comparative analysis. But it makes sense to compare our policies with those of countries most like us in level of development, character of economic and political systems, and cultural traditions. Those most often used are Great Britain, France, West Germany, Canada, Japan, and Sweden, although

Italy, Denmark, the Netherlands, and Norway will appear from time to time.

Next, we explore the changing conditions and events that define the problem area today. We expect to find controversy over what the "facts" of each situation are, because the facts will be understood differently by contending groups. Responsible scholarly analysis following principles of social science will help us to some extent, but it cannot resolve all the issues. Indeed, one of our interests will be in noting the limits of social science analysis and the part necessarily played by values and priorities.

Finally, our focus will shift to the major alternatives that are urged as solutions and to the issues involved in choosing between them. Some of our attention follows the details of the alternatives, their probable consequences, and who or what would be relatively advantaged or disadvantaged thereby. But we shall also want to consider the moral and ethical, as well as the practical, aspects in the choice of alternatives. Policy choices are not just applications of purely private value preferences, in which all values are to be treated as equally appropriate. Some choices may be rationally or morally better than others. We shall try to raise such issues in each case.

Chapter 4

Managing the Economy: Strategies and Policies

The first problem in analyzing the policies involved in "managing the economy" is *conceptual* in character. What we *are* and *are not* looking at needs to be clear. The conceptual framework must tell us what basic policies *do* and how they relate to each other, and give us confidence that we have a "handle" on this subject. We *can* grasp the basic facts[1] and the essentials of policy alternatives in this area without being schooled in economics. This point is vital: understanding and choice do *not* require technical skills. Moreover, economic policies are too important to be left to the economists, even if the "experts" were not so divided and uncertain about both causes and cures for today's problems. We shall first outline what managing the economy means, and then note some special features of the policy-making system involved, before taking up current policies and how they evolved.

GOVERNMENT AND THE ECONOMY

The United States government is integrated with the "private" economy in many ways. It gets its revenues, its agenda, and many of its officials *from* that economy, mainly from the large corporation and banking sector but to some extent from the competitive smaller firms and other governments as well. It gives direction *to* that economy in a variety of purposeful and some not-so-purposeful ways. And it is also a *part* of the national economy, the largest employer and purchaser in it.

This chapter and the next focus on the goals and policies involved in the process of trying to affect the general level of prosperity in the private economy. Much of what the national government does, such as the regulation of various industries or environmental protection or monitoring affirmative action, is relegated to the background by this focus. These activities have real economic impacts, but will have relevance for us only insofar as they have *general* effects on production, prices, wages, or employment. Similarly, government purchasing, subsidy, and loan guaranteeing practices, and management of public enterprises such as the Tennessee Valley Authority (TVA), will be largely ignored except when they have economy-wide impacts.

Three goals predominate in the area of our concern. The first is *stability*, particularly of prices but also of labor and other factors affecting the economy. Inflation cheapens dollars, posing both immediate and long-term dangers to economic stability. Some benefit but more lose as the value of earnings, interest, and profits erodes. Resentments touched off by reductions in living standards can generate social and political unrest sufficient to threaten the whole structure of the economy and society. One study of the period 1963–1973, for example, found that of forty countries whose inflation reached 15 percent, thirty-eight "abolished their democratic institutions in one way or another."[2] Moreover, much economic activity—investments, trade, purchases, saving, etc.—depends on confidence that it will produce a profit or some other kind of gain. To maintain that confidence, stability in the value of the *measure* of that profit or gain (money) is essential. Without it, economic transactions of every kind will be inhibited. Strikes and other work stoppages also threaten stability and predictability in the economy: government seeks to prevent them as well.

The second major goal is economic *growth*, the expansion of total production of goods and services by the economy. Growth as an overriding goal has recently been challenged on the grounds that (1) it threatens the quality of life, both environmental and social; and (2) it is undesirable in a time when various resources, particularly fossil fuels, are on the verge of exhaustion and/or very costly. This controversy will be considered in Section III of Chapter 5. There is little doubt, however, that growth has been and still is a dominant goal of American economic policy. Orthodox thinking maintains there must be expansion to provide new jobs for an increasing population, to enable business to make profits and pay off past debts, and to have something left over to maintain military spending and provide services for the less fortunate. The need for expansion is closely linked to the imperative that profit be earned at every stage of the production/consumption process. Growth also makes possible the granting of claims of the "have-nots" without taking from the "haves." Expanding the pie is always easier than cutting its pieces differently.

The third goal is maximizing *employment*. People need jobs to earn income to satisfy their needs. Their income assures the consumer demand necessary to keep production and profitability at high levels. Without jobs, people require more governmental assistance. And sustained joblessness may lead to social and political unrest.

The three goals are closely related and mutually reinforcing. Stable prices encourage investment and growth, which assure jobs and income. Consumer demand encourages investment and production, and hence growth. The government's responsibility for achieving these goals was first declared in the Employment Act of 1946, which created the President's Council of Economic Advisers, mandated the President's annual *Economic Report*, and established the Joint Economic Committee of the Congress to consider the President's recommendations. The Full Employment and Balanced Growth Act of 1978 further elaborated on the nature of the government's responsibility with respect to these goals, requiring a number of specific short- and long-range targets to be set. Although both statutes assert that the key to prosperity is the free economic market, they also clearly imply governmental responsiblity for some degree of overall planning to achieve these goals.

Four types of policies are employed for the purpose of affecting general levels in the economy as a whole and thereby promoting the basic goals.

1 Fiscal Policies What the government does with its own revenue-raising, spending, and indebtedness comprises its fiscal policies. How much the United States government takes from the economy, and from whom, profoundly affects what people and corporations do. When the government changes the level or targets of its revenue-raising, people and corporations act differently. The ratio between revenue and spending has had powerful effects in spurring or slackening overall demand in the economy. When more revenue is raised than is spent, money has been withdrawn from the economy, demand reduced, and expansion slowed. When more is spent than is raised, money is injected into the economy, demand increased, and expansion spurred. Purposeful manipulation of fiscal policies can thus serve as an important tool for achieving the assigned goals.

2 Monetary Policies What the government does to affect the supply of money and credit in the economy comprises its monetary policies. In theory, there is a level of steady increase in money supply appropriate to the natural increase in population and a desired expansion in the production of goods and services. Increasing the supply of money and credit beyond that level induces further expansion—and probably inflation. Decreasing the supply induces contraction—and probably unemployment. Money and credit supplies can be affected by simply printing more or less money, by regulations regarding the reserves banks must keep on hand, by the level at which interest rates are set, and by direct controls on consumer credit.

3 Incomes Policies Through its income policies, the government intervenes more directly in the economy to allocate shares of the national income produced to different sectors of the economy. Wage and price controls are the principal means, and have usually been employed to stop inflation. The government normally "freezes" wages and prices (sometimes profits, rents, and interest as well) at present levels. Then it sets up ways that all requests for change can be reviewed and approved or rejected. Whatever goals the government has can be implemented directly. Historically, wage-price controls have held the line on wages more firmly than on prices, but have been followed (after their removal) by periods of catch-up inflation. As a result, they are not generally popular and are reserved for periods accepted as emergencies.

4 Market-Supplementing Polices To keep the free economic market working as well as possible and/or induce the provision of social goals as well as private ones, the government designs a variety of market-supplementing policies. This very large category of policies includes efforts to promote competition between, or otherwise control the effects of, large economic concentrations, to maintain demand through unemployment compensation and overseas sales programs, and to reduce business costs through funding research and development, providing worker training, and guaranteeing loans and mortgages. The underlying assumption is that an essentially free economic market could or does exist and its workings should result in harmonious progress and efficient use of resources. The task of government is to remove impediments and otherwise help to keep it working properly. Sometimes this means compensating for its failures, and at other times, for its successes (as when the competitive success of imported steel or cars results in calls from business and labor for increased tariffs).

"Managing the economy" is thus a process in which the national government employs four types of policies in search of three basic goals with respect to the prosperity level of the economy as a whole. It is an entirely comprehensible process, in part just *because* it is not (and cannot be) a primarily scientific or rational one. Each of these types of policies depends on accurate factual knowledge and proper timing to produce the desired effects. But the causes of inflation, unemployment, and low growth—and therefore the proper remedies—are matters of dispute. Each set of policies also has significant reallocating effects, shifting burdens and benefits from one sector of the economy to another. Who pays the costs of fighting inflation, for example, is a crucial question: jobless workers and wealthy corporate stockholders may well disagree as to the extent that either should be required to suffer. Which policy should be applied, and how, who wins and who loses, is finally decided by the political power of each side. As such, the policy choices are less technical economic questions than value judgments and power struggles. Citizens have every reason and every right to take part.

SPECIAL FEATURES OF THE POLICY-MAKING SYSTEM

In the area of *managing the economy*, the President shares responsibility with a major independent agency, the Federal Reserve Board, and with the Congress (particularly certain key committees). Three units within the executive branch itself are the President's primary means of deciding upon or seeking to implement policy in this area. The Office of Management and Budget (OMB) is part of the Executive Office of the President, the closest advisers and consultants. Its function is to review budget requests for future years with the various independent agencies and executive departments, trying to fit them into the overall totals and priorities set by the President. The hardest decisions over major program expansion or retention are usually made by the President, the President's staff, and the appointed Secretary of the appropriate department, or perhaps even in open discussion among the assembled Secretaries of all the departments (the President's Cabinet). But many far-reaching decisions are taken at the sub-Cabinet level, between budget staff members of OMB and departments or agencies. When the budget is complete, a process that normally takes a year or more, it is proposed to the Congress by the President.

Because the federal budget now involves revenues and expenditures of more than $600 billion, or 21 percent of the total Gross National Product (all goods and services produced in the country), it has profound effect on how the economy is managed by the government. The sources and objects of revenue and spending in Fiscal Year 1980 are shown in Tables 4–1 and 4–2. Clearly, such massive transfers have major consequences on the economy. Purposeful manipulation of them (at least in theory) can contribute to the United States government's ability to "manage" the economy in one or another direction.

The second executive body that the President employs is charged with

Table 4-1 U.S. Revenue Sources, Fiscal Year 1980 (current dollars)

Revenue	$ billions	% of total
Individual income taxes	244.1	47.0
Social Security taxes	136.5	26.5
Taxes on corporate profits	64.6	12.5
Excise taxes	18.3	3.5
Crude-oil excise tax	6.0	1.0
Unemployment insurance tax	15.3	3.0
Estate and gift taxes	6.4	1.0
All other revenue	28.8	5.5
Totals	$520.0	100.0

Note: Although dollar totals are rising rapidly, proportionate shares of the tax burden change only slowly over time as major legislative changes in tax laws are made.

Source: U.S. Office of Management and Budget, 1981.

formulating proposals for integrating budget decisions with assessments of economic conditions and basic goals for the economy. This is the Council of Economic Advisers (CEA), a three-member body of (usually) prominent economists appointed by the President. Its functions are to conduct studies of economic trends and make an annual report to the President proposing goals for the next years and policies to achieve them. The President in turn makes essentially the same economic report to the Congress, and sets budget proposals in the context of that analysis and prescription.

The third unit involved in presidential policy in this area is the Department of the Treasury. Decisions taken by the Secretary of the Treasury, always an appointee and usually a close adviser of the President, can affect the amount and value of money in circulation, tax policies, and the way the massive national debt is handled—all matters that have important economy-managing consequences. Normally, the heads of OMB, CEA, and Treasury agree on the basic directions that presidential policy should take. Where they do not, however, the struggle can be bitter and protracted, perhaps forcing the President to replace one or more of these key advisers in the midst of crucial policy-making processes.

Standing outside the executive branch itself, but holding full legal powers (hence the term "independent agency") over the vital area of the availability of money and credit in the economy, is the Federal Reserve Board (Fed). The Fed's Board of Directors and Chairman are appointed by the President, but for fourteen-year terms, so that an incumbent President may be forced to try to work with a Fed controlled by persons appointed long before. Normally, Fed appointees are people with long banking or other financial experience, and may see the public interest quite differently from the elected branches of government. Their powers include setting the levels at which banks belonging to the Federal Reserve System (all major banks) must maintain reserves (cash on hand to meet depositors' demands or other obligations), affecting the total amount of money in circulation, and controlling credit. The prospect of conflict with the President's economic advisers is substantial, but in this case the legal independence of the Fed is such that the President may be forced to accept a compromise or see his policies undercut by Fed actions.

Much of the real decision-making power over how the economy is to be managed lies with the Congress, particularly with respect to the final character of the government's annual budget. The budget submitted by the President in January of each year, after preparation by OMB in the manner just described, is often the real focus of Congress' own decision making—and likely to become the major way in which Congress makes itself felt in national public policy generally.

Congress acts in two stages, as we noted in the previous chapters: the "authorization" process and the "appropriations" process. In the authorization process, it enacts legislation establishing new programs, agencies, or requirements. Here, the "standing," or subject-area, committees hold hearings and bring forth a bill reflecting a compromise among the interests represented on that committee. In the subsequent appropriations process, however, Congress makes the harder and more consequential decisions about how much money shall be granted to actually carry out such functions. These decisions are made by the Appropriations Committees in each house, which may reflect wholly different interests or ideologies from those represented on the standing committees. By decisions over the amount of money appropriated for each activity of the government, and through amendments specifying in detail for what purposes the money may and may not be spent, Congress effectively asserts its will over that of the President. Unless willing to veto the appropriations act and see the usually long process start all over again, the President is obliged to live with such modification.

Two major consequences flow from this congressional power to set spending levels and specify the purposes for which the money may be used. One is that the Congress tends, by the end of the fiscal year, to appropriate more money than the President originally proposed and thereby to upset the revenue-expenditure relationship initially projected. Where the budget was at first balanced (spending equal to estimated receipts), it is thrown into deficit (spending greater than receipts). Where it was at first expected to show a small deficit, it ends with a much larger one.

Together with the President's tendency to be excessively optimistic in

Table 4-2   U.S. Government Spending Patterns, Fiscal Year 1980 (current dollars)

Object	Millions	% of total
Defense	135.9	23.4
Social Security benefits	117.1	20.0
Interest on debt	74.8	13.0
Medicare and other health	58.2	10.0
Public assistance, food stamps, and other aid	36.7	6.0
Education, manpower, social services	30.8	5.0
Aid to veterans	21.2	4.0
Aid to transportation, commerce	27.2	4.6
Civil service retirement	14.7	2.6
Unemployment compensation	18.0	3.0
International, economic, and military	10.7	1.9
Energy	6.3	1.0
Commercial and regional development	10.1	2.0
General revenue sharing	6.8	1.0
Rivers, dams, natural resources	8.3	1.2
Science, space technology	5.7	1.0
Pollution control	5.5	1.0
Aid to agriculture	4.8	0.8
Post Office subsidy	1.7	0.3
All other spending, less earnings and interagency transfers	- 14.9	
Total Spending	$579.6	101.8

Source: Derived from U.S. Office of Management and Budget, 1981

estimating revenues (so as to maintain or expand politically popular programs and still show the "fiscal conservatism" of a balanced budget), this congressional practice puts steady upward pressure on national spending, deficits, and debt. It comes about even though the first congressional reaction to a President's proposed budget is often one of determination to cut it. Senators and representatives rally to the defense of programs that the President has proposed to cut, or to the pet projects for which they have worked before or that benefit constituents. New problems arise or new legislation is passed during the year after the first appropriations bills have been passed, and a variety of "supplementary appropriations" are enacted that add steadily to the total actually appropriated.

The newly created Congressional Budget Committees have sought to rationalize the first appropriations process by setting goals for each subcategory of appropriations. Previously, several appropriations bills, each applying only to one component of the total budget for all government spending, would be sent to the full house from its Appropriations Committee in such a way that members would not know the full spending total until the last bill had been passed. By relating each appropriations bill to a target total, it was hoped that Congress could gain better control over its own spending. But the new Budget Committees have not yet been able to assert such controls, and the Congress as a whole has yet to meet its own timetables for setting goals and/or for consideration of totals and components.

The other consequence of congressional power over government spending is that one- or two-member subcommittees of the Appropriations Committees of each house become specially influential over appropriations for particular sectors of government activity. An Appropriations Committee, whether of about fifty members (House) or twenty members (Senate) has a massive problem of understanding where some $600 billion of federal money is going and for what it is being spent. On the average, each member of the larger House committee would be responsible for tracing the present and possible alternative uses of $10 billion. Out of necessity, these committees divide such labor, assigning major areas to such one- or two-person subcommittees. Normally, the full Committee follows the recommendations of those who have studied their subfields intensively, and then the houses follow their committees. There are exceptions, of course, for certain high-visibility or controversial programs. But by and large the necessity of specialization means that one or two members of each house, and the interests or ideology they represent, become specially determinative of the practices and priorities of major bureaus, agencies, or programs.

There is little the President can do to contain spending or modify its purposes once Congress has appropriated the money. President Nixon sought to "impound" (set aside and not spend) money appropriated by the then-Democratic Congress for purposes of which he disapproved. But later congressional action clarified the respective institutional powers in this respect so as to oblige the executive branch to carry out congressional purposes in almost all cases.

Another factor that takes the total of government spending out of the immediate control of both President *and* Congress is the nature of budgetary "entitlements." These are rights that people or corporations have been given in previous legislation which automatically come into play when certain specified conditions occur. If unusually good weather conditions or new fertilizer should produce greater than average crop yields, for example, government price-support mechanisms would be triggered and

Table 4-3   Major U.S. Government Units with Fiscal Responsibilities

The Executive Branch

1. The President: Establishes final budget-proposal levels in annual budget presented to Congress. Receives and passes to Congress the report on the economy from the Council of Economic Advisers.
2. Office of Management and Budget: Acts on behalf of President to conform agency budget requests and appropriations to program standards.
3. Council of Economic Advisers: Advises President regularly and in formal annual report of economic trends and appropriate policy responses.
4. Department of the Treasury: Implements President's policies in credit, borrowing, currency, and tax fields.

Independent Agencies

1. The Federal Reserve System: Controls amount of money in circulation, interest rates, member-bank reserve requirements, and consumer credit.

The Congress

1. Joint Economic Committee: Reviews President's Economic Report, recommends congressional action.
2. Standing (Policy Area) Committees: Recommend to respective houses the authorization of expenditures for various programs.
3. Budget Committees: Develop overall budget ceilings to be recommended to each house, to serve as guidelines for later program appropriations actions.
4. Appropriations Committees: Decide upon levels of funding to be recommended to respective houses for effectuation of authorized programs.
5. Ways and Means Committee (House) and Finance Committee (Senate):   The former initiates all revenue-raising bills and sends them to the House floor; the latter recommends Senate response to House actions.
6. The Congressional Budget Office: Serves as neutral source of analysis of budget proposals and consequences of various present policies and possible alternatives.

billions of dollars added to the expenditure side of the budget. Similar entitlements exist in the area of civil service and veterans' pensions and social welfare programs.

When the President has made his economic report, the congressional Joint Economic Committee reviews it and tries to translate its understanding of economic prospects into broad goals for congressional action. The budget is only one of these. Others include monetary policy goals, with respect to which the Congress (or its financial committee members) may want to put pressure on the Fed, or matters requiring new legislation. The latter might include tariff measures affecting imports, for example, or standby authority for the President to impose wage and price controls.

In identifying policy-making units in this area, we have only touched on the most visible public bodies. Many other congressional committees, independent agencies, and presidential staff positions might also have been included. Outside of government, many private organizations (the Business Roundtable, the Committee for Economic Development, the AFL-CIO) and individuals (key bankers, leading economists, former government officials) play important parts. The manner in which the economy is managed is so vital that there are many contestants for policy-making influence. How well they succeed can be seem from analysis of existing policies.

I CURRENT POLICIES

The policy problems of the 1970s led to the coining of a new word: "stagflation." The term expresses the simultaneous presence of low growth, high unemployment, and inflation. An unprecedented combination, stagflation challenges the basic assumptions that lie behind fiscal and monetary policy management. In the past, high economic growth, low unemployment, and inflation *or* low growth, high unemployment, and deflation had occurred together. Fiscal and monetary policy is designed to promote or prevent each set *as a unit*, and cannot deal with them separately.

But inflation persisted throughout the last decade, reaching 13.5 percent in 1980 and totaling more than 100 percent over the ten-year period.[3] It was barely slowed by the mild recession of 1970 or the more severe one of 1974–1975. And inflation was accompanied by unemployment levels of from 5 percent to 8 percent, equally unprecedented since the immediate postwar adjustments of 1946. In the 1980s, 8 percent unemployment by official government figures means that about 9 million people are out of work. This figure, however, understates the impact of unemployment in some important ways. First, the official figures do not count people who have given up looking for work, are working only part-time, or are in jobs below the levels for which they are qualified. Second, the total of the unemployed is made up of different people from month to month, so that well over 9 million people would be out of work at some time during the year. Even more people face the day-to-day prospect of losing their jobs. Finally, some groups within the population feel the effects generated by the unemployment far more than others. Blue-collar workers are hit much harder than higher-status workers. Women averaged 50 percent higher unemployment rates than men. Blacks' unemployment is normally double that of whites. Younger people are particularly affected, with black teenagers reaching unemployment levels of 35 percent and more.[4]

As if the twin problems of inflation and unemployment were not enough, the decade also saw the emergence of the Organization of Petroleum Exporting Countries (OPEC) as a force capable of driving the price of oil up from $2.70 per barrel in 1969 to $34 in 1980. The value of the dollar dropped precipitously abroad, and the United States began to run a continuing deficit in its balance of trade with other countries. Partly as a result of these developments, the crucial but fragile system of international finance and money exchanges was endangered. The task of managing the American economy in this combined context was as difficult as it was important. Not only must inflation be controlled and new jobs found, but both had to be accomplished amidst continuing danger of sustained recession or depression.

The Nixon Administration

President Nixon's administration had the distinction of deploying the greatest variety of economy-managing policies in this period. Both fiscal and monetary policies were used in an effort to control the nearly 5 percent inflation inherited from the 1960s, but modest budget surpluses and tightened money supply succeeded only in pushing unemployment up to 6 percent. These conditions were joined in 1971 by deficits in the balance of payments between imports and exports and declining value of the U.S. dollar in relation to other world currencies. This led to a sudden use of incomes policies. A ninety-day wage and price freeze was ordered by the President under already-existing legislative authority. After the ninety days, procedures were established to permit rises, if they could be justified. The controls remained in effect until 1973. At the same time, fiscal and monetary policies were highly stimulative. Budget deficits were incurred; taxes were cut; and the money supply was expanded briskly.

Reduction of inflation to less than 4 percent during the period of controls and a spurt in growth and employment resulted. 1972 was a boom year. But as soon as controls were removed, inflation jumped back to levels approaching three times those before—14 percent. Once again, fiscal and monetary policies turned restrictive. By the end of 1973, growth had slowed precipitously and unemployment was back around 6 percent. Oil shortages and price rises contributed to the general economic decline. But inflation continued high even as the economy headed into the steepest recession since the Great Depression of the 1930s. The official definition of a recession is decline in the total output of goods and services for two consecutive quarters of a year. In 1974, total output after inflation dropped for three consecutive quarters, but inflation remained at "double-digit" levels throughout.

The Ford Administration

President Ford saw inflation as the priority problem, but sought initially to cope with it through voluntary means. The recession helped to bring inflation down to 6 percent by mid-1975, a level still higher than that preceding the government-induced expansion of 1972–1973. But the costs in unemployment were high: in early 1975, more than 8 percent of the labor force were without jobs. With this number of people unemployed and growth slow in picking up, inflation dipped below 5 percent in 1976. Fiscal policies were highly stimulative in both 1975 and 1976, with record-setting peacetime budget deficits.

The Carter Administration

President Carter initially faced another period of expansion, and with it the steady rise of inflation to not only double-digit levels (1979) but an annual rate of 18 percent for the first three months of 1980. Unemployment hovered near 6 percent, however, despite budget deficits not much below those of the Ford years. As inflation climbed in 1978 and 1979, monetary policy turned more and more restrictive. In particular, interest rates and bank reserve requirements were raised and credit limited. By 1980, this policy had produced record high-interest rates for all kinds of loans in the country. The lack of money for home mortgages meant that the housing industry, and with it a good share of the lumber industry, went into sharp decline. Unemployment rose again, and the economy headed into another recession.

The policy dilemma should be clear. Inflation seems built into the current economy. Though its causes are hotly disputed, as we shall see in Section II of Chapter 5, few doubt its dangerous character. But none of the remedies available have as much effect on inflation as they do on increasing unemployment and inhibiting economic growth. Increasingly deep recessions with attendant suffering appear to be the only means, and then inadequate ones, of controlling inflation. The dilemma is mirrored in passages only a few sentences apart in President Carter's *Economic Report* of 1979:[5]

> The corrosive effects of inflation eat away at the ties that bind us together as a people. . . . We will *not* try to wring inflation out of our economic system by pursuing policies designed to bring about a recession. That would be unfair. It would put the heaviest burden of fighting inflation on those who can least afford to bear it.

Unfair, probably, but nevertheless precisely what policies later that same year sought to do.

In looking at what policies are used, we should not overlook some important aspects that are not always explicit. For example, an incumbent President may turn to expansionary policies more by the calendar than by economic analysis. The prospects of coming elections in 1972, 1976, and 1980 clearly influenced policies and timing in the eighteen months prior to each. The goal has always been to have the greatest possible appearance of prosperity as November nears, even if later inflation is likely.

Not to be overlooked is the part played by the Congress. Congress is usually reluctant to vote new taxes or reduce spending for favorite projects, particularly in election years. Much presidential authority depends on prior legislative grants, which may simply not be forthcoming. For example, President Carter did not have power to order wage and price freezes in 1979 or 1980, even if he had wanted to use it. And everything the Congress does, particularly reconstructing the President's proposed budget (and thereby setting its own fiscal policy) normally takes substantial time.

In our final category of market-supplementing policies, the 1970s saw a long swing of the pendulum from enactment of new environmental, safety, and antidiscrimination standards to their deferral or reduction and even elimination of some other regulations of long standing. Policies concerning free trade (the opportunity for foreign-made goods to be sold in the American market without special taxes or quotas being imposed) were generally permissive of competition—with some important exceptions.

In the early years of the decade, Congress passed a number of prohibitions against air pollution and other forms of environmental degradation, and created the Environmental Protection Agency (EPA) to administer them. New requirements for safety at work were established, and the Occupational Safety and Health Administration (OSHA) created to monitor them. New requirements for "affirmative action" to reduce discriminatory practices against women and minorities were implemented by various federal departments and agencies.

By 1977, however, continued inflation gained a sympathetic hearing for business claims that such standards had gone too far and were either impossible or too costly to meet. Automobile pollution and safety standards were deferred; strip-mining limits were eased; and work-safety rules loosened. Challenges were mounted to the OSHA itself, and to the regulatory powers of the Federal Trade Commission (FTC), on the grounds that excessive costs (and thus inflationary pressure) were being imposed on the corporations and other businesses involved.

The late 1970s also saw major pressures from both business and labor, particularly in the automobile and steel industries, for restrictions on imports into the American market. The Carter administration responded by seeking voluntary limits on the quantity of goods shipped by Japanese manufacturers to the United States. The danger usually seen in taking stronger "protectionist" action is that other countries will retaliate by barring American exports from their markets. Extensive protectionism can sharply curtail trade and thus production and employment; it is generally thought to have been one of the major factors behind the Great Depression of the 1930s. And, of course, protectionist tariffs, quotas, or prohibitions are *supportive* of an *American* market only in the sense of helping producers at the cost of increased prices to the consumer. And they are distinct *denials* of an *international* market.

The Reagan Administration

President Reagan's administration opened with perhaps the greatest shift of direction in regard to managing the economy since the early days of Franklin Roosevelt's New Deal in the 1930s. It came to office facing inflation at a rate of 13 percent, low economic growth of just over 1 percent, 7 percent unemployment, and a federal budget whose expenditures had been rising at the rate of 16 percent per year from 1979 to 1981 and seemed headed out of sight. President Reagan decided to focus on promoting economic growth as the route to curing inflation and reducing unemployment, but to do so by placing primary reliance on the private economy. Multiple incentives for business expansion and investment, and a major effort to curb "inflation psychology" (the belief that inflation is likely to continue, and consequently the practice of buying now in order to avoid higher prices later, which of course increases demand and fuels inflation in a self-fulfilling manner) were built into a three-part package of actions and legislative proposals to the Congress.

The first part consisted of reductions in the rate of increases in federal expenditures that had been projected because of the provisions of existing statutes and prospective inflation. The rate of increase was to be slowed to 6 percent in fiscal year 1982 (the year ending September 30, 1982) by means of cutting $41.4 billion from the budget previously proposed by President Carter (see Table 4-4). Certain basic social programs (the essential "safety net" for needy and deserving people, in the administration's eyes), such as Social Security retirement benefits, Medicare, and

Table 4-4   The Reagan Spending Cuts, Revenue, and the Elusive Balanced Budget (in billions of current dollars)

Fiscal Years	1982	1983	1984
Total spending	$695.5	$733.1	$771.6
reduction below Carter estimate	41.4	79.7	104.4
Total revenue	650.5	710.2	772.1
Deficit/surplus	−45.0	−22.9	+0.5

Source: White House Fact Sheet, February 18, 1981, as reported in *New York Times*, February 19, 1981, p. A11.

veterans' benefits, were left untouched. But nearly every other area of government activity was cut back, sometimes sharply. The deepest cuts were focused on social programs such as federally funded jobs, education, food stamps, school lunches, and long-term unemployment benefits. Military spending, however, was slated for substantial increases.

The second part was a proposal for major reductions in business and personal income taxes. Businesses were to receive accelerated depreciation allowances as a means of spurring investment in new plants, technology, and other ways of increasing productivity and expanding output. Personal income taxes were to be reduced by 10 percent at all levels each year for a period of three years, in hopes that such savings would find their way into new investment in productive capacity. Substantial losses in government revenue were anticipated from such reductions, with accompanying increased federal budget deficits, but the administration argued that the economic expansion likely to follow such cuts would produce new revenues that would in time more than make up the difference.

The third part was an effort to reduce the burden and cost to business of federal regulations, particularly those involving health care, the environment, and energy. This was to be achieved by cutting the budgets of regulatory agencies, postponing or abandoning new regulations, and appointing a Presidential Task Force on Regulatory Relief to review and simplify or eliminate existing regulations.

Congressional action is essential to implement any proposed federal budget, change the tax laws, or modify provisions of existing laws that give businesses, agriculture, or individuals legal claims to federal financial aid. Orthodox fiscal conservatives of both parties, and many Democrats in the House (where the Democratic party remained in the majority), were opposed to the tax cut and its implications for budget deficits and inflation. Most of the rest of President Reagan's program, however, was generally accepted with only minor changes. Because these sweeping proposals amount to a major new direction of government policy in the 1980s, we shall take up their broader implications in our later section on alternatives for the future.

II THE ORIGINS OF CURRENT POLICIES

The policies of the 1970s, and in a certain way the Reagan program as well, owe their character to two parallel lines of development in American history. One is the practical experience of the twentieth-century growth of the role of government, both as a taxing-spending factor in the economy and as the vehicle for serving the needs of a nationalizing private economy and its citizens. The other is the dramatic shift from 1936 to 1946 in the theoretical perspective on the proper role of government in the economy.

In one of the great upheavals in American political-economic thinking, the principles of the British economist John Maynard Keynes entered the mainstream of American thought and provided a new rationale for government management of the economy. We shall look at each of these lines of development briefly and then examine their combined impact in the economic context of the relatively stable and prosperous postwar period (1946–1968).

The Growth of the Role of Government

From the earliest days of the Republic, the national government has played a significant role in supporting the "private" economy. During Washington's first administration, Secretary of the Treasury Alexander Hamilton initiated a comprehensive program for stabilizing the value of money, establishing a national market, and promoting the growth of manufacturing. As capitalism and industrialization took hold in the nineteenth century, however, the official ideology of *laissez faire* ("let alone") developed as a rationale for nonintervention in what was taken to be the naturally self-regulating economic market. In fact, the federal government was still promoting various nascent industries by elaborate tariff protections, giving lands to the railroads, and vigorously helping to put down strikes. And the national Supreme Court developed new doctrines in the 1880s and 1890s to enforce laissez faire principles against state governments which sought to limit business practices in what they thought to be the public interest.

What distinguishes the twentieth century is: (1) the expansion of the government's own size and direct activities; and (2) the expansion of government management of the economy even beyond Hamilton's aspirations. At the turn of the century, the national government was still an inconsequential collection of soldiers, clerks, and customs collectors. It required only $587 million per year in tax revenues, employed only 239,000 persons, and regularly ran budget surpluses. By contrast, the United States government in 1979 raised $456 *billion* in taxes, employed 4,814,000 persons, and ran a budget of $493 billion. One out of every fifteen people in the population, and one out of every seven employed persons, worked for some level of government—national, state, or local.[6] Even more people worked for industries that in part or in full depended on government contracts.

Much of this new activity is attributable to the development of a much larger military capability and the assumption of new social services, such as education and welfare. But a good share of the expansion came from the assumption of new regulatory responsibilities requiring oversight and enforcement personnel. The Federal Trade Commission, for example, was created in 1914 to monitor business practices and keep competition free and fair. By the late 1970s, fourteen major new statutes and countless amendments had added new responsibilities and thousands of employees to the agency. Sixty analogous new agencies had been created, and a wide variety of new regulatory functions assigned to existing executive branch departments and their bureaus as well.

The pressures leading to this sort of expansion came from two different directions: the power and practices of the regulatory agencies represent a kind of trade-off between them. One source of pressure was the vigor of social reform movements.[7] Scarcely had the radical demands of the agrarian Populists been deflected by the election of 1896 and its aftermath than two new movements developed in the early twentieth century. One was the rise of the Socialist party of Eugene Debs, with its call for comprehensive reconstruction of the American social order. The other was the principally urban and middle-class movement that gave its name to the period, the Progressives. Both movements voiced moral outrage and resentment against the hardships, corruption, and open greed that seemed to characterize the workings of the new industrial economy. Workers in particular suffered from low wages, long hours, and unsafe working conditions. At the same time, "muckraking" journalists publicized unsanitary conditions in food industries and a variety of other profiteering excesses on the part of large corporations.

The second source of pressure for new government regulation was the large corporations and banks themselves.[8] They needed stability and predictability in the national market, which could be provided only by overall monitoring of competitive practices and financial arrangements. And the national government was the only source of the powers to accomplish these ends. Besides, the corporate-banking sector of the economy could not take the risk that Socialists and/or Progressives might use the combination of popular protest and government inaction to gain power and implement drastic reform.

The result of the congruence of these potentially conflicting interests was a series of statutes creating new government responsibilities. The reformers saw them as welcome steps in the direction of popular government control over corporate excesses. The leading corporations and banks, which had participated in drafting the statutes, gaining their major goals in the process, saw them as helping to rationalize the economy and to mute public resentments. The Federal Reserve System, for example, was established in 1913, after the banking panic of 1907 and protracted negotiations among bankers had led to a bill that the President and Congress could accept. The System created national supervisory authority not unlike that proposed decades before by the Populists. But the management of the System was almost entirely in the hands of private bankers, and it had legal independence from both President and Congress.

The process by which these first regulatory statutes came into being is important because it established a kind of model which later policy making would follow. Reform pressures and big business needs combine to produce new government responsibilities. The appearance of reform and popular government control may not be matched by the reality because (1) the new policies would not have been enacted without big business concurrence; (2) their substance is acceptable to big business, though quite possibly not to the smaller and more competitive businesses of the economy; and (3) over time, policies as implemented become more and more consistent with the needs of big business. Two reform periods, the Progressive Era and the New Deal, reflected this model and set up the framework of today's government-business "partnership." Each was followed by a World War, in which the need to mobilize resources provided an opportunity for developing the partnership further. Growing integration of the (expanding) national government with the corporate-banking part of the economy, and mutual dependence of each upon the other, resulted. Conflict between reformers and business is still characteristic, with the balance shifting from one side to the other on any given issue.

The Rise of Keynesian Principles

Before the late 1930s, American thinking assumed that the economic market, if left free of government intervention, would automatically provide full employment of people and resources. Government was viewed as a parasitical drain, merely withdrawing funds otherwise productively spent by private hands. And each regulatory function had to be justified independently. The emergency measures of the early Depression years did not imply revision of this basic perspective. But the sustained suffering of the Depression years, with their 25 percent unemployment rates, business failures, and evident inability of the economy to restore itself, prepared the way for dramatic change.

John Maynard Keynes was a British economist teaching at Cambridge University when he published *The General Theory of Employment, Interest and Money* in 1936.[9] Looking at the world around him, he argued that the economic market could reach equilibrium at *any* level of employment, including high *un*employment.[10] He denied, again with strong factual support, that unemployment was understandable only as *frictional* (the result of technological change leaving workers temporarily out of jobs until they learned new skills or moved) or *willful* (the deliberate choice of lazy people). Instead, he saw unemployment as *systemic*, produced by the way that the capitalist economic system necessarily worked when demand and investment were low.

Demand and investment are closely linked. Demand is created when workers have jobs and thus income with which to purchase the goods and services they need. If some people have more than enough money to fulfill their immediate consumption needs, they may hold the remainder as savings. They also make choices as to whether or not to invest their savings. Those choices determine the level of investment—and thus the extent to which new jobs (and workers' incomes) will become available. Their investment choice is based on the future expectation of profit, which in turn depends on the level of future demand.

Both demand and investment must be present to make for full employment of people and resources. Each depends on the other. But investment is more variably subject to human choice, depending on expectations about others' investment intentions and future demand levels. The existence of basic food, clothing, and shelter needs, combined with the possession of income, generates demand. As people make more income, they tend to spend somewhat less than all of it on immediate consumption; however, at all but the highest levels, income translates consistently into demand.

As the more variable factor, and as the key to initiating multiplied effects upon national income and employment, Keynes focused on investment. Investment has multiplier effects because new jobs produce demand, which creates more new jobs, and so on, throughout the economy. Each dollar invested in some job-creating productive enterprise might eventually result in an additional two dollars in national income. *Real* investment (factories and machines, not stocks, bonds, or other speculative paper transactions) had to be promoted in order to restore prosperity.

These principles run directly counter to the idea of government as something outside and basically irrelevant, if not harmful, to the private economy. Instead, government becomes central, with a greatly expanded, purposeful, and legitimate role in managing the economy. Investment might be promoted by official exhortation or assurances about a "good business climate" and future profits. Or it could be induced by favorable allowances and deductions in the tax laws, and/or by forms of taxation on the uninvested portion of savings. More directly, interest rates could be managed so as to promote real investment.

But the most effective route to expanded investment and income was public works financed by government deficits. In Keynes' eyes, this was far superior because, unlike its apparent equivalent of commensurate reduction of taxes, it put the whole of the new investment into socially determined uses. Tax reductions might not all be used for productive real investment. In any event, increased private control might direct funds into production of less socially desirable goods and services. Direct investment in public works, for economy-spurring purposes, symbolizes how sharply Keynes's principles constrasted with the prior laissez faire thinking.

The Keynesian analysis primarily addressed public policy in a time of low investment, demand, and employment. But it could be, and was, generalized into a rationale for government action at any stage of the business cycle. Particularly in the intellectual background of the Employment Act of 1946, a set of routine strictures emerged in the form that was described on 61–63.

But the dominance of the Keynesian rationale for such use of national government policies is not owed to its success in the latter stages of the Depression. Instead, it is owed to the dramatic demonstration of the prosperity-inducing efficacy of government deficits and spending during World War II. "Public works" investments of billions of dollars in war material and "public employment" of more than 11 million people in the armed forces built an unequalled economic engine. Thus ended the worst American depression—all in validation of Keynes' arguments if not his preferences.

The other factor in establishing Keynesianism was its success in capturing the minds of most American economists. As the new orthodoxy of a rising generation of scholars and activists, it became firmly embedded in public policy at least through the mid-1970s. As government efforts to control inflation were increasingly seen to fail, however, the older free market doctrines were revived and major questions raised about the efficacy of Keynesianism. The issues were not entirely clear, because economists disagreed on the causes of this apparent failure—whether it lay in a lack of strong and consistent government action along Keynesian lines despite political pressures, the special nature of the unprecedented stagflation, or the inapplicability of Keynesianism itself amidst public demand for a profusion of social services.

In his speech announcing his economic program, President Reagan declared his intent to abandon use of government taxing power for social purposes, saying: "The taxing power of government must be used to provide revenues for legitimate government purposes. It must not be used to regulate the economy or bring about social change. We've tried that and surely must be able to see it doesn't work."[11] This led some observers to declare that Reagan sought "to repeal the Keynesian revolution."[12]

But there was no question of Reagan's intent to spur investment by means of changing the tax laws to allow new business depreciation allowances and reduce personal income taxes, much as Kennedy had done in his administration under the Keynesian label. And it seemed unlikely that the massive revenue/expenditure patterns of a government committed to military spending, Social Security, and other social economic functions amounting to at least 20 percent of the total GNP could ever *not* have powerful impact on the economy. The federal budget remains a vital tool for accomplishing a President's purposes (see Table 4-5), as do the tax laws and economic regulations. What was really different about the Reagan

Table 4-5　U.S. Presidents and Budget Deficits, 1930–1980 (billions of current dollars)

President	Total years in office	Total deficits	Total deficits as % of GNP	Largest deficit and year
Hoover	4	$ 5.1	1.7%	$ 2.7, 1932
Roosevelt	12	197.0	14.0	54.9, 1943
Truman	8	4.4	0.2	6.5, 1953
Eisenhower	8	15.8	0.5	12.9, 1959
Kennedy	2	11.9	1.1	7.1, 1962
Johnson	6	42.0	0.9	25.2, 1968
Nixon	5	68.7	1.2	23.4, 1972
Ford	2.25	124.6	3.6	79.4, 1976
Carter	4	180.5	2.1	59.0, 1980

Source: Derived from U.S. Department of Commerce data reported in *U.S. News and World Report,* January 19, 1981, pp. 58–59.

program was its free market rhetoric and the sharp change in direction of the deliberate value choices involved in decisions about who or what interests are to be favored or burdened, and how much, by federal government spending, revenue-raising, and other activities. Business had clearly won a major victory, but the implications for economic theory lay well in the future.

Public Policies in the Postwar Context, 1946–1968

The United States emerged from World War II as the dominant economic power in the world. But this fact was not fully appreciated by many thinkers concerned that peace would bring a return of the Depression. Initially, policy focused on establishing mechanisms for implementing Keynesian principles to prevent depressions. In essence, this meant assuring jobs, with government (if necessary) as the "employer of last resort." The Employment Act of 1946, previously described, provided the vehicle. However, conservative opposition to the act stopped it short of committing government policy to full employment. Instead, the act committed the government to such support of the private economy as would maximize the number of jobs available. But in practice, with an established process of annual review and recommendation to Congress, the assumption of responsibility by government was clear.

The anticipated slide into depression did not occur. After a sharp jump during the postwar adjustment of 1946, prices stabilized. Growth was steady if unspectacular, and employment remained relatively high. The Korean War briefly pushed inflation, growth, and employment, but after the readjustment recession of 1953, all three returned to 1950 levels. The Eisenhower administration saw inflation as a first-priority danger, and followed fiscal and monetary policies that controlled it effectively. Those same policies, however, resulted in restrained growth, unemployment at rates of 4 percent to 6 percent, and short recessions in 1957 and 1960.[13]

In the meantime, the economies of Western Europe and Japan, many of them rebuilt with American public and private investment, were establishing a better record. Growth was much faster, unemployment much lower, and prices remained roughly stable. Moreover, the American edge in productivity, technology, and scientific capability seemed to be diminishing. The new factories of Western Europe and Japan were cutting competitively into American sales, both at home and abroad. The greater profitability of foreign investment, chiefly in Europe but also in the Third World, was drawing American capital overseas. The Soviet launching of the first earth satellite in 1957 seemed to threaten the end of American scientific superiority as well.

All of these factors gave rise to a sense of the need for renewed government leadership. But it was not until the Kennedy administration took office that a coherent development program was instituted. This took the form of a series of measures straight out of the Keynesian textbook. First were investment tax credits, soon followed by increased depreciation allowances that made more profits available for investment. Regular budget deficits were incurred, and monetary growth steadily expanded. But the centerpiece of the program was a large tax reduction enacted in the face of a growing federal budget deficit. Proposed by Kennedy but not enacted until 1964, the tax cut was designed to remove potential tax limits on the then-expanding economy and let the demand and investment money thereby kept in private hands continue to provide pressure for expansion.

This vigorous application of Keynesian principles met with apparent success, at least for seven or eight years. The nation's Gross National Product nearly doubled in this period, while unemployment was cut in half as more than 10 million new jobs were created. At the same time, prices remained remarkably stable: from 1961 to 1965, the inflation rate was a mere 1.3 percent per year. To be sure, the beginning of government spending for the Vietnam War in 1965 and 1966 provided some of the impetus, but much seemed to have been achieved by deliberate stimulation of the private economy. The status of Keynesian principles was never higher. The focus of concern seemed to have left depressions forever for the more complacent task of maintaining the boom.

In retrospect, however, the year 1968 marked the end of what had been perhaps the most sustained period of relative prosperity in American history. Inflation, spurred in part by the Johnson administration's decision to finance an unpopular war through expanding the money supply and incurring large deficits, began to exceed 4 percent. New taxes were both late in being proposed and delayed in enactment. The drainage of American gold reserves and the rise of balance-of-payments deficits helped to undermine the value of the dollar. American manufacturers found the competitive challenge of European and Japanese producers more and more difficult to meet, in both domestic and foreign markets. And the continuing involvement (and lack of military success) in Vietnam caused both allies and Third World countries to be more independent and wary of American leadership in all things.

The context and conditions for economy-managing policies were clearly changing. Whether they would still permit—and respond to—the familiar or any other remedies remained to be seen. Much of the answer, as we shall see, depended on the *reasons* for the new condition of high inflation–high unemployment–low growth, or "stagflation." And the rest of the answer depended on what priorities people preferred to see implemented in their society.

NOTES

1 The basic data are available from a few authoritative sources readily available to all Americans. These include the *Economic Report of the President* (published annually in January) and the *Statistical Abstract of the United States* (published annually). Both are for sale by the Government Printing Office in Washington, D.C., and are stocked in United States Department of Commerce offices in major cities around the country. Both contain useful international comparisons. For further analysis of contemporary trends in the United States and among the European countries, Canada, and Japan, the best source is the Organization for Economic Cooperation and Development's semiannual *Economic Outlook*, published in July and December and available from the OECD's Washington, D.C., office. The day-to-day policy actions of the United States Government can be followed readily in *Congressional Quarterly*'s Weekly Edition. These sources may be supplemented by following the business pages of the *New York Times*, particularly on Sundays, and using *Fortune* and *Business Week* magazines to be alerted to other data developments. All of these sources are available in libraries in even the smallest cities and colleges, with the possible exception of the *OECD Economic Outlook*. But it should be stressed that the *data*—the numbers in tabular form—are what are generally reliable; interpretations, conclusions, and forecasts are notably subject to assumptions, biases, etc., with which the reader may or may not agree. Even the way certain measures are defined or constructed must be examined skeptically on occasion, as we shall note in the chapter. In illustration of the point made in this note, note, all data in this chapter (with only one or two exceptions) are drawn from these sources. Other materials are listed in the bibliography.

2 *New York Times*, February 3, 1980, sec. 3, p. 1.

3 Unless otherwise noted, data in the following paragraphs are drawn from the *Economic Report of the President* (Washington, D.C.: Government Printing Office, annually). The *Report* is actually prepared by the Council of Economic Advisers and its staff.

4 *Economic Report of the President* and *New York Times*, February 3, 1980, sec. 3, p. 1.

5 *Economic Report of the President*, 1979, p. 7.

6 Data in this and the prior two sentences are drawn from the *Statistical Abstract of the United States*, various years.

7 Richard Hofstadter, *The Age of Reform* (New York: Knopf, 1955).

8 See Gabriel Kolko, *The Triumph of Conservatism* (New York: Free Press, 1963), and James Weinstein, *The Corporate Ideal in the Liberal State* (Boston: Beacon Press, 1964).

9 John Maynard Keynes, *The General Theory of Employment, Interest and Money* (New York: Harcourt, Brace, 1936).

10 For the best contextual interpretation of Keynes' arguments, see Robert Lekachman, *The Age of Keynes* (New York: Random House, 1966), from which this section is drawn.

11 *New York Times*, February 19, 1981, p. 1.

12 Ibid., February 20, 1981, p. 1.

13 Unless otherwise indicated, all data in this section are drawn from the *Economic Report of the President*, various years.

Chapter 5

Managing the Economy: Crisis and Conflict

This chapter focuses on the deepening economic crisis of the late 1970s and early 1980s, and on the range of alternatives urged to cope with it. Not surprisingly, analysts disagree sharply about the causes—and therefore the cures—for the worst inflation the United States has ever known. Basic values and ideology appear to be as important as any factual analysis in shaping understanding of the problem and what to do about it. Moreover, the combination of inflation and unemployment, or "stagflation," was a worldwide phenomenon. We shall survey the experiences of other countries before exploring the economic crisis in the United States and the alternative policies among which choices must be made.

I UNITED STATES POLICY IN COMPARATIVE CONTEXT

In general, the government of each of the other industrial democracies plays a larger role in economy management than does the United States government. There are individual differences, of course, but in one way or another government involvement is greater. At least until 1973, their success in achieving growth and employment without inflation was greater. After 1973, all industrialized countries, including the United States, began to experience similar problems. None seemed able to handle what began to be recognized as a growing crisis. We shall first look briefly at the other countries' approaches to economy-managing and then at their periods of prosperity (1946–1973) and crisis (1973–present).

Approaches to Managing the Economy

The greater economic impacts of the other governments stem from both their own taxing, spending, and entrepreneurial activities and from their guidance of their private economies. Almost uniformly, there is more *government ownership* of key sectors of the economy and higher *government spending* than in the United States. Figure 5-1 summarizes the government's share of the economy for most of the major countries. Only Japan approaches the United States in extent of private ownership. Other countries generally thought of as capitalist, such as West Germany and Canada, actually have considerable public ownership. France and Italy have about the same extensive public ownership as does Great Britain. Therefore, governments in these countries can affect their economies simply by the way they conduct their own enterprises—expanding or contracting, setting prices and wages, etc.

Nearly all the other countries also spend more, despite their relatively lower military budgets. In some cases, such as Sweden and the Netherlands, the government spends almost a 50 percent larger share of the GNP than in the United States. Only Australia and Japan (which had negligible military expenditures at the time) showed a lower government share of spending than in the United States. Moreover, between 1960 and 1975, the *rate of increase* in every country, including Japan and Australia, outpaced

Table 5-1   Economic Growth and Defense Spending, 1960–1977

% Growth in GNP, 1960–1977	Country	% of GNP devoted to Defense, 1961–1977
3.4	United States	7.8
3.2	Britain	5.3
5.1	France	4.7
3.9	Germany	3.9
4.4	Italy	3.0
5.1	Canada	2.8
8.8	Japan	0.9

Source: Derived from World Bank and U.S. Arms Control Agency data, reported in *New York Times*, October 15, 1980, p. D2.

The Government's Share of the Economy

Who owns how much?
Privately Owned: ☐
Publicly owned: ◰ 25% ◧ 50% ◼ 75% ■ All or nearly all

	Postal service	Telecommunications	Electricity	Gas	Oil output	Coal	Railroads	Airlines	Autos	Steel	Shipbuilding	Government spending (percent of gross domestic product) 1962	1975
Australia											†	24.0	32.0
Austria											†	32.1	40.2
Belgium					†							30.7	43.2
Britain												34.2	44.4
Canada												29.4	40.9
France					†							36.3	40.3
Italy					†	†						32.4	41.9
Japan					†							19.0	23.4
Netherlands					†	†						34.4	51.2
Sweden					†	†						32.7	49.4
United States							*					29.5	34.0
West Germany												33.6	42.1

† Not applicable or negligible production   *Including Conrail
Shading indicates countries in which the rate of government spending grew most rapidly.

Sources: The *Economist* and the Organization for Economic Cooperation and Development

Figure 5-1 Government's role in the economy of certain major countries. (*From the New York Times International Economic Survey, February 4, 1979, p. 12.*)

the United States. These totals reflect the much more extensive and rapidly increasing social welfare programs in all the European countries. But for economy-managing purposes, it means that the government can exercise immediate and far-reaching impact by its funding and implementing practices.

The contrast between the United States and the other countries is almost as great in the scope and character of purposeful guidance of the private economy. Perhaps the greatest difference is in the extent of planning. Even before the development of the European Economic Community, most European countries set up institutions for the purpose of developing and executing long-range plans for economic growth. Levels of investment in particular industries might be set, or work force needs prepared for, or research and development programs initiated, in order to harmonize the factors of production and maximize jobs and output. For several years, France was the model of successful planning: government planners were able to gain the willing cooperation of business leaders to produce the highest growth rates of the major European countries over the period 1960–1976. The French averaged 4.3 percent per year over that time, 60 percent higher than the United States. In other countries, planning is conducted less by official government agencies and more by organizations of businesses, sometimes with the participation of trade unions. Coordination may be by government action or through the consistent decision making of dominant financial institutions.

The greater use of long-range planning in Europe parallels a longer and stronger commitment to full employment. Where the American commitment stopped short in the Employment Act of 1946, the European countries almost all abandoned the idea that the market could be counted on to provide full employment. They vigorously applied Keynesian principles and managed their own enterprises to put growth and employment first. Characteristically, European governments take action to prevent unemployment more quickly than the United States, in part because Europeans have been less tolerant of unemployment than Americans.

Much of the difference between European and American practice stems from the American commitment to the free economic market and limited government. Where Europeans, such as the Germans, or the Japanese, talk in capitalist market terms, their businesses and banks often act in closely coordinated ways. The leading study of capitalist world economy-managing is that of a British economist. He sums up the distinctiveness of the American approach by saying that the United States has a

> popular tradition of shouting "Hands off!" as soon as it looks as if the Federal Administration may be about to move in anywhere with a positive policy. The

Table 5-2   Tax Burdens and Marginal Rates, 1976, for Selected OECD Countries

Country	Percent of gross earnings*	Marginal rate†
Denmark	33	55
Germany	27	34
Netherlands	31	42
Norway	27	42
Sweden	35	63
Britain	26	41
United States	17	32

*The percentages of gross earnings paid in national/state/local income taxes and social security taxes combined, by the average production worker (married with two children and receiving average earnings in the manufacturing sector).

†The combined tax rates that would be applied to the next 10% of gross earnings by the same worker.

Source: Theodore Geiger, *Welfare and Efficiency* (Washington, D.C.: National Planning Association, 1978), p. 28.

only exception is when there is a manifest crisis, as in Franklin Roosevelt's "hundred days" during 1933. Then the Government is allowed, indeed expected, to interfere everywhere. But that is only on the theory that the body of the nation is temporarily crippled. As soon as it recovers its faculties, the nursemaid in Washington is supposed to be sent away to her normal menial duties in the back part of the house.[1]

The Record of the Postwar Years

The industrial democracies enjoyed the most sustained period of prosperity in their history during the nearly three decades from 1946 to 1973. With the exception of Great Britain, major countries' growth rates averaged almost twice that of the United States until the Kennedy tax program took effect. Japanese growth averaged more than 10 percent per year throughout the entire period. Unemployment was negligible on the European continent, with many countries having to import immigrant workers from sources as far away as Turkey. Prices rose at modest 2 percent to 4 percent levels. GNP per capita climbed steadily toward American levels, until Sweden, Canada, and West Germany achieved comparable or higher standards in the mid-1970s. The European countries also had fewer and shallower recessions than the United States. While it cannot be demonstrated conclusively that these achievements were due to the comparatively greater scope of government management of these economies, that

implication seems warranted. The need to rebuild war-shattered economies might have given initial impetus to the economic takeoff, but it could
not account for the sustained prosperity of the period. Only Britain, with
its special import dependency and history of "stop and go" policy shifts,
failed to share fully in the continuing boom.

But the picture changed sharply after 1973. Tables 5-3 and 5-4 show
the contrasts in each category for major countries. Growth was much
lower, unemployment higher, and inflation sharply higher. Japan and
Germany maintained the strongest growth with lowest unemployment, but
Japan temporarily suffered high inflation. Italy, France, and particularly
Britain were hit by the newly characteristic stagflation. Unemployment and
growth levels were worse than at any time since the Depression of the
1930s, and inflation was well into "double digits" (nearly 20 percent for
Britain for a period of years). The United States experienced the sharpest
recession since the 1930s in 1974–1975, but still suffered somewhat lower
inflation than most of the others. Canada, dominated as always by the
economic situation in the United States, experienced similar patterns.

The reasons for this shared slump were several. The oil embargo and
price rises set by the OPEC countries have received most of the blame.
Some of it is certainly deserved, for most of the industrial countries of
Europe and Japan were importing more than 90 percent of their oil. But
other factors were also involved. In particular, the growth of international
trade and finance and the globalization of major corporations have created
an interdependence among the industrial economies such that they tend to
affect each other strongly and quickly. The Europeans charged that the

Table 5-3   Economic Growth, 1959–1980 (in percents)

Country	GNP		Real Growth		
	Per capita ($ in 1976)	Total (billions of 1979 $)	1959–1973	1974–1979	1980
Sweden	9030	NA	4.1	1.8	3.0
Canada	7930	222	5.1	3.0	−1.5
United States	7880	2,369	4.2	2.3	−1.3
West Germany	7510	762	4.9	2.2	2.3
France	6730	573	5.9	3.0	2.5
Japan	5090	1,022	10.9	4.0	4.3
Britain	4180	NA	3.3	1.2	−2.3
Italy	3220	292	3.4	2.3	3.7

Source: OECD Economic Outlook, December 1980.

Table 5-4   Inflation and Unemployment 1960s vs. late 1970s (in percents)

Country	Inflation			Unemployment		
	1960–1973	1974–1979	1980	1962–1973	1974–1979	1980
Sweden	4.6	9.7	12.2	2.1	1.9	2.0
Canada	3.0	8.9	10.9	5.1	7.5	6.9
United States	3.0	8.1	13.5	4.6	6.8	7.5
West Germany	3.3	4.2	5.1	0.6	4.3	3.6
France	4.5	10.1	13.5	2.2	4.2	6.2
Japan	6.2	7.3	7.5	1.2	1.9	2.0
Britain	4.7	15.5	15.7	3.1	4.8	7.0
Italy	4.5	15.8	20.5	3.5	5.8	7.9

Source: OECD *Economic Outlook, December 1980.*

American inflation of 1968–1973 had cheapened dollars that they were holding as bank reserves; thus, the United States had "exported inflation" to them. Apparently, there were also other, less understood, causes of inflation at work as well. Neither oil prices nor the export theory accounted for the size or persistence of the inflationary pressure.

By 1980, inflation clearly posed the focal problem for economy-managing policies. Figure 5-2 traces the experience of the major countries through the decade of the 1970s. It shows the ominous upward thrust that led to the generally shared near-record levels of 1980. Because in most countries inflation of this magnitude was accompanied by low growth or recession and rising unemployment, the Keynesian principles themselves were called into question. The only apparent way to control inflation was to force a serious recession, exactly what some countries thought it necessary to do. But induced recession might be almost as politically risky as suffering prolonged inflation. And it was certainly risky in economic terms. Not only was the danger of depression always present, but there was no assurance that inflation would not start up again as soon as restrictive measures were relaxed.

The challenge to Keynesianism began to take two forms. One argued that Keynesian principles were applicable only to periods of classic depression, where the task was to promote growth and employment, and inflation was not present or threatened. In this view, the flaw in Keynesian strategy was that it was much more difficult (for both political and economic reasons) to *reduce* spending or *raise* taxes than it was to do the opposite. Thus Keynesianism was really applicable only to one side of the business cycle, the downturn. It was essentially useless on the upturn, when excessive expansion had to be checked.

The Global Price Squeeze

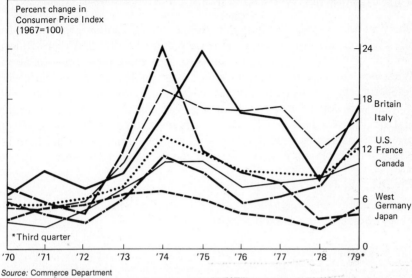

Source: Commerce Department

Figure 5-2 Effect of consumer price index on various countries in the 1970s. *(From the New York Times International Economic Survey, February 3, 1980, p. 31.)*

The second argument held that Keynesianism simply contemplated a different economy than the ones that now existed. Economic concentrations were such that they could defy market pressures or government inducements, raising prices as they wished to protect profit margins. And the integration of economies in the world prevents policies from having their intended effects; for example, raising interest rates is less likely to restrict credit than it is to attract short-term capital from abroad. Much more drastic controls over credit, capital, and investment would be necessary, and growth itself might have to be reexamined as a principle of policy.

In both cases, the tools for restoring prosperity and relieving widespread suffering were neither economically nor politically available. Most governments still followed the old methods, amidst growing crisis and concern about the prospect of depression. Popular reaction in Europe took the form of resistance to further increases in public spending, much as it did in the United States. General skepticism and distrust of government economy-managing capability was also apparent. But what policy makers feared most was the demand for protection of local industries and jobs against foreign imports—and the resultant prospects of trade wars. If protectionism were widely implemented, most feared, there would be no way to avoid a depression.

II CONTEMPORARY CONDITIONS: ISSUES OF FACT AND INTERPRETATION

Many of the conditions that give rise to current policy problems have already been identified. We shall review these briefly, and then explore possible explanations for the most insistent of these problems—inflation. What we shall see is that interpretations of available facts, particularly with respect to the causes of inflation, contrast sharply with each other. And they do so in consistent ways, linking up with coherent groupings of values and beliefs sketched in Chapter 2. Understanding of the facts of our present problems is thus partly shaped by the premises we hold. In all probability, both will flow consistently toward related remedies.

The Defining Features of Our Times

We shall note but five of the major problems that make up the agenda for policy choices in the United States today.

1 Inflation   American inflation has risen steadily for most of the 1970s and 1980s. It pauses only briefly during recessions, and then starts up again from beginning points that are higher each time. At 13.3 percent in 1979 and 13.5 percent in 1980, inflation was higher than at any time since 1946. Real wages (per capita income after allowing for inflation) were declining. And, perhaps surprisingly, relatively little inflationary pressure could be attributed to the rise in OPEC oil prices. (See accompanying box material) Those prices have proceeded at a rate only somewhat higher than American inflation, to which they are particularly sensitive because all are fixed in terms of the American dollar. The best technical estimates of the contribution of all energy price increases to inflation range between one-quarter and one-third of the total.

OPEC and Inflation

The increase in the price of imported oil . . . represents less than 0.5% of the 8% average yearly inflation from 1972 to 1980. . . . The actual quantity of oil imported in 1980 constituted only 1/31 of total GNP (it was 1/274 in 1972) and the spectacular price increase of imported oil has therefore failed to produce a major inflationary impact.

From an article by Philip Opher, economist, in *New York Times*, March 1, 1981, p. E19.

---

2 Low Growth and High Unemployment   With the exception of the mid-1960s and 1972–1973, economic growth in the United States has lagged consistently behind Europe and Japan. Substantial proportions of productive capacity have remained unutilized and millions of people have been out of work. In 1980, unemployment neared 8 percent, meaning that around 10 million people were without jobs at some time during the year.

3 Profit Squeeze and Low Investment   With the prominent exception of the oil industry after 1973, most American corporations experienced difficulty in maintaining profit margins in the 1960s and 1970s. One major reason was the growing competition of foreign manufacturers. Another was the growing age of the American industrial plant; and perhaps a third was slack demand resulting from continued unemployment and underemployment. In many cases, only the repatriated profits from capital investments overseas enabled corporations and banks to keep profits up; the proportion that such profits bore to total profits rose steadily in the 1970s. All of these trends point up a central problem for the American economy: capital investment in new productive facilities has been low for the last decades. This explains the age and reduced competitiveness of American industry. Low capital investment itself is explained in part by the greater profits to be made from investments in Europe or the Third World.

4 The Instability of Growing Indebtedness   Two kinds of debt raise specter of inability to repay and resultant collapse: domestic United States debt and Third World international indebtedness. The recovery of 1976–1978 was financed chiefly through a vast growth of business and consumer debt, to more than $4 trillion, or 50 percent more than that of 1974. The use of savings and new debts is credited with having delayed the recession of 1980 for a year or more, but the cost was potentially ruinous if recessionary unemployment or reduced profits prevented repayment. The Third World problem was that of debt-ridden poor countries faced with drastic price increases for the imported oil on which they depended for development. Failure to repay would endanger the industrial world's largest banks, many of which were cornerstones of the American financial system.

5 Balance of Payments and Dollar Difficulties   As inflation cheapened the dollar, it set off fluctuations in world currency values and threatened the stability of world trade. At the same time, it made American exports more competitive in world markets and reduced demand for suddenly higher-priced imports. Accordingly, the drain on American reserves resulting from more imports than exports was temporarily eased. But then came the OPEC price rises, and the balance tilted unfavorably again— setting off another round of decline in confidence in the dollar. The point is: the level of inflation, the balance of payments, and the value of the dollar are inextricably linked. Trouble for one means trouble for the others—and inevitably, trouble for the prosperity level and manageability of the American economy.

The term "crisis" is increasingly applied to the economic situation in part because it is the worst combination of conditions since the Depression of the 1930s. In steepness of decline and extent of suffering by jobless people, the recessions of 1974–1975 and 1980–1981 were the worst in that forty-year period. Yet they had only momentary effects on slowing inflation. The apparently intractable economic problems were accompanied, moreover, by growing lack of confidence in leaders and their policies.

The other reason for the term "crisis" is the sense of helplessness that seems to grip policy makers and citizens alike. What the Keynesian tool kit offers to prevent inflation only contracts growth and produces unemployment. What it offers to promote growth and employment only intensifies already-virulent inflation. The known cures for inflation—prolonged recession, even depression—seem impractical politically and undesirable socially. In this context of uncertain knowledge and wide foreboding, policy choices must nevertheless be made.

Inflation as the Central Problem

If inflation were eliminated, many of the other problems would be removed or greatly reduced as well. While most would agree with this premise, much less agreement exists on what *causes* inflation, and, not surprisingly, on what cures it. We shall use the argument over the causes of inflation as a case study of how values and beliefs connect to analysis and prescription. Three categories of possible causes of inflation will be examined: (1) what the government has done or not done; (2) external sources; and (3) characteristics of the economy itself. Three schools of thought take consistent positions in each category, reflecting positions on the right, center, and left of the "continuum of conflict" depicted in Figure 2-1. The right is made up of the strongest believers in individualism, the free market, and freedom.[3] The left consists of those who believe in social responsibility and purposeful government intervention to replace the nonexistent market with a more egalitarian distribution system.[4] The center is composed of post-Keynesians, committed to maximizing profit in the private economy through direct government intervention while still maintaining most social services.[5] Table 5-5 summarizes the positions of each school of thought.[6]

The Right The right puts the blame for inflation primarily on the government. The most important failings have been overexpansion of the money supply and excessive government spending and regulation. The right tends to be "hard money" and monetarist in approach. This means

Table 5-5   The Continuum of Conflict and the Causes of Inflation

Social responsibility	←————————————→	Individual responsibility
Social (governmental) management	←————————————→	Free market determination
Equality	←————————————→	Freedom

The Causes of Inflation

(Left)	(Center)	(Right)
	A. What government has done or not done	
failure to enforce competition or otherwise control monopoly corporations failure to employ wage-price controls	Johnson administration failure of Vietnam taxes	overexpanded money supply excessive social spending stimulative budget deficits overregulation
	B. External sources	
loss of American hegemony in Third World oil company profiteering	OPEC price rises	OPEC price rises coupled with "do nothing" government policy
	C. The economy itself	
concentration of power in corporations and industries	low productivity excessive consumer demand	excessive regulation low productivity minimum wage laws unions

that it takes maintenance of a stable-value dollar, perhaps linked to a constant value in gold, as a first priority and believes that control of the money supply is an important key to managing the economy. Controlling the money supply is particularly appealing because it gives the greatest effect to free market forces and keeps the government in the background. Changes in the amount and value of money, if any, appear neutral and noncoercive in character. The right also blames the government for promoting inflation by spending too much for social services. Because of these expenditures, and its deliberately stimulative approach to the economy, the government regularly runs inflation-causing federal budget deficits. Finally, excessive government regulation is an intolerable *and* costly interference with the economic free market.

The right concedes that such external factors as oil price rises have played an important part in our current inflation. However, it charges the government with encouraging or tolerating such effects through its "do-nothing" policy. Complete and immediate deregulation of all domestic oil and gas production might help to encourage exploration and production from domestic sources. More effective would be the deployment of military power to assure continued supply of foreign oil at stable prices.

With respect to the economy itself, the right sees another significant push to inflation stemming from artificially rising costs of production. Some come directly from government regulations and social programs, such as safety and pollution standards or affirmative action guidelines. More come from wage pressures. Some artificial costs are government-created in the form of minimum wage laws. But others are created by unions, in both the private and the public sector, often with the support of government authorization in the form of collective-bargaining statutes.

A final cause is the problem of declining productivity (the units produced per hour that a person works). When productivity increases and more units are produced in the same number of hours worked, the employer can grant wage increases without having to raise prices. But if productivity only slightly increases, or decreases, wage increases can be granted only if prices are raised. Steadily increasing productivity thus holds inflation down; decreasing productivity spurs inflation. The United States once had steady productivity increases, but in the last several years the situation has reversed. The right argues that productivity has been declining due to a lack of incentives for private investment and because unions have prevented more efficient work standards.

The Left   The left sees inflation as grounded in the basic structure of the new economy, primarily in the newly concentrated power of corporations and banks. Prices and terms for credit can be set with almost exclusive regard for profit margins. The corporate-banking sector is essentially unaffected by market forces or government efforts at manipulation. Government's failures are chiefly those of omission, as in refusal to impose sweeping price, interest, profit, rent, and wage controls—or business-biased implementation when they are imposed. Government is also blamed for being too much the captive of the corporate-banking sector. It can neither enforce competition by means of the antitrust laws nor otherwise control corporate power.

The left denies that OPEC oil price rises are more than a minor factor in United States inflation. Not only are they running only modestly ahead of inflation, but it is domestic oil and the transporting, refining, and marketing profits of the major oil companies that are taking the biggest bite from the American consumer. After years of ardently promoting energy usage and buying up all the various alternative energy sources, the oil companies are the source of the energy increment to inflation. But they are able to use the OPEC actions as a cover for their own profiteering in part because it is true that the United States no longer has the economic, political, and military dominance in the world that it did between 1946 and 1968. The decline in United States economic strength, moral leadership, and military superiority, symbolized by the failure of the Vietnam War, was really brought about by the simultaneous rise of competition from Europe and Japan and other economic problems, the growth of Soviet military strength, and the insistent demands of the Third World peoples for independence. Denied the opportunity to exploit the Third World via raw materials or direct investment or loans, the United States is forced to pay for what it gets—and to suffer the inflationary consequences.

The left puts the primary blame for inflation squarely on the fact of economic concentration in the new economy, as previously noted. With two, three, or four companies dominating many industries, competition is replaced by tacit cooperation and prices are "administered" upwards in defiance of the illusory economic market. An example is: in 1980, in the face of the worst sales in sixteen years, all three auto manufacturers substantially increased new car prices.

The issue of productivity is viewed on the left as either a cover under which to excuse poor management and/or cut back the unions' power and gains, or a natural result of the system of capital seeking the greatest return. Some deny the accuracy of productivity measures entirely, particularly when they are applied to noncomparable activities. Others see productivity as a polite word for "speedup" of workers. Where decline in productivity is accepted, the blame is put on the lack of investment in new technologies in American plants. Instead, it is argued, investors (including United States corporations) went in search of the higher returns to be made from investment in European or Third World facilities.

The Center   The center sees inflation, and indeed the entire range of current problems, as arising from a combination of historical accidents or mistakes and persistent mass desire for greater and greater consumption. The Johnson administration's error in not raising taxes earlier to fight the Vietnam War, using greater debt and expanded money supply instead, is widely acknowledged. Also acknowledged is the impact of the oil price increases, for which the OPEC countries alone are blamed. But after these coincidental causes are identified, the major cause of inflation remains the continuing rise of expectations on the part of masses of people. The center believes government has done what it can in this context. With the exception of reduction of some of the more onerous regulations and standards, change in popular values and expectations must occur before government can do more.

The center sees OPEC-generated energy costs as the principal cause of inflation. Because the primary cause is external to the United States economy, moreover, it is essentially uncontrollable in the usual ways.

The center is more likely to understand the economy as having an excess of demand coupled with declining productivity. The excess of demand results from the apparent assumption on the part of people generally that they ought to have a steadily rising standard of living. Post-Keynesians argue that this is an expectation fostered in the current generation by the specially prosperous postwar period. In our new economic situation, such expectations are no longer appropriate.

The center blames the decline in productivity for a good share of American inflation. The causes of this decline are seen as an aging plant, the reasons for which are not really examined, and balky union leadership that does not understand its own interests.

Table 5-5 summarizes these positions against a background of a condensed version of the "continuum of conflict" described in Chapter 2 (Table 2-1). As stressed in the text, analysis of the causes of inflation closely follows the premises (values and beliefs) the analyst brings to the task. In the next section, we shall see that preferred alternatives flow directly from (indeed, are often implicit in) the premises assumed and analyses made by each school of thought.

III ALTERNATIVE POLICIES FOR THE FUTURE

Too much can be made of the role of values and beliefs in linking premises, analysis, and preferred alternatives. The facts of a situation and the demonstrability of probable consequences often temper or prevent pre-ferred policy choices. But the three contending schools of thought that we have just seen in action clearly dominate the public discussion of policy questions. And, just as clearly, they mesh with present practices to set the beginning framework within which policy choices are actually made. In this section, we shall first show briefly how widely the schools apply. We then focus on the principal issue of 1980s economy-managing policy choice: "reindustrialization."

Implications for Other Vital Debates

The vigorous arguments of the three schools of thought are not limited to the question of the causes of inflation. Their clashing interpretations carry over into many other important areas where policy choices have to be made. While the three different positions are not always explicitly argued, major issues necessarily engage each way of looking at the world. We shall briefly examine four critical issues with economy-managing significance from the conflicting standpoints.

1 Government "bailouts" of Financially Troubled Cities and Corporations Should the United States government provide loan guarantees to enable New York City or the Lockheed or Chrysler corporations to avoid bankruptcy? The center sees no alternative, but tries to force conditions upon the failing enterprise that will prevent repetition in the future. To do otherwise threatens the whole economy. For example, in the case of New York City, not only the big banks of New York but a large number of banks across the country holding New York's bonds stood to lose seriously from the city's bankruptcy. The financial system of the country might have been affected adversely, if only in terms of investors' confidence in state and municipal securities. Working together, the big banks, the state of New York, and the national government fashioned a new layer of government for New York City. Boards, staffed by bankers or their representatives, now exercise final authority over all major financial matters—displacing the elected officials of the city on a permanent basis.[7]

In the case of Chrysler, the collapse of the nation's tenth-largest corporation would have meant the loss of hundreds of thousands of jobs, millions of dollars of investment in Chrysler plants and dealerships, and a major blow to economic confidence in the country. Called "the most complex financial operation in United States history" by the Secretary of the Treasury,[8] the government provided $1.5 billion in loan guarantees. The conditions were: (1) that Chrysler obtain another $1.5 billion from private banks; (2) that all 400 of the banks then holding Chrysler obligations agree to the refinancing scheme; and (3) that Chrysler accept stringent government monitoring. Even then, however, there was no way to be sure that Chrysler might not eventually fall into bankruptcy.

The right opposed both "bailouts" on several grounds. New York was seen as profligate with services, corrupt, and deserving of whatever happened to it as a lesson in prudence to other cities. Chrysler should be left to the workings of market forces. In the words of one senator during the Chrysler debate, "What we are doing is rewarding bad management, ignoring the decisions of the marketplace, and distorting the forces of competition."[9]

The prospect of deep government involvement in private enterprise is particularly distressing to the right, but it is only slightly less disturbing to the left. The left worries that government is taking one more step toward the integration of the state with corporate capitalism—on the corporate-banking sector's terms. In New York City, intervention not only saved the banks, but the bankers gained control over city decision-making. At Chrysler, the bailout was to save investors (and jobs, to be sure) at taxpayers' risk and expense. In both situations, the government is put in the position of shoring up a flawed capitalist economic system, using the people's money to assure continued private profit.

2 Commitment to the Principle of Economic Growth as a Necessity Both center and right, and much of the left, accept the idea that economic growth is necessary to provide jobs for an expanding population, assure profits and ability to pay debts, and have something left to provide for military and social expenses. As noted earlier, a growing total product permits fulfilling the demands of the "have-nots" without threatening to take away from the "haves." The principle has been virtually unquestioned for centuries. The only arguments have been over how the goal of growth might best be achieved.

In the 1980s, however, two new developments made the idea of economic growth a matter of major controversy. First, concern on the right with rising inflation and the government's inability to contain it led some to a radical new emphasis on growth. Only dramatic new economic growth, it was argued, could put people back to work, reduce government budget deficits and increase revenues, and increase productivity enough to stabilize prices again. And only dramatic tax cuts could provide the investment capital to spur such new growth.

Second, environmental and energy problems have led to a challenge to the growth principle from a small but vigorous part of the center and left. One version argues simply that the environmental destruction and resource exhaustion (or escalating costs just prior to exhaustion) wreaked by industrial growth and waste (whether capitalist or socialist) is no longer tolerable. Not just the amenities of life, but physical health today and economic and social survival tomorrow, are said to be at stake. Another version sees *social* rather than physical limits to growth. What good is it to have a comfortable fast car if the roads are constantly clogged with other people's equally comfortable fast cars? Opportunities for individual advancement in education, income, or possessions are reduced in significance when they are widely shared; in qualitative terms, achievements carry less meaning. Only the aspirations remain, doomed to frustration for all but a few.

The remedies that emerge from these views range from far-reaching controls over the use of all resources to preserve the essential features of the present system as long as possible, to small-scale capitalism with limited population and concern for the renewability of nature, to versions of steady-state democratic socialism with environmental priorities. Characteristic of all developing arguments, the antigrowth position has many forms—most of which lack concern for political feasibility or even implications. But the argument is undoubtedly here to stay and can only grow in its challenge to center and right commitments to maintaining capitalist profitability.

3 The Nature of the Soviet Threat The center sees the growth of the Soviet Union's military strength and the intentions of its leaders as requiring a substantial buildup of American weapons in the next decade. The right holds a more cataclysmic view: the United States faces a period of Soviet military superiority, calling for a crash program of military expenditures double that of the center. In both cases, large new expenditures would be added to the military side of the federal budget. Equal reductions in other spending, or new tax revenues, would have to be found to compensate for these shifts in priorities.

The left charges that other motives lie behind the newly discovered Soviet "threat." One is the desire to stimulate the United States economy by massive new expenditures that are ideologically acceptable and unlikely to disturb existing economic relations as might similar investments in public works or social services. Another is the need to develop mobile military forces (the "Rapid Deployment Force") capable of inserting United States power into Third World situations to protect United States economic interests. A third is the use of "knee-jerk" anticommunism and the threat of war to divert Americans' attention from their own deteriorating economic situation.

4 International Interdependence and Trade This is a major point of contention between center and right in which the left is little involved. The center is convinced that global corporations and banks have a paramount interest in maintaining close cooperation between themselves, their counterparts all over the world, and their national governments. Mutual consultation and assistance, and coordinated policies, are essential to preserve this fragile system in the face of oil price rises, potential shortages and nonpayment of Third World debts, and other economic problems. Above all, free trade must be preserved and protectionism avoided, lest retaliatory measures drive the world into another depression.

The right is much less convinced of the extent or importance of interdependence, focusing instead on the needs of industries based primarily in the United States. One way to preserve their shares of the United States market is to keep foreign competition under control, even if protective tariffs or quotas raise prices to consumers and add inflationary pressure to the United States economy. The right argues that protectionism is not particularly risky because the United States economy and consumer market are still stronger than any other. Furthermore, no other country will want to risk potentially ruinous trade wars by retaliating against the United States.

On each of these (and many other) major issues, a contrast of policy preferences is clear. Substantial differences for the economy as a whole—in particular, its rates of growth, unemployment, and inflation—are at stake in the choices that flow from each perspective. Thus, almost every major issue engages the three schools of thought. More importantly, the differing proposed solutions carry wide economy-managing effects.

"REINDUSTRIALIZATION" AS THE CENTRAL ISSUE OF THE 1980s

"Reindustrialization" means the development of a whole new and techno-logically advanced capital base (plants, machinery, transportation systems, etc.) for the production of goods and services in the United States. It is an all-encompassing approach to managing the economy that would direct fiscal, monetary, and other policies toward this single, overarching goal. Both center and right advocate reindustrialization as essential to restoring United States productivity and competitiveness, and thereby profitability and jobs. Though agreeing upon reindustrialization as the only long-term solution to inflation (together with "energy independence"), center and right differ sharply over whether it should be accomplished by purposeful government management or by letting private investors and market forces work their will. On the other hand, the left views reindustrialization skeptically. They see it as a vast extension of the "trickle-down" principle in which most people are forced to undergo austerity in wages, public services, and standards of living generally, in order to finance the new investment (and profit) necessary to generate future jobs.

The center position on reindustrialization argues that excessive con-sumption and lack of investment have led to low productivity. Add energy price rises, and one completes the explanation for our persistent stagfla-tion. The solution that follows from these premises is to embark on a program of government-managed development of key sectors of the economy and encouragement of private business investment generally. The means are: expanded military spending and transportation programs; a tax policy consisting of depreciation allowances, fast write-offs for certain investments, deferral or reduction of taxes on interest or profits from such investments, etc.; and reduced social services and consumption ("belt-tightening").

Overall tax reduction is an essential component of the center strategy because continued inflation pushes people into higher tax brackets and produces too much revenue for the government—retarding recovery from recession as well as antagonizing voters. Reindustrialization implies a deliberate policy of maximizing reductions for particular business and investment decisions deemed desirable. This contrasts with the usual 2:1 ratio of consumer to business reductions and with letting the reductions be made across the board (e.g., 10 percent in every category). The center is concerned about profitability of the major corporations and banks. It believes in purposeful government assistance to them rather than reliance on the economic market to direct investments to their best use.

Wage and price controls have no part in the center strategy, however, because the market image still plays a large enough role to make controls seem inevitably ineffective. Despite public opinion polls showing a 65 percent majority for controls in early 1980,[10] center economists and political leaders continued to resist such a step.

The left's critique of reindustrialization is both philosophical and practical. The left opposes the idea that private profitability should be enhanced by popular sacrifice. If people are going to bear the burden of declining real wages, reduced services, and lower standards of living, they should share in the rewards that are produced thereby. And the left emphasizes the everyday problems of people suffering from joblessness, poverty, and lack of health care. The standard of social justice and equality is raised against designs which would place the profitability of private investment and production first among policy priorities. The left calls instead for a complete freeze on prices, rents, profits, wages, etc., followed by democratic national planning to direct investment in key industries in socially desirable directions. Some vital industries, such as the oil companies, might have to be nationalized in order to fully control their wide-ranging effects.

The critique of center reindustrialization from the right focuses on the extent of government direction rather than the goal itself. The right accepts the need completely. But it would leave all choice-making to private wealthholders and corporations. Government should simply give up prospective revenues—across the board, from whatever source derived—and let their use be dictated by market inducements. Concurrently, government should reduce its needs for revenues by cutting back on nonessential services (those not connected to military defense or promoting the economy). Whether the center or the right version prevailed, services would be cut and austerity imposed on large numbers of people. The right would expand military spending, and related jobs, in a manner that would compensate, in a way, for the center's preservation of relatively more services.

As inflation continued to remain high and growth low in 1980–1981, the sense of economic crisis on the right deepened. Severe budget deficits seemed indicated for years ahead, as previously legislated entitlements drained the Treasury and the stagnant economy kept revenues low. Efforts to stop inflation through such monetary policies as high interest rates and tight money supply restrained growth and raised the unemployment rate without significantly affecting inflation. At this point, "supply side" advocates (people who stress capital investment and productivity as opposed to "demand side" proponents, who stress jobs and purchasing power) rallied to the new commitment to economic growth as the solution that was noted earlier. Rapid and substantial growth was seen as the only way to a permanent cure for inflation that would not cause unemployment, sustained recession, and vast government expenditures along the way.

THE REAGAN GAMBLE

The Reagan economic program described briefly in the last chapter is an expression of the analysis and goals of the right. It is also a major gamble, on the success or failure of which American prosperity in the 1980s will depend, and whose costs will be borne primarily by the poor, the young, the unemployed, and other recipients of federal social service programs. Much has also been sacrificed in the process of deregulation, including workers' safety, clean air standards, consumer protections, and energy costs.

The gamble turns on whether real economic growth of the level projected by the Reagan administration planners can be attained soon enough, and sustained long enough, to produce the budget-balancing new revenues and reduced inflation that were promised by the President in early 1981. The Reagan program foresees economic growth of more than 4 percent per year from 1982 through at least 1986, but this level has been reached only occasionally, and never sustained, by the United States since the end of World War II. The years after the Kennedy tax cut of 1964 (including the Vietnam War buildup) and the years 1972 and 1978 saw growth of more than 4 percent in total GNP. The average for the period 1966 through 1977 however, was 2.8 percent; the average for 1978 through 1980 was 2.5 percent. Partly because of its expectations of rapid and sustained economic growth, the Reagan administration projected a decline in the inflation rate to 8.3 percent in 1982 and 5.5 percent in 1984. Both growth and inflation estimates are necessary to the achievement of its projected federal budget surplus by 1984. If *either* the growth *or* the inflation target is not achieved, the budget will be in deficit. If *neither* target is achieved, the budget will be in very serious deficit. And inflation will be spurred accordingly.

Reaching the inflation target involves several uncertainties besides the growth requirement. The commitment to add substantially to military spending over the next several years is clearly a boost to inflation, as are new Social Security taxes and minimum wage requirements. So is the fact

**Table 5-6 The View from 1981: Two Presidents'
Estimates of the Future**

	Calendar years			
	1981	1982	1983	1984
Real economic growth				
Reagan	1.1%	4.2%	5.0%	4.5%
Carter	0.9%	3.5%	3.5%	3.7%
Inflation*				
Reagan	11.1%	8.3%	6.2%	5.5%
Carter	12.5%	10.3%	8.7%	7.7%
Unemployment				
Reagan	7.8%	7.2%	6.6%	6.4%
Carter	7.8%	7.5%	7.1%	6.7%

*Consumer Price Index
Source: Derived from data in New York Times, February 19, 1981.

that consumers will have an additional approximately $60 billion in tax-cut funds to spend per year in 1981 through 1984. How much of this will go into savings rather than increased demand will depend on how fully "inflationary psychology" is arrested and whether people's real needs can be satisfied by spending less than the full amount of new income. The prospect of substantial budget deficits as the tax cuts go into effect, inflation continues, and growth is slow to pick up adds additional inflationary pressure to the economy.

Reaching the growth target also involves uncertainties beyond its unprecedented character. Businesses and other investors must use their substantial new tax savings to increase American productivity and expand American output. But short-term profit opportunities are probably greater from investments other than plants, technology, or equipment in the United States—i.e., from speculative transactions or from Third World investments. If inflation does not dip promptly from its 1979–1980 levels, the Federal Reserve Board will be strongly tempted to raise or maintain high interest rates, which will severely hamper economic expansion.

Thus it is far from assured that the Reagan program will succeed. The growth and inflation targets are optimistic, and the program's projected consequences unprecedented. Perhaps the best defense of this alternative is that the economic crisis facing the United States government in 1981 was patently very severe, and no previous policies seemed to be working. Underlying the crisis, the failure of previous remedies, and the uncertainties involved in the Reagan program is the question of *why* high inflation, low growth, and high unemployment have occurred together, persisted, and grown worse. The Reagan analysis is that government taxation, regulation, and social spending make for low growth, and that government deficits are primarily responsible for inflation. Most economists dispute this focus on government as the major problem and deny that "unleashing" the private economy with commensurately lower concern for the poor is either economically or socially a sound remedy.

If the Reagan program is *not* successful, inflation will jump to new and unprecedented levels—pushed by new demand from the tax cuts, growing federal expenditures and widening deficits, increased military spending, and a renewed inflationary psychology. Unemployment will rise as expansion slows, population increases, and various federal job programs and aids to education are terminated. With the curtailment of long-term unemployment benefits, Medicaid, food stamps, and a variety of other social programs, new pressures will be placed on state and local welfare systems and new hardships experienced by the people affected. Significant social unrest might follow, with resulting need for greater government efforts to maintain order or deflect resentments in some other direction. In short, a great deal is at stake in the choices among alternatives in the area of managing the economy.

NOTES

1 Andrew Shonfield, *Modern Capitalism* (New York: Oxford, 1965), p. 17.

2 *New York Times*, February 3, 1980, sec. 3, p. 8.

3 Among economists in this category the most prominent is Milton Friedman; among political leaders, Ronald Reagan.

4 Among economists the leaders are Gar Alperovitz and Jeff Faux of the National Center for Economic Alternatives; political spokespersons include Barry Commoner, presidential candidate of the Citizens party.

5 Economists include Charles Schultze and Wassily Leontief. Political leaders number Jimmy Carter and John Anderson.

6 Each position is built from the writings and platforms of the persons named in notes 3–5 and those closely associated with them.

7 For a full analysis, see Robert Greenblatt et al., "The New Governance of New York City: Financiers, Administrators, Politicians, Labor Unions, Communities, Minorities," paper presented at the annual meeting of the American Political Science Association, Washington, D.C., 1979.

8 *New York Times*, June 29, 1980, p. F19.

9 Ibid.

10 Ibid., February 3, 1980, p. F18.

Chapter 6

Making Energy Policy

The problem of assuring an adequate energy supply at stable and afford-able prices nearly equals in complexity, while forming a major part of, the problem of managing the economy. But energy does not seem to lend itself to the same right/center/left analyses and prescriptions. Conflicts abound over what the basic facts are as well as what should be done about them. However, such debates tend to focus on particular issues (for example, nuclear safety, environmental imperatives, or solar feasibility) rather than comprehensive interpretations and alternatives. "Solutions," though many, often are offered piecemeal—for one fragment of the total problem at a time. In these chapters, we shall try to highlight the controversies as they arise. Consideration of their potential coherence is reserved for the concluding section.

Once again, however, we need some organizing conceptualization—a "handle"—with which to grasp the elements of our energy crisis. Without such a framework, little can be understood of the strengths, weaknesses, or other implications of public policies. One helpful framework approaches our energy problem in terms of two closely linked topics: *consumption patterns*, including both forms and sources of energy and end uses; and *solution premises*, the assumptions and preferences that shape proposed alternative policies.

As a result of oil shortages and price prices, the consumption versus supply picture is probably the most familiar to Americans today. Table 6-1 shows the shares of total consumption represented by various forms of energy in 1960, 1973, and 1980. As total consumption increased steadily over the period, natural gas and coal declined in proportions, while oil rose to nearly half of all energy.

But the vital change occurred in the *source* of oil: in 1960, only 17 percent of all oil was imported; by 1978, the proportion was 42 percent, down from a high of 47 percent the previous year. Rising demand and decreasing domestic production had led to a situation where about a quarter of all American energy needs had to be filled from imports.

What made this situation so damaging was the fact that oil-producing countries acted together to raise prices from roughly $2 per barrel in 1971 to more than $34 per barrel in 1980. The price jump drained billions of dollars out of the American economy and spurred inflation and balance-of-payments problems all around the world. Moreover, supplies might be cut off at any time by politically motivated embargoes or internal unrest, particularly in the Middle Eastern oil-producing countries. Nor was oil the only energy source in short or threatened supply. Natural gas was limited in amount; hydro power was at its maximum; and the dangers of nuclear fission provoked opposition. Only coal was plentiful, but its development posed many problems. In this context, the term "energy crisis" was well justified.

Consumption rose 74 percent over the last two decades, slowed only by the massive price rises of the late 1970s. Partly because energy was

Table 6-1   U.S. Energy Consumption, Selected Years

	1960		1973		1980	
	Quads*	%	Quads*	%	Quads*	%
Oil	19.9	45.2	34.8	46.6	37.3	47.2
Natural gas	12.4	28.1	22.5	30.2	20.5	26.0
Coal	10.1	23.0	13.3	17.8	15.1	19.1
Nuclear	—	0.0	0.9	1.2	2.8	3.5
Hydro, other	1.6	3.7	3.1	4.2	3.3	4.2
TOTAL	44.0	100.0	74.6	100.0	79.0	100.0

*Quads =quadrillions of British thermal units (BTUs, the standard measure of heat) are used for comparability among sources of energy.
Source: U.S. Department of Energy, *Monthly Energy Review*, January 1981.

initially so inexpensive, Americans became heavy users. Residential and commercial heating and lighting account for about 37 percent of all energy used. Industrial needs draw 36 percent and transportation a relatively high 26 percent of available energy.[1] The transportation figure is produced chiefly by the high number of private automobiles—117 million in 1978, almost twice as many as in 1960. Extensive private auto use in the United States puts particular pressure on oil supplies.

Two important assumptions about American energy demand patterns must be examined in order to understand this side of the equation. One is that there is a close link between growth in energy usage and economic growth generally. In other words, it is often assumed that energy demand *must* continue to rise or else economic growth cannot be achieved. Events of the past decade and comparison with other countries, however, have seriously challenged, if not refuted, this assumption. From 1968 to 1973, energy consumption rose 22 percent and the economy grew by 17 percent; but from 1973 to 1978, energy consumption rose only 5 percent and the economy grew by 12 percent.[2] The energy consumed per dollar's worth of Gross National Product (GNP) produced in other countries is also sharply lower than in the United States. The proportions in 1976 ranged from about half in France to 73 percent in West Germany and 82 percent in Sweden.[3] As if in confirmation that energy usage could be much more efficient, the amount of energy used in the United States to produce each dollar of GNP has declined each year since 1970.[4] Thus, even if growth is assumed to be necessary and desirable, strong evidence indicates it can be achieved without increased energy usage. We shall explore this issue more fully in Section II of Chapter 7.

The second assumption is that electricity is appropriate to so many uses that demand for it will continue to rise steadily. Between 1960 and 1978, demand for electricity did nearly quadruple. Electricity generating absorbed all the nation's hydro and nuclear capacity, most of its coal, a sixth of its natural gas, and increasing amounts of oil (nearly triple its usage in 1960). But the need for such intermediate conversion in the energy supply-usage process is very costly. Much primary energy (anywhere from one-half to two-thirds) is wasted in making electricity. The giant plants involved require massive capital investments to build. In the case of nuclear facilities, serious safety issues arise.

In the late 1970s, the high cost of such conversion, reflected in prices to consumers, led to sharp reductions in the rate of increase in demand for electricity. It also led to greater emphasis on the concept of "end use," the ultimate use to which energy would be put. By looking at the actual tasks to be done (heating rooms and water, lighting, powering cars and industrial machinery, etc.) and trying to connect them to forms of energy *required* to do them, the real need for electricity could be shown (at least theoretically) to be much lower than that projected. The relatively low temperatures required for space heating, for example, do not justify the thousands of degrees of temperature involved in nuclear fission or hundreds of degrees in burning of oil and gas that are requisite to producing electricity. One authority argued that *all* lighting, electric motors, electronics, etc., that *required* electricity actually constituted no more than 8 percent of all United States energy usage.[5] And a 1979 government report noted that only 57 percent of United States energy resources actually provided energy in end-use forms; the remaining 43 percent was lost in conversion, transmission, and so forth.[6]

This brings us to consideration of some of the contrasting solution premises involved in responses to our energy crisis. As already indicated, it makes a great deal of difference whether demand patterns and their components (i.e., the demand-growth link, electricity) are taken as "givens" of the situation. If they are, attention focuses almost exclusively on the supply side. Efforts are made to assure access to foreign oil, encourage domestic exploration and production through price decontrol or other inducements, and develop alternative energy sources, such as coal, nuclear, and synthetic fuels, with crash programs involving tremendous capital investments. Such solutions imply centralized means and high technology as well as great expense for every unit of energy ultimately produced.

In contrast, a balanced emphasis including systematic questions about the demand side makes possible a wider range of alternatives. Conservation and low-technology alternatives (particularly solar) play a much larger part. The means are local rather than central, for they depend on widespread changes in popular values and practices. Changes in sources of energy supply still have an important role in the total response, but there is more time, a greater range of choice among alternatives, and perhaps less necessity for massive new expense. One version of this combination of premises has been called the "soft path," in contrast to the "hard path" involved in the other set of premises.[7] As we shall see, the initial American policy response—such as it was—was primarily a hard path solution.

I PRESENT POLICIES

Americans had their first encounter with their "energy crisis" in late 1973. Gasoline shortages produced long lines at service stations and heating oil shortages were severe in the winter of 1973–1974. These apparently resulted from an Arab oil embargo imposed in October 1973 to pressure the United States and certain other countries against aiding Israel in the Mideast war of that time. It later appeared that actual shortages were few and lack of supplies to consumers developed in anticipation of price rises.[8] No one doubted, however, that a strong signal of a very real impending crisis had been given.

Quite properly, the focus was on oil. Domestic oil production was declining steadily after peaking in 1970 at about 11.3 million barrels per day. Demand was running at 16 million barrels per day, however, and was projected to rise each year. The growing gap could only be made up by imported oil (which totaled 33 percent of supplies in 1973, and sold for less than $3 per barrel), at least until alternative sources could be found or developed. Although future embargoes and price rises were thought possible, very few observers had any idea of the capacity of the OPEC to drive prices toward the $30 per barrel level reached by the end of the decade.

The Illusion of Energy Independence

The American policy response was slow, and subject to several enduring conflicts between vested interests. Within two weeks of the Arab embargo, President Nixon announced "Project Independence," a series of proposals designed to end energy dependence on all foreign countries by 1980. But the proposals were not really very far-reaching.

Congress created the Federal Energy Administration (FEA) to manage fuel supplies in emergencies and the Energy Research and Development Administration (ERDA) to develop nuclear and other alternative energy sources. The old Atomic Energy Commission and other energy functions were replaced by ERDA, which was to handle research and development, and by the new Nuclear Regulatory Commission (NRC), which was to be responsible for licensing and safety.

Senators and representatives sympathetic to the oil and gas industries blocked windfall tax proposals but sought deregulation of natural gas and accelerated procedures for building energy projects and leasing the outer continental shelf. Those responsive to environmentalists and the urban poor opposed deregulation of gas and removal of environmental standards and sought windfall taxes and price controls on domestic oil. Action was further constrained first by attention to the Watergate scandal and then by a declining sense of immediacy of the crisis.

In January of 1975, President Ford sent Congress a proposed Energy Independence Act, together with a description of actions he intended to take. The Democratic Congress struggled all year with the issues raised by these proposals, finally producing the Energy Policy and Conservation Act in December. The act required continuation of domestic oil price controls, and even extended controls to certain kinds of oil not previously covered. It also set fuel efficiency standards for cars, created the strategic oil reserve, and granted the FEA and the President many of the requested powers over utilities and fuel allocation. Standby rationing authority was made subject to congressional veto.

In 1976, the President proposed another sixteen energy measures. Only four (extension of the FEA, speeding up the Alaskan gas pipeline, heating standards, and weatherization assistance) were passed by the Congress. Refused or ignored were proposals to deregulate natural gas, grant powers to allocate supplies during shortages, and develop synthetic fuels. The major energy funding measure of the year was a bill authorizing almost $8 billion for research programs to be conducted by ERDA.

The pattern of funding for ERDA clearly shows the nuclear priorities of the time. In its first full year of operation, ERDA received $4.5 billion. Less than 2 percent was for solar energy, and less than 1 percent for conservation. Nuclear research and development, and nuclear weapons, made up most of the expenditures. The larger appropriations for fiscal year 1977 raised solar energy to about 4 percent of the total, but were still heavily devoted to nuclear development. In particular, funds were committed to nuclear fusion research ($275 million), nuclear fission reactors ($630 million), uranium enrichment ($925 million), and nuclear weapons ($1.36 billion).

One major project receiving nuclear research and development funds was the liquid-metal-cooled fast breeder reactor (LMFBR) at Clinch River, Tennessee. A "breeder" reactor creates more fuel than it uses, thus theoretically going on forever. If energy self-sufficiency were to be obtained, a great part of the production of electricity by means of nuclear breeder reactors seemed essential. In 1970, Congress funded a demonstration project. The project was supposed to establish that breeder reactors were practical for electric utilities and to encourage development of a related commercial industry.

By the end of the 1970s, hundreds of millions of dollars had been invested in the breeder reactor project. Delays had postponed the date by which the plant would be operational by several years. Cost estimates had tripled to more than $2 billion. The project was locked in controversy, in part because a byproduct of breeder reactors is plutonium, the fuel for nuclear weapons. ERDA was forced to defend its safety, security, and disposal procedures against charges that creating such amounts of highly dangerous plutonium would create a series of excessive risks. Throughout 1977–1980, the Congress and President Carter struggled over whether the project should be funded or terminated.

The Road to Price Decontrol

In 1977, President Carter proposed a series of 113 measures under the title of the National Energy Plan. Both he and congressional leaders asserted that it would be their top priority for the year. In the renewed atmosphere of crisis generated by rising oil imports and prices, Carter proposed to extend oil and gas price controls; induce conservation by businesses and homeowners through a variety of new standards, requirements, and tax incentives; and create a new Department of Energy to centralize federal government energy efforts and make them more effective.

In August 1977, Congress created the Energy Department, giving it nearly all the energy functions then scattered among other departments and agencies. But no other parts of the program, or alternatives to it, were enacted in 1977. Observers assigned responsibility for the failure variously to lack of administration political sensitivity and leadership, congressional disagreements over deregulation, special-interest tenacity, and the inherent difficulty of the problem.

Eighteen months after it was first proposed, what was left of the National Energy Plan was enacted by the Congress. Carter had sought to extend regulation of prices to gas produced and sold within a single state as well as to gas transported for sale elsewhere. Controls over interstate gas prices had led to sharply higher prices for intrastate gas and shortages in interstate supplies. Instead, Congress provided for a doubling of prices on newly discovered gas and the end of all controls by 1985. Where Carter sought power to order switches to coal, and taxes to penalize use of oil and gas, Congress provided standards only for newly constructed utility plants and an extended period during which conversion to coal would be encouraged.

In other 1978 actions, Congress established procedures for bidding on and leasing rights to oil and gas drillings on the outer continental shelf, and the East Coast was opened up to exploration and possible production. A major effort to develop coal slurry pipelines was defeated by a combination of railroad interests, liberals concerned about federal "giveaways" to

Table 6-2   Price Comparisons, 1950–1980

	1950	1960	1970	1973	1975	1978	1980
Retail price, gallon of regular gas	$0.27	$0.31	$0.36	$0.39	$0.57	$0.66	$1.21
OPEC oil, price per barrel*	$1.75	$1.80	$1.80	$5.18	$12.38	$13.66	$34.16
Consumer Price Index (1967 = 100)	72.1	88.7	116.3	131.1	161.2	195.4	230.9

*Based on year-end price of Saudi crude oil, the standard pricing measure for OPEC countries.
Source: Dollars and Sense, July–August 1980, pp. 14–15.

private industry, conservatives devoted to states' rights, and westerners worried about scarce water supplies. (Coal slurries are pipelines in which pulverized coal from Western surface mines would be mixed with water and transported hundreds of miles to Midwestern users and/or transfer points for Eastern shipment.) Pipeline developers would have been granted power to acquire rights-of-way by eminent domain (the legal procedure by which owners can be forced to yield their property for just compensation). Some consider coal slurries essential to bring coal transportation costs to an economical level and avoid repeated snarling of traffic by long trainloads of coal in many Western towns. They are opposed by the railroads, which hope (after restoring their roadbeds and rolling stock with federal support) to regain profitability through carrying massive amounts of coal. Environmentalists, ranchers, and others concerned about land damage and water supplies also oppose coal slurries.

When President Carter turned to the worsening energy crisis again in 1979, it was with an entirely different strategy. In April, he announced that he would use his existing powers to phase out price controls on domestic oil, beginning on June 1, 1979, letting prices rise to the then-current world levels. At the same time, he proposed to Congress a major "windfall tax" program on this now much more valuable oil. Not long after, another gas shortage developed, with resulting long lines at service stations and major price increases to consumers. Some blamed the shortage on reduced production by revolutionary Iran; others on deliberate oil company policies to legitimate price increases. In any event, the Carter administration held an unprecedented series of discussions with leaders of various sectors of the society and emerged in July with a vast new program to use the windfall revenues to develop energy alternatives.

Estimates of the amount of new revenues to be raised by 1990 under the windfall tax provisions as ultimately passed depended greatly on the actual world price for a barrel of oil during those years. Carter originally estimated that about $140 billion would become available. He proposed to devote the bulk of it ($88 billion) to the proposed Energy Security Corporation. This was to be an independent public corporation run by a seven-member board appointed by the President to develop its own energy production facilities or invest in private enterprises. Its purpose was to promote a synthetic fuels industry, in which oil would be produced from shale rock or coal liquefaction and gas would be made from coal or waste products ("biomass"). The technology already existed, but government support was thought necessary to encourage large-scale private investment in the field.

Other uses of the windfall revenues included promoting conservation, developing solar alternatives, helping utilities to convert to coal, and finding "unconventional" ways to produce oil and natural gas not otherwise likely to be recovered from existing wells. Two major projects were the development of mass transit facilities ($16.5 billion) and aid to the poor for payment of higher energy bills ($24 billion).

One other important proposal would have created an Energy Mobilization Board. This three-member board in the Executive Office of the President would have had the power to cut through federal and state licensing and environmental procedures to expedite energy projects. Another proposal not involving new spending would have imposed import quotas to assure that the United States would never use more foreign oil than it had in 1977.

None of these proposals was passed in 1979. President Carter eschewed further proposals in 1980 in hopes that action would be completed on the 1979 ones. In February, the windfall tax provisions were enacted. Based on then-current price forecasts,[9] more than $227 billion was estimated to become available by 1990. This left the oil companies with about 22 percent of the net profits derived from price decontrol alone. Of the sum raised, 25 percent was committed to helping the poor pay their bills to the oil companies; 15 percent was earmarked for energy develop-

Table 6-3   The Legislative Basis of U.S. Energy Policy

1. *Emergency Petroleum Allocation Act of 1973.* Establishes pricing and allocation power over petroleum supplies in the hands of the President.

2. *Energy Supply and Environmental Coordination Act of 1974.* Requires new utility plants to be designed to burn coal rather than oil or gas to make electricity.

3. *Energy Policy and Conservation Act of 1975.* Continued price controls on domestic oil, but authorized President to remove controls after June 1, 1979. Granted emergency powers to President, set standards for automobile fuel efficiency, established strategic petroleum reserve.

4. *Energy Conservation and Production Act of 1976.* Set standards for energy efficiency in new buildings, encouraged conservation through new electricity rates.

5. *Natural Gas Policy Act of 1978.* Ends price controls on natural gas in several stages to be completed by 1985.

6. *National Energy Conservation Policy Act of 1978.* Requires utilities to aid customers' conservation efforts in various ways, sets efficiency standards for appliances, grants conservation aid to schools and hospitals.

7. *Powerplant and Industrial Fuel Use Act of 1978.* Prohibits new utility plants from burning oil or gas, requires existing plants to convert by 1990, and grants authority to government to order conversion to coal under certain conditions.

8. *Energy Tax Act of 1978.* Gives tax credits for energy-saving modifications to homes and businesses, including solar and wind equipment but not wood stoves. Applies taxes to newly manufactured "gas guzzling" cars of less than 15 mpg rating in 1980.

9. *Energy Security Act of 1980.* Establishes Synthetic Fuels Corporation to promote that industry through loans and guarantees.

10. *Crude Oil Windfall Profits Tax of 1980.* Applies taxes to new profits realized through decontrol of domestic oil prices, allocates to new energy developments, mass transit, and assistance to the heating costs of the poor.

ment and mass transit, as determined by future legislation; and 60 percent was set aside for future tax reduction.

By June, the Synthetic Fuels Corporation had been approved. Originally planned for a $20 billion capability, the "synfuels" effort was charged by Congress with producing 2 million barrels of fuel per day by 1992. With such optimistic goals, even the Congress foresaw costs closer to $70 billion.[10] But at almost the same time, Congress defeated the third major component of the latest energy plan, the Energy Mobilization Board. A coalition of conservatives and liberals, fearing greater government intervention and overriding of state and local procedures, managed to prevent passage of an apparently broadly-supported bill. Nuclear energy development remained stalled as Congress and the President stayed deadlocked over the breeder reactor issue and public opposition mounted in the wake of the near-disaster at the Three Mile Island reactor in Pennsylvania.

One of President Reagan's first acts upon taking office was an Executive order to completely remove all remaining price controls on domestic oil. He also made it clear that his administration would be sympathetic to the needs of the struggling nuclear power industry. The development of synthetic fuels received a sharp setback, however, when the Department of Energy's funding for support of research and demonstration projects was substantially reduced. Indeed, the Department itself (and perhaps the national government) seemed slated for a much lesser role in seeking to cope with the energy crisis. Table 6-4 reflects these and other initial policy decisions. President Reagan's faith in the free economic market, particularly as regards development of new domestic oil once all price controls were removed, appeared to be the cornerstone of his administration's energy policy.

The Lessons of the First Stage of the Energy Crisis

The result of the first eight years of energy crisis policy making was a modest package: tax incentives to encourage conservation; ongoing decontrol of oil and gas prices with a portion of the new profits from oil devoted to finding other energy sources; and a variety of speeded-up opportunities for energy companies to develop new sources and distributing capacity. Although presidential proposals seemed to escalate with the deepening crisis, congressional action trailed well behind. Both President and Congress evinced a special concern for the extent to which existing patterns of business and social life would be affected.

The basic method by which public policy (understood as deliberate action *or* inaction) sought to cope with the crisis was to raise prices for consumers. That this was ultimately a very effective conservation device is shown by the most dramatic energy development of the late 1970s; demand for gasoline, and thus for imported oil, actually dropped in 1978 and 1979.

Table 6-4 Proposed Energy Reductions, First Stage of Reagan Economic Program, 1981 (in millions of current dollars)

	1982			1984		
	Current base*	Cuts	New total	Current base*	Cuts	New total
Solar development	$589	$365	$224	$657	$406	$251
Energy supply (various programs to develop new means of supply and storage)	605	156	449	572	170	402
Energy conservation (technology, regulation, financial aid)	799	310	489	776	589	187
Alcohol fuels (subsidies and loans)	133	123	10	29	29	—
Solar subsidies	149	149	—	147	147	—
Synthetic fuels	864	864	—	676	676	—
Fossil energy research (technology for coal, oil, and gas recovery)	799	361	438	895	549	346
Mass transit	876	96	780	1168	600	568

*"Current base" is a figure based on the current law used by the Reagan administration in its projections of February 18, 1981.

Source: *New York Times*, February 20, 1981, pp. A11–A16.

The developing recession helped to refute all the earlier forecasts of ever-rising demand. The major cause, however, was undoubtedly the system of rationing by price implemented by the unlikely coalition of OPEC price rises, oil companies pass-alongs of refinery, transportation, and marketing profit increments,[11] and government inaction. Though effective, the burden of such a policy falls most heavily on those least able to pay.

The implications of the changing American demand pattern are potentially far-reaching, perhaps extending to a redefinition of the nature of the "energy crisis" itself. In 1980, the United States imported 18 percent less oil than it did in 1979—the largest year-to-year decline in history.[12] Domestic output inched upward, mainly from Alaskan production but partly because of a substantial slowing of the rate of decline in production from the lower forty-eight states. The number of new wells drilled and the level of new exploration set records. The ratio of energy used to each GNP dollar produced continued its steady decline. Still, imports amounted to 40 percent of all United States petroleum needs in 1980. The impact of price increases (and recession) on both energy usage and energy efficiency was much greater than anticipated, and led some experts to revise substantially their projections of future demand patterns.

Perhaps ironically, the conflicts and delays of the first decade of the energy crisis—and the semideliberate grant of the power to shape energy policy from public authorities to the pricing mechanisms of OPEC and the oil industry—provided time during which the nature of the problem began to change. Price increases forced changes in people's lives and energy usage, ranging from severe hardships to mere inconvenience depending on their relative affluence. These changes may have been those immediately possible, and further adaptation might be much more difficult. The price of a barrel of oil rose from an average of $19.81 in 1979 to $31.89 in 1980, and stood at $34.16 in December 1980; further price increases seemed likely, with renewed pressure on usage patterns. But the implication seemed to be that the oil component of the energy crisis was less a problem of *actual shortage* of supplies than it was an *economic problem* (for people to be able to pay such prices for necessary heating and transportation) and a *political problem* (the threat of an embargo that might disrupt vital supplies and lead to war).

Shining through the discord of this period are three major assumptions shared by Presidents of both parties and the Congress. One is the acceptance of the structure of the energy industry as it is: a small number of giant companies with interests in all phases of several forms of energy production and marketing. Their independence and profit needs are taken for granted despite the consequences for consumers and the rest of the economy. Quite possibly, it is just assumed that by now there is no practical alternative. But it is noteworthy that in a period of growing crisis and record oil company profits, the only serious challenge to the structure of the industry was an occasional call for promoting competition by forcing companies to convert their "integrated" functions of production, transportation, refining, and marketing into independent companies specializing in just one such function.

Another major assumption is that the market is the best primary allocator of goods and services. Somehow, socially desirable ends must be adapted to market workings. Price increases, if large and prolonged enough, will shape behavior—and, not incidentally, restore or enlarge profit margins for major suppliers of necessities. Government strategies for changing supply or use patterns depend on making certain investments safer or more profitable for private industry. For example, government may undertake research and development itself, guarantee loans, or subsidize costs. Or, it may penalize some energy uses and encourage others by means of tax surcharges or credits.

Finally, there is the assumption that crash programs utilizing new technology and involving massive investments are the means to solution— if only they are undertaken in the proper "American spirit." Long a cultural assumption, validation rests on the evidence of the World War II effort, particularly the Manhattan Project, which developed the atom bomb, and, more recently, the space program. Next in line, and potentially the most expensive peacetime project ever undertaken, stands the Synthetic Fuels Corporation and associated coal-production projects. Not far behind are still-supported nuclear projects and high-technology solar satellite proposals.

These assumptions are not necessarily conscious, considered commitments. They are all the more significant because they function below the surface, widely shared but often unrecognized shaping forces. For an understanding of how such assumptions became operative, we must turn to the history of past policies.

II THE ORIGINS OF PRESENT POLICIES

Understanding of the origins of present United States energy policies begins (and nearly ends) with a history of the development of the world's largest industry, the international oil industry (Table 6-5). Of the seven leading companies that dominate this "private planning system operating on a global scale,"[13] five are based in the United States (Exxon, Mobil, Texaco, Gulf, Standard of California) and two in Britain (British Petroleum, Royal Dutch/Shell). Ranked by assets, the five American companies are among the seven largest of all American industrial corporations; only General Motors (second) and Ford (fourth) are comparable.

For the history of the rise of these and the other major oil companies, and the current structure of the industry, we shall rely primarily on Dr. John M. Blair's sober and definitive *The Control of Oil*.[14] Blair was for thirty-two years a United States government economist with the Temporary National Economic Commission, the Federal Trade Commission, and the United States Senate. He is the author of several major studies of economic concentration, particularly in the oil industry. Other works will be cited from time to time, usually when they present data and interpretations from authoritative government reports or oil company sources.[15]

The oil industry was born in 1859 when oil was first produced by drilling in western Pennsylvania. As its uses multiplied from lighting to powering steam engines to heating and automobiles, the production of crude oil steadily rose. In 1909, United States production was 500,000 barrels per day, more than the rest of the world combined.[16] The major United States companies marketed their products throughout the industrialized world and also sold crude oil to other companies. As late as the 1920s, American firms supplied nearly three-fifths of total foreign demand.[17]

The operations of the United States oil industry were prominent among the targets of antitrust-law litigation almost from the first enactment of such laws. In 1911, the Standard Oil Trust (put together by John D. Rockefeller in 1882) was broken up. However, the four resulting companies (currently Exxon, Mobil, SoCal, and Standard of Indiana) still operated, still dominated their markets, and are still controlled by Rockefeller family individuals, trusts, foundations, and banks.[18] The vital principle established by the Rockefeller Trust era remained clear: cooperation was more profitable than competition, although the latter was a strategy to be applied vigorously when the opportunity arose to eliminate or absorb a smaller company.

When oil was discovered in the Middle East just before World War I, British and Dutch interests cooperated to secure exclusive rights to production in Iraq. Thus, the power of British Petroleum (BP) and Royal Dutch/Shell in world markets was established. Because oil was already such a strategic necessity and there had been temporary shortages during World War I, the United States government strongly supported the American companies' postwar efforts to move into the Middle East. Exxon and Mobil bargained their way into part-ownership of the BP-Shell Iraq Petroleum Company in 1928. In the early 1930s, SoCal and Texaco acquired concessions in Bahrain and Saudi Arabia. Saudi Arabian oil was such a large find that the Arabian-American Oil Company (Aramco) was formed to develop it. Exxon and Mobil were ultimately allowed to buy into

Table 6-5 The Oil Industry, 1980

U.S.		International	
"Top eight"	"Lesser majors"	"Seven sisters"	Leading "independents"
Exxon	Getty	Exxon	Compagnie Française
Mobil	Phillips	Mobil	Pétrole
SoCal	Signal	SoCal	Continental
Stand. (Ind.)	Union	Texaco	Marathon
Texaco	Continental	Gulf	Amerada Hess
Gulf	Sun	Royal Dutch/Shell	Occidental
Shell	Amerada Hess	BP	
ARCO	Cities Service		
	Marathon		

the project. Also in the early 1930s, Gulf and BP acquired concessions in Kuwait, contracting to supply Exxon and Shell as well. Concessions covering five-sixths of Iran had been secured in 1931; in 1933, the concessions were acquired by the Anglo-Iranian Oil Co. (BP), which promptly made supply agreements with Exxon and Mobil.

In this way, the principle of cooperation focused on *supply*. In each of these cases, agreements were made covering how much oil would be produced, where it would be marketed, and at what prices. To be avoided wherever possible was potentially ruinous price competition between major companies. At the same time that the new Middle Eastern oil was being divided between the "seven sisters" of the industry, agreements were made to cover *marketing*. After a brief price war between Mobil and Shell in 1927, one that started in India and spread rapidly to the United States and Britain, the famous "As Is" agreement of 1928 was negotiated by the heads of Exxon (ever the voice of Mobil as well), BP, and Shell. Meeting at Achnacarry, Scotland, they drew up a document, dated September 17, 1928, that provided for: (1) accepting and maintaining the market shares of each company; (2) making their facilities available to each other; (3) drawing supplies from nearby producing areas and not using surpluses to affect prices elsewhere; and (4) not expanding except to meet growing consumer needs.[19] This agreement was followed by three detailed agreements in the early 1930s that fixed quotas and prices for various markets, provided for exchange of information, and set the compensation to be paid by one company to another in the event of a violation. By 1932, Mobil, Gulf, and Texaco were also formal participants. Finally, principles were established for dealing with troublesome "outsiders," i.e., independent refining or marketing companies.

One of the factors giving the major companies such predominant influence in the industry was (and is) their *integrated* character. Oil is one of the very few industries where the same company produces, transports, refines, and markets a product. This enables their control to be far more effective. They can manage *supply*, preventing too much oil from becoming available and undermining prices. They can simultaneously manage *marketing*, keeping prices stable at profitable levels. By undertaking each function themselves, they can both realize profit from each stage of the process and keep any independent companies from developing new markets through competitive price-cutting. If an independent company should try to expand its operations in one of these areas by such price-cutting, the integrated majors can shut off supplies, boycott or otherwise refuse to supply services, and/or undercut its prices for the period required to put it out of business.

For the most part, the oil companies were able to control supply and manage the terms of marketing entirely through their own actions. But at certain key points, government assistance was necessary. In the 1920s and 1930s, the national government helped by restricting access to United States oil sources unless other countries permitted the American companies to explore within their jurisdictions and by pressuring the British government to open up its Middle East protectorates. During World War II, lend-lease assistance was provided to the King of Saudi Arabia to protect Aramco interests there; the four-company partnership in Aramco was cleared against United States antitrust action on national security grounds; and additional payments to the King were facilitated by means of a credit against United States income taxes, in a kind of taxpayers' subsidy of Aramco operating costs. But perhaps the most important assistance was provided by state governments in the form of controls over how much oil could be produced from within their borders. For example, the Texas Railroad Commission, acting ostensibly on grounds of conservation, engaged in detailed management of production so that supplies would never reach the point of an excess that would encourage price-cutting.

After World War II, the national government intervened ever more supportively to protect sources of supply. Half the world's oil was still being produced within the United States in the early 1950s, but cheap Venezuelan and Middle Eastern oil was starting to be much more profitable. When the Iranian government sought to nationalize BP properties in 1951, the majors were able to use their 98 percent control of the world oil market to boycott Iranian oil and replace it with production elsewhere. The Central Intelligence Agency (CIA) helped to reinstall the Shah at the head of a new Iranian government. The United States then arranged a consortium of the major oil companies to develop and market Iranian oil (and not incidentally, thereby provide financial support to the Shah). Later in the decade, the national government imposed import quotas on the less-expensive foreign oil to prevent it from disrupting price and supply patterns of domestic oil produced for the American market.

The mid-1950s were probably the high point of oil industry influence and prospects in the world. The five United States majors produced two-thirds of the oil for the world oil market, and the two British majors almost all the rest. The countries in which the oil was produced played little or no part in the process. They merely accepted the royalties granted them by the majors' unilateral pricing decisions. Vast programs of suburban housing development in the United States, subsidized by government-guaranteed mortgages, were creating new demand for automobiles and gasoline. A massive new interstate highway system funded by the federal government would add thousands of miles of superhighways (and gasoline demand) in the next decade. Utilities were switching to oil to generate electricity to meet their steeply rising demand. Oil-state senators and representatives dominated the leadership and key committees of the

Congress. Oil influence in the executive branch was strong regardless of which political party was in power.[20]

In this context, the majors were able to keep prices stable and relatively low. Their profits were grounded solidly on a carefully managed growth of total world sales of about 9.5 percent per year and great expansion of production of very inexpensive Middle Eastern oil. Investment in new exploration shifted sharply from the United States to the Middle East and Africa after about 1957. United States reserves, including offshore sources, were estimated to be plentiful. Access to foreign oil appeared to be entirely secure.

In the 1960s, three developments occurred to change, but not immediately threaten, this rosy picture. One was the formation of the Organization of Petroleum Exporting Countries (OPEC) in 1960. Two successive cuts in crude oil prices paid to oil-producing countries, implemented by the majors without consultation, led to a meeting of Iraq, Iran, Saudi Arabia, Venezuela, and Kuwait, and to the formation of a permanent organization of oil producers. Although ignored by the majors and the world press, from the beginning OPEC's early leaders had the intent to allocate production in just the same manner that the oil companies then did.[21]

Second was the rise of independent producers and marketers, particularly those drawing on new supplies from countries like Libya and Algeria. These countries had the foresight (and power) to grant their concessions for oil discovered in the 1950s to many different companies in competitive bidding. By supplying the European market from directly across the Mediterranean, the independents could undersell the majors and noticeably affect their markets. For this reason, and because production in the United States was relatively expensive, in the 1960s the majors experienced unaccustomed profit reductions—to about the average of all American industrial corporations.

Finally, the frustration of American military power in Vietnam and the dilution of financial strength and diplomatic leadership that followed, undermined one of the industry's less visible props. It should probably be added that the military strength of the Soviet Union was by now sufficient to make overt use of American power risky in any event.

The first sign of the weakening of the major's grip came in 1970 when a Middle Eastern pipeline failure interrupted supplies to Europe. Libya moved swiftly to pressure an American independent with no other source of crude oil, the Occidental Petroleum Company, into sharp price increases. Other companies were forced to follow. In 1971, the leadership of the Shah of Iran helped OPEC to obtain a then-large 50-cent-per-barrel increase. At the same time, it should be recalled, American domestic production had leveled off, while demand (and hence imports) rose steadily. The oil-producing countries were on the verge of reaching parity with the Western oil companies that had controlled their resources for so long.

But the oil industry was far from ready to yield its role in energy production. A series of mergers had increased the size and power of the companies just below the majors. All of them moved aggressively into alternative fuel sources. Standard of Ohio, with BP support, led the way into Alaskan development of both oil and natural gas. Because gas is usually found with oil, the majors already produced about 75 percent of America's natural gas. In the 1960s, the oil companies acquired coal companies, to the point where half of the top-ten coal producers of the early 1970s were oil companies. The oil companies also controlled about half of the known coal reserves in the United States, the world's leading source of coal. Similarly, the oil companies dominate in the nascent synthetic fuels industry—both in coal gasification and liquefaction and in extracting oil from shale rock. They also mine about 60 percent of domestic uranium and control 72 percent of high-quality uranium reserves, so that they are deeply involved in the nuclear alternative as well. Just to complete the story, they have recently begun to move into solar research and technology.

The principal focus of the oil companies, however, is still the production and marketing of oil. Nor are they about to be replaced in this regard, despite the new power of OPEC. What has developed since the embargo and price increases of 1973 is a new relationship—not a reduction in overall significance. For one thing, the relatively thin profit margins and high cost of American production in the early 1970s had made clear that expanded domestic exploration and production would require sharp price increases before it would become economical. For another, much oil company profit occurs *after* oil has been withdrawn from the ground, in transportation, refining, and marketing—very little of which is now, or is likely to come, under OPEC control. And, every time the OPEC price rises, so does the value of the companies' American reserves, and with no added costs. In short, the oil industry may not have *wanted* the embargo and OPEC assertiveness of the 1970s, but the price increases have been highly functional and the newly equal relationship at least tolerable. A look at the record-setting profit levels of the industry in the last half of the decade of the 1970s (Table 6-6) more than adequately proves these conclusions.

The United States–based portion of the oil industry retains firm control over energy supplies and prices. And it still powerfully influences the United States government and American values and beliefs generally. The shortages of 1973–1974 and 1979, and the price rises associated with them, are promoted chiefly as the result of Arab greed and profligate American usage. And even when Congress makes efforts to tax or

Table 6-6   Major Oil Company Sales and Profits, 1979 and 1980 (in billions of current dollars)

	1979				1980			
	Sales	% Change	Profits	% Change	Sales	% Change	Profits	% Change
Exxon	84	+30	4.3	+ 56	110	+30	5.7	+32
Mobil	48	+28	2.0	+ 78	64	+32	3.3	+63
Texaco	39	+34	1.7	+106	52	+34	2.6	+50
SoCal	32	+29	1.8	+ 64	43	+34	2.4	+35
Gulf	26	+30	1.3	+ 68	29	+10	1.4	+ 6
Standard (Ind.)	20	+23	1.5	+ 40	28	+38	1.9	+27
Arco	17	+31	1.2	+ 45	24	+45	1.7	+42
Shell	15	+31	1.1	+ 38	20	+37	1.5	+37
Conoco	13	+32	.8	+ 81	19	+44	1.0	+26
Sun	11	+42	.7	+ 69	13	+22	.7	+ 3

Source: *New York Times*, March 19, 1980, and March 2, 1981, p. D3.

otherwise limit oil company supply and pricing power, the capable coalition of oil and gas lobbyists and sympathetic elected officials normally turns them back. In number of lobbyists and extent of campaign contributions, the oil and gas industry is the national leader.[22] No other industry approaches its influence.

For all these reasons, United States energy policy tends to be an extension of oil industry practice. It would be very difficult for serious policy makers to even formulate, let alone enact or implement, policies that did not take into account the structure and needs of the oil industry. To be sure, occasionally the industry loses a round in Congress—as when it was forced to surrender its unique "depletion allowance" (tax credit for a share of the oil removed from the ground in a given year). But routinely, and characteristically, the U.S. and state governments endorse and enforce the decisions made within the oil industry. Variously known as a private planning system, or as a private government, in the affairs of the world the international oil industry is a force greater than most governments.

III UNITED STATES POLICY IN COMPARATIVE PERSPECTIVE

The energy policies and problems of the other industrialized countries differ from those of the United States in two basic ways: each has reached greater energy intensity or efficiency, often with variations in national style, supply mix, and end uses; and all profoundly depend on United States energy policy and performance. We shall highlight some of the contrasts in efficiency of usage first. Then we consider variations of national style and the extent of dependency on the energy practices of the United States.

The most obvious contrast in energy efficiency arises in the transportation sector. The United States is distinguished by decentralized patterns of residence, distances traveled from home to work, number of automobiles and propensity toward single-person use, and general commitment to personal mobility in a large country. Partly as a result, the United States (and Canada) lead the world by a wide margin in the share of energy devoted to transportation. The United States uses four times as much energy per person for transportation as West Germany, for example.[23] Such ratios may change, of course, as the price of gasoline in the United States rises. European gasoline usage has been much more energy intensive because of much more fuel-efficient cars and prices per gallon two to three times those of the United States. Japanese gasoline usage has been even more energy intensive, for essentially the same reasons, plus extensive mass transit systems.

This contrast carries over into other areas. In space heating, for example, the United States uses twice as much energy per person as West Germany.[24] The United States comes closest to European standards in the energy intensity of industrial production, where we lead some countries and trail others. Overall, the European countries still uniformly produce more dollars worth of GDP (Gross Domestic Product) per person for the same amount of energy used. Per capita energy consumption in the United States in 1976, for example, was roughly two and one-half times that in France and almost twice that in Germany. These differences in consumption are *not* due to the greater total output in the United States.[25] When the energy required to produce $1 million worth of Gross Domestic Product is compared, France uses only about half as much and Germany three-quarters of that used in the United States. Americans apparently just use more energy than people in countries where it has been more expensive for much longer.

Variations in National Style

Variations tend to follow lines marked out by special features of each country's supply situation, but there are exceptions reflecting cultural or economic differences. We shall consider the major economies: West Germany, Great Britain, France, and Japan.[26]

West Germany has the largest industrial base and the largest energy consumption of the European countries. Its energy sources are about half oil, almost all of which is imported, about 20 percent natural gas, and 20 percent coal. Nuclear technology is well advanced; Germany leads the European countries in production, but still derives only a tiny proportion of its primary energy from this source. Natural gas reserves are limited, but coal is relatively plentiful. The danger of dependence on oil imported from OPEC is viewed as very high.

German energy policy has sought to minimize this danger in several ways. The government has invested heavily in a national oil company, which is conducting explorations all over the world and seeking closer mutual exchange relations with the Middle Eastern countries. Oil might also be available at some point from British North Sea exports. Natural gas supplies have been augmented by substantial imports from the Soviet Union. Coal production has been expanded, although at rates lower than hoped. The official targets for expanded nuclear power called for raising nuclear electricity-generating capacity from 4 percent of the total in 1975 to 25 percent in 1980 and 45 percent in 1985. But delays resulting in part from popular opposition make these targets unlikely. And energy usage was rising in 1980, despite slowing growth. The picture remains one of continuing dependence on imported oil.

Great Britain has had relatively poor economic performance throughout the postwar years. Forced to import almost all her raw materials and more than half her food, Britain has had chronic balance-of-payments problems, rising indebtedness, and persistent inflation. Coal was plentiful but very difficult for an antiquated industry to extract. For decades, all oil had to be imported; and by 1970, oil represented nearly half of all energy supplies.

In this context, discovery of oil under the North Sea represented a dramatic opportunity for turning around both the energy situation and the economy as a whole. Britain formed a national oil company to conduct exploration and production *and* to oversee development of other tracts. A national gas monopoly was created as well. Production was estimated to reach 2 million barrels per day in 1980 and 3 million by 1985, with the possibility that enough would be available for exports sufficient to relieve the balance-of-payments drain. Delays and technical problems were encountered, but production goals still seemed within reach.

Coal remains a major British energy resource, although steadily replaced by cheap imported oil in the postwar decades (from 96 percent of all energy sources in 1946 to little more than 33 percent by 1974). Expanded production will be necessary to enable exports of both coal and oil to produce any income. Coal too is a national enterprise in Britain. Thus, all the main sources of energy are under direct government control. Nuclear power development has never gotten seriously underway. Quite probably, it never will. In prospect for Britain, alone among the industrialized nations, is energy self-sufficiency—at least for one or two decades.

France follows the general European pattern of initial postwar dependence on indigenously produced coal followed by steady seduction by inexpensive imported oil. In 1950, 70 percent of French energy was produced at home, most of it by coal but a significant and growing proportion by hydropower; France remains today the European leader in hydropower. By 1973, however, France was importing more than three-quarters of her energy supplies, 80 percent of which was petroleum. In 1959, for example, fuel oil accounted for barely 5 percent of electricity production, but had reached 40 percent in 1973 and was expected to exceed half by the early 1980s.

The French response to the embargo and price rises of 1973–1974 was distinctive in its nuclear emphasis. To some extent, this was foreshadowed by the nationalist commitment to the development of an independent nuclear weapons capability. But early development of nuclear electricity-generating plants was slow, studded with equipment and construction failures. A four-year moratorium resulted in 1966–1970. New technology was introduced thereafter, and momentum increased after the crisis. By 1980, France was installing the world's first commercial-sized fast breeder reactor. Scheduled to enter service in 1983, the "Super-Phoenix" will produce more nuclear fuel than it uses. However, that fuel will be in the form of plutonium, the most deadly radioactive of the nuclear family and the basic ingredient of modern nuclear weapons.

The managers of the French nuclear program point out that French uranium, converted to unending stores of plutonium in fast breeder reactors, would be worth 50 billion tons of oil, or something comparable to Middle Eastern oil reserves.[27] Certainly France has the most ambitious nuclear program in the Western world. The nuclear share of electricity generation is projected to reach more than 60 percent by 1985 and 85 percent by the year 2000. Opposition to French nuclear development from the French people has been negligible. Much more vigorous objections were voiced by the Carter administration in the United States, arguing that the production of plutonium on this scale increases the danger of the spread of nuclear weapons. Nevertheless, France has projected several more fast breeder plants.

Japan has enjoyed the world's fastest-growing economy of the postwar years. From 1960 to 1972, economic growth averaged a staggering 12 percent per year. But Japan has no significant oil, gas, or coal. In those same years, therefore, nearly all energy supplies had to be imported: total energy consumption trebled; oil and gas quintupled; and coal and electricity rose about one and one-half times. Like the European countries, Japan too was switching from coal to the cheaper oil. In 1962, coal represented 36 percent of primary energy, oil 46 percent. Ten years later, coal stood at 17 percent and oil at 75 percent. Japan imported 86 percent of all its energy in 1972. It was therefore the most vulnerable of all the industrialized nations to the OPEC strategy.

The Japanese response was to impose an immediate 10 percent cut in consumption of both oil and electric power. Further, it initiated a long-range program of developing oil supplies from its own outer continental shelf and from direct government-to-government agreements with oil-producing countries. More aggressive exports were projected as a means of increasing the foreign exchange necessary to pay for higher-priced imported oil. Japan can do little else given its lack of indigenous resources. Nuclear power generation has been developed on a small scale. However, strong popular opposition exists, and a number of geological, climatological, and technical factors have also made progress difficult.

The Impact of the United States

Summarizing this brief review: Germany is looking for oil while trying to develop more coal; Britain has found oil and envisions self-sufficiency; France has committed itself to the nuclear alternative; and Japan is preparing itself to export enough to pay the price for imported oil. All of these efforts, including the British, are undertaken with a kind of desperation under the shadow of what the United States will do in the way of energy policy and performance. No alternative to imported oil exists; it will continue to be the primary near-term source. The American demand is so great that it is more than that of all the other countries combined. Thus, American consumption levels will do more to affect the supplies and prices of imported oil to the other countries than anything they themselves can do. The European countries and Japan are already using energy far more intensively than the United States, and there is much less that they can do by way of conservation. But continued rise in American demand for imported oil will stretch existing and projected supplies beyond their limits and push prices steadily upwards throughout the world. These are the stark facts that lie behind repeated European criticism of the United States for failure to enact a comprehensive energy policy.

Table 6-7 compares the energy usage of the major countries and the growing part played by imported oil for each. It may serve to summarize the points just made. Notice first the absolute size of American oil consumption: 55 percent of the oil used by the noncommunist industrialized world is consumed by the United States, even though oil is still less than half of all United States energy usage. The next largest oil user, Japan, consumes less than one-third of the American total.

Next, the table shows the high reliance of the other countries (except Canada, and very recently Great Britain) on imported oil. In the final column, the growing portion of all energy usage that is represented by imported oil is very clear. West Germany, France, Italy, and Japan all depend on imported oil for more than half of total energy supplies; in the case of Japan, the proportion is more than 70 percent. These are trends of

Table 6-7 Major OECD Countries' Energy Usage and Oil Shares

		Total energy usage*	Total oil usage*	Oil as % of energy	Imported oil as % of all oil	as % of all energy
United States	1960	1,014	453	45	14.6	6.5
	1970	1,570	688	44	22.2	9.7
	1978	1,842	889	48	46.2	22.2
Canada	1960	96	41	43	33.7	14.4
	1970	155	71	46	2.1	1.0
	1978	207	89	43	13.7	5.9
Japan	1960	95	30	32	100+	31.6
	1970	284	195	69	100+	70.9
	1978	359	259	72	100+	70.5
France	1960	90	27	30	94.4	28.1
	1970	150	88	59	90.4	53.0
	1978	185	111	60	94.8	57.1
West Germany	1960	146	31	22	86.6	18.6
	1970	236	128	54	94.7	51.2
	1978	271	146	54	96.4	51.8
Italy	1960	50	21	41	94.1	38.8
	1970	117	83	71	97.7	69.2
	1978	143	96	67	88.1	58.8
Great Britain	1960	170	44	26	100+	26.7
	1970	213	100	47	100+	47.2
	1978	213	97	46	43	19.6

*Millions of tons of oil equivalent; 1 million tons = 20,000 barrels/day.
   Source: Organization for Economic Cooperation and Development, *Economic Outlook*, 1979, Tables 32 and 33, pp. 63–64.

long development, the product of the extended period during which oil was so inexpensive. They cannot be reversed within a period of shorter duration: alternative supplies are sometimes not available, and always require long lead times for development. In the words of one leading student of Western energy policy,

. . . what must be an inescapable conclusion for all energy planners in the Western world, is that, whatever efforts may be launched to realize these alternatives, the brute fact is that OPEC and Saudi Arabia in particular are likely to remain the residual source of energy for the foreseeable future, probably for most of the balance of this century.[28]

The world outlook for oil availability, and the pressing need for conservation, has been cogently set forth in various publications of the Organization for Economic Cooperation and Development (OECD) and the International Energy Administration (IEA). Formed in 1960 at the urging of the United States, OECD includes all the major noncommunist industrialized nations of the world, twenty four countries in all. It serves as a framework for the exchange of information and the beginnings of cooperative planning. The IEA is a sixteen-country body set up in 1974 within OECD to promote energy restraint, emergency sharing, and long-range self-sufficiency. The principal thrust of these two bodies' analyses is: (a) world oil demand, even at reduced levels of expansion, will exceed world production capacity sometime in the 1980s; and (b) the key to narrowing the gap to manageable proportions, if it is possible at all, lies with conservation where it would have the greatest effect—in the United States transportation and space heating sectors.

One factor in world demand is the prospect that the Soviet Union will switch from being a net oil exporter to being a significant importer sometime in the 1980s. This would bring the total world demand on OPEC resources to something like 50 million barrels per day. With all states producing at capacity, Saudi Arabia, with the largest reserves and greatest potential capacity, would have to reach about 20 million barrels per day. This is far beyond present and even projected capacity. Moreover, Saudi Arabia is likely to lose its role as price moderator within OPEC when it loses its capacity to increase production. All of these projections, of course, assume that the Middle East in general, and Saudi Arabia in particular, remain at peace and internally stable for the entire decade. Neither OECD nor IEA anticipate the breakup of OPEC solidarity or the advent of major new production in the 1980s.

United States production, including Alaskan, is expected to decline in this period even with price decontrol and new fields and extraction methods. Perhaps 9 million gallons per day will be the maximum available from domestic sources unless there are dramatic new discoveries on the Alaskan North Slope, the Beaufort Sea, or the outer continental shelf.[29] With demand running at 18 million gallons per day, even very sharp reductions through conservation would leave the United States drawing heavily on OPEC sources.

These demand prospects underscore the OECD proposals for conservation in the United States. Citing the transportation sector particularly, OECD argued in 1977 that the United States could cut its consumption between 48 percent and 53 percent by such measures as mandatory fuel economy standards, higher fuel prices, greater efficiency and payloads in the trucking and airline industries, car pools, and expanded mass transit. Savings of up to 16 percent were seen possible in the residential/commercial space heating sector, principally through insulation.[30] OECD holds that the combination of American conservation and development of new supplies would amount to 55 percent of all savings possible within the twenty-four member countries.[31]

This may seem like a bleak projection for the coming decades. What it really stresses, however, is the extent of interdependence among the industrialized countries and the centrality of energy policy to their economic, social, and political futures. And we have not even mentioned the potentially ruinous effects of ongoing inflation, balance-of-payments problems, currency fluctuations, and inability to repay debts on the part of developing countries that follow in the wake of the shortfall and price increases of imported oil. In 1980, the seven leading countries of OECD pledged to cut the place of oil among their energy sources from 53 percent to 40 percent by 1990, doubling the use of coal and building more nuclear plants. However, they displayed little confidence that this would be possible without internal unrest and perhaps new political arrangements.[32]

Some unexpected breathing space was made available in 1981 and 1982 when high prices and low growth combined to reduce world demand, and continued high Saudi Arabian production kept supplies up. In this context, the world experienced a "glut" (or oversupply) of oil, and prices even slipped a bit. And the CIA acknowledged that its long-asserted conviction that the Soviet Union would become a net importer of oil in the 1980s was inaccurate; Soviet resources were newly estimated to be adequate to prospective needs for the foreseeable future.[33] But these developments do not change the basic picture, which remains one of vulnerability and dependence on the part of the Western industrial countries. Let us return to the specifics of the American situation.

NOTES

1 Data in this paragraph are drawn from the *National Journal*, July 21, 1979, p. 1200.

2 *New York Times*, February 20, 1980, p. E20 (citing a National Academy of Sciences study report).

3 Robert Stobaugh and Daniel Yergin, eds., *Energy Future: Report of the Energy Project at Harvard Business School* (New York: Random House, 1979), p. 143.

4 *National Journal*, July 21, 1979, Loc. cit.

5 Amory B. Lovins, *Soft Energy Paths: Toward a Durable Peace* (New York: Harper

& Row, 1979), p. 39.

6 U.S. Department of Energy, *Domestic Policy Review of Solar Energy* (Washington, D.C.: Government Printing Office, 1979), p. iii.

7 Lovins, *Soft Energy Paths*. Lovins defines "soft energy paths" as those low or soft technologies that are "flexible, resilient, sustainable, and benign" (p. 38). The contrast with "hard" paths is grounded on "the technical and sociopolitical *structure* of the energy system" (p. 38).

8 For detailed analysis of this "shortage," see Robert Engler, *The Brotherhood of Oil* (Chicago: University of Chicago Press, 1977). Unless otherwise indicated, however, this account rests on the authoritative *Energy Policy* (Washington, D.C.: Congressional Quarterly, 1979).

9 *New York Times*, March 2, 1980, p. E5.

10 Ibid., June 29, 1980.

11 *Dollars and Sense,* September 1979, citing *Fortune* magazine.

12 Data in this paragraph are drawn from *New York Times*, January 16, 1981, p. D4, and January 29, 1981, p. 23, and from *Oil and Gas Journal*, January 26, 1981, pp. 102–103.

13 Engler, *Brotherhood of Oil*, p. 18.

14 John M. Blair, *The Control of Oil* (New York: Pantheon, 1976).

15 The best of these are Engler, *Brotherhood of Oil*, and Anthony Sampson, *The Seven Sisters* (New York: Viking, 1975). See also the applicable chapters in the authoritative Stobaugh and Yergin, *Energy Future*, and Barry Commoner, *The Poverty of Power* (New York: Knopf, 1976).

16 Stobaugh and Yergin, *Energy Future*, p. 14.

17 Blair, *Control of Oil*, p. 33.

18 Ibid., p. 149. The next paragraphs rely on this account.

19 Ibid., pp. 55 ff.

20 Engler, *Brotherhood of Oil*, chap. 3, provides the details.

21 Stobaugh and Yergin, *Energy Future*, p. 25.

22 *Congressional Quarterly Weekly Report*, November 3, 1979, p. 2455.

23 Lovins, *Soft Energy Paths*, p. 33.

24 Ibid.

25 Stobaugh and Yergin, *Energy Future*, p. 143.

26 Except where indicated, this account is based on Douglas Evans, *Western Energy Policy: The Case for Competition* (London: Macmillan, 1978), Leon Lindberg, ed., *The Energy Syndrome: Comparing National Responses to the Energy Crisis* (Lexington, Mass.: Lexington Books, 1977), and *World Energy Outlook* (Paris: Organization for Economic Cooperation and Development, 1977).

27 *New York Times*, May 21, 1980.

28 Evans, *Western Energy Policy*, pp. 9–10.

29 Stobaugh and Yergin, *Energy Future*, p. 42.

30 *World Energy Outlook*, p. 69.

31 Ibid., p. 36.

32 *New York Times*, June 29, 1980.

33 *New York Times*, June 18, 1981.

Chapter 7

Energy: The Problem and Some Alternatives

We have seen that, as serious as the energy crisis is for Americans, it is much more serious—and has caused much greater efforts at conservation —in Europe and Japan. The contrasts in extent of dependence on imported oil, and in efficiency of energy usage per person, are very instructive. Even though our own usage of energy and of imported oil was dropping steadily in the early 1980s (partly because of high costs and recession), we still had not approached the European or Japanese efforts. The focus of the noncommunist world's energy problem, therefore, remains the United States—its usage patterns and energy policies.

This chapter begins with analysis of the American side of this problem, examining the problems and possibilities involved in each of the energy sources that are now known. Finally, we examine the implications involved in some of the major alternative solutions.

I THE CURRENT AMERICAN POLICY DILEMMA

Much of the American energy problem has already been described. Essentially, it consists of heavy and at least temporarily unavoidable dependence on imported oil, a significant share of which comes from the potentially turbulent Middle East. About $78 billion was drawn out of the United States economy in this way in 1980, widening the dollar-undermining trade deficit that had been developing for years. The actual sources of imported oil are shown in Table 7-1. Much United States oil comes from relatively secure and possibly expandable African and Latin American sources. But there apparently will be an unavoidable dependence for the foreseeable future on Middle Eastern oil. In any event our OECD trading partners are utterly dependent on the latter source. If world demand exceeds available oil-producing capacity, as it is projected to do in the late 1980s, serious economic and social dislocations and/or military conflicts appear inevitable.

Secondly, a sharp disjunction between United States energy usage and domestic supplies seems to point the way to any real approach to self-sufficiency. Oil and gas make up about 75 percent of energy usage, while coal supplies about 18 percent. But oil and gas represent only about 7 percent of known United States energy reserves, and coal stands at 90 percent. Self-sufficiency and national security would seem to require reversal of this relationship. The United States is adequately supplied with uranium, at least to the end of the century. In that respect nuclear power is a viable option.

Table 7-1 Sources of Imported Oil, 1980*

Country	Thousands of barrels per day	Country share as % of total
Saudi Arabia†	1,254,900	18.4
Nigeria†	862,800	12.6
Libya†	547,200	8.0
Mexico	535,700	7.8
Algeria†	487,400	7.1
Canada	435,100	6.4
Venezuela†	433,200	6.3
Virgin Islands	379,000	5.5
Indonesia†	340,600	5.0
Netherlands Antilles	221,100	3.2
United Arab Emirates†	196,200	2.9
Trinidad & Tobago	179,200	2.6
Bahamas	85,300	1.2
Puerto Rico	79,000	1.2
Other OPEC‡	128,200	1.9
All other countries	674,800	9.9
Total	6,839,900	100.0

*Average through October 1980.
†OPEC member countries.
‡Ecuador, Gabon, Iraq, Kuwait, and Qatar.
Source: U.S. Department of Energy, Monthly Energy Review, January 1981, pp. 32—33. Figures may not add due to rounding.

The American energy problem clearly involves finding ways to reduce the growth of demand, perhaps even reducing demand itself, *and* developing alternative sources of supply. So far, tax incentives for conservation measures and sharp price rises have been the principal approach to reducing demand. They have had (together with an economic recession) demonstrable effects. For example, about eight and one-half barrels of oil equivalent were consumed per $1,000 of GNP (in 1975 dollars) in the 1960s. By 1978, 6 percent less energy was required per unit of GNP, equaling a demand reduction of 2 million to 2.5 million barrels per day. And in 1980, imported oil fell back to 1975 levels.[1]

In this section, we shall focus on the serious dilemmas involved in trying to expand each of the possible sources of additional energy supplies. In the next section, we shall contrast these "hard path" possibilities with the "soft path" alternatives and look at other types of solutions to the evolving energy crisis.

Coal

The size of American coal reserves—30 percent of the world's supply—has led to calling the United States "the Persian Gulf of coal" and coal itself "the great black hope." But serious practical problems stand in the way of realizing such hopes. These have to do with the reconversion of electricity-generating utilities to burning coal, the locations and mining practices involved in producing coal, and the environmental and health problems surrounding each.

The principal uses of coal are the production of electricity by utilities (about three-quarters), production of industrial heat (particularly in the iron and steel industries), and industrial steam. After World War II, oil replaced coal in many industries and utilities. Only the rapid increase in electricity consumption assured coal of a steady market. Public policy, in the form of exceptions to oil import quotas and clean air standards, helped to encourage the switch to oil. The development of nuclear power also contributed to reducing coal's role in supplying utilities.

The reversal of public policy after the 1973 embargo included inducements and some requirements for utilities to switch back to coal, and a requirement that new generating plants use coal. Along with greatly increased prices for oil and gas and a slowing of nuclear development, coal seemed ready for a comeback. But the utilities were slow to switch back again. One reason was that the steep increases in electricity costs after 1974 had led to equally steep declines in consumption growth rates. Utilities that had once based their plans on historically steady growth rates of 7 percent or more per year in demand for electricity were now unable to predict their future capacity needs. The recession of 1974–1975 cut into industrial usage, which constituted about 40 percent of all power generated. Another reason was that the environmental requirements for burning coal required installation of expensive "scrubbers" to prevent sulfur from being discharged into the air. Until federal financial aid was forthcoming, many utilities delayed their reconversions, eyeing instead nuclear possibilities and even partnerships with independent domestic oil producers. In 1980, the Congress appropriated $3.6 billion to assist in conversion of 38 plants, a reduction from President Carter's request for $10 billion to convert 107 plants and a blow to the goal of doubling coal usage by 1990.

The long-term prospects of coal still seemed strong, however. Exports of the coal used to generate electricity quadrupled in 1980, taking up some of the slack from the sluggish rise in domestic demand. Furthermore, many new coal-fired utility plants were projected for the United States.

But even these long-term prospects present some problems. About 60 percent of American coal deposits are located west of the Mississippi, relatively near the surface, where they can be "strip-mined." To strip-mine means to blast or dig off the soil and shovel the coal up with bulldozers and power shovels. This process leaves the land devastated unless careful and costly efforts at reclamation are made. Federal and state laws both provide for reclamation, but neither coal companies nor environmentalists are satisfied with the requirements. Strip-mining goes on under continuing controversy.

Western coal is much more efficiently strip-mined than Eastern coal, which is produced from underground mines. Strip-mining succeeds in extracting about 90 percent of the coal available, while underground mining produces only about half. Safety hazards, a history of poor working conditions, and labor-management conflict also inhibit reliance on underground production. Western coal has a lower heat content, therefore providing less energy per pound. On the other hand, it also has less sulfur, presenting less threat of air pollution. Over the past two decades, there has been a decided shift to the use of strip-mined coal, to the point where it now represents 60 percent of all coal used in the United States.

On balance, even greater usage of Western coal might seem more economical—if only it could be brought to the predominantly Eastern markets that use it. Transportation is the final factor in this complicated equation. The railroads are willing, but their equipment and roadbeds may not be equal to this massive task without basic reconstruction requiring federal assistance. And repeated blocking of Western towns with frequent long trainloads creates opposition. The alternative is the construction of hundreds of miles of coal "slurries"—pipelines in which crushed coal mixed with water can be carried to transshipment points. Opposition to such projects, as noted earlier, unites the railroads, ranchers concerned for water supplies, and environmentalists.

Finally, both coal production and burning present significant environmental and health hazards. Coal production is famous for the "brown lung disease" of miners; various forms of "acid rain" and cancer are attributable to the burning of coal. Environmental dangers include not only the effects of strip-mining but also the pollutants and threat to the stability of the upper atmosphere produced by burning. Where available, remedies and protections for these hazards have proved to be costly. The great availability of coal, in short, has yet to be translated into a practical energy alternative.

Synthetic Fuels

The major possibilities for developing synthetic fuels lie in extracting oil from shale rock, making oil or gas from coal (liquefaction and gasification), and making gas, particularly methanol, from waste products ("biomass"—wood wastes, or farm or municipal wastes). The technology largely exists. Oil was produced from shale before it was drilled from underground wells. Germany made oil from coal and methane gas from organic wastes during World War II; South Africa does so today in significant amounts. The problem has been to establish that it could be done on a large scale in the United States at costs and with market prices that would assure a profit for private industry. The goal set for the Synthetic Fuels Corporation created in 1980 was to produce 2 million barrels per day by 1992. Many thought that goal beyond reach, except at staggering costs approaching $100 billion. As Roger Loper, President, Chevron Oil Shale Corporation, said in an interview with the *New York Times*, August 4, 1980:

> A lot of spear shaking and saber rattling goes on about how shale is now clearly economical. It's absolute balderdash. Nobody has proven we can do this, and a lot of blood, sweat, and tears have to come down the river and go over the dam before we can be sure.

The processes for recovering oil from shale rock involve heating the fractured rock, either in above-ground plants or in its original underground setting. The potential is vast, with shale rock reserves exceeding all known petroleum reserves in the world. Most American shale is located on federal lands in the Western states, and the oil industry has invested heavily in leases since the early 1970s. Capital investments to build the necessary facilities will be huge, as will be the need for water for cooling purposes, which will be drawn from scarce Western supplies. Cost estimates for a facility capable of producing 45,000 barrels of oil per day begin at $2 billion and go as high as $5 billion or $6 billion. With imported oil at $35 per barrel in 1980, however, some companies believed they could produce and sell shale oil profitably. Therefore, efforts to perfect recovery techniques were proceeding.[2]

Coal gasification and liquefaction involve heating under pressure, with similar high capital investments and need for cooling water. Plants would be located in the West, near ready coal supplies (also located chiefly on federal lands). But transportation problems would be solved by the use of existing or supplementary oil and gas pipelines. The lure of synthetic fuels attracted the oil companies to acquire coal companies and leases in the 1960s, but to date the costs of extraction have been prohibitive.

Conversion of agricultural, forest, and urban waste to methanol or other liquid fuels is of particular interest because it offers the possibility of use in the vital transport sector, which requires portable liquid fuel. Both burning and bacterial or enzyme methods are possible, with the latter preferred for environmental reasons. The basic principle would be the same as that for making beer or wine, but of course the scale would be vastly larger. Most methods are in a very early experimental stage.

The task before the Synthetic Fuels Corporation is thus one of encouraging private investment, through loans and guarantees, sufficient to in effect create several major new industries. The probable risk-takers are the oil companies, which hold leases on much of the coal capacity and have undertaken most of the research in the area so far. About 10 percent of all oil company research and development expenditures in the last few years has gone into coal gasification and liquefaction.[3] There are no major competitors in sight. The same is true of the nascent shale oil industry.

Nuclear Power

While the dilemmas in developing coal and synthetic fuels as alternatives to oil involve massive costs, serious practical and environmental problems, and opposition from contending industry and other groups, they appear modest indeed in comparison with the problems confronting further development of nuclear power. Indeed, the question in the early 1980s seemed to be whether there would ever be a significant nuclear contribution to solution of the American energy crisis.

This situation represented a dramatic reversal from the height of the nuclear industry's status and prospects in the late 1960s and early 1970s. The first American nuclear reactor connected to commercial electricity generating and distributing was a prototype that went into service in 1957. It employed fission reaction (the splitting of uranium 235 atoms) to heat water to run steam turbines and generate electricity. The water was kept under pressure to raise its boiling temperature in some reactors, and allowed to boil off immediately into steam in others. In both cases, the water served also as a coolant for the reactors. Both types are known as light water systems.[4] In 1963, the first commercial contract to build a light water system was signed by General Electric and a New Jersey utility company. Several more contracts with GE and the other three manufacturers soon followed. By 1967 nearly fifty systems were on order totaling about 40 GWe ("gigawatts," or billion watts) of electrical generating capacity.[5] Nuclear energy appeared to be about to create a revolution in the production of cheap energy.

The euphoria continued into the 1970s. In 1972, the government estimated that nuclear power would provide 1200 GWe of electricity by the year 2000.[6] The Project Independence Report of 1974 estimated that nuclear power could provide 40 percent of electricity-generating capacity by that year, instead of the 6 percent (about 50 GWe) that it then provided. In the five years between 1970 and 1974, 145 orders for new reactor systems were placed; only 15 were canceled. By 1975, however, estimates of capacity by the year 2000 had been cut a third, to 800 GWe. In 1977, estimates were reduced by more than half again, to 380 GWe. In the five years between 1975 and 1979, only 13 orders for new reactor systems were placed; 47 were canceled outright; and many more were postponed.

The problems encountered by nuclear power included the drop in electricity demand during and after the recession of 1974–1975, sharp increases in construction costs, and serious deficiencies (fuel reprocessing and waste disposal) that heightened safety questions, leading to wide public opposition. These problems were all mounting in severity well before the near-disaster at the nuclear reactor at Three Mile Island in Pennsylvania in 1979. But Three Mile Island crystallized the opposition and brought the whole idea of nuclear fission as a source of energy into question. A brief description of nuclear power generation as a *system* will help to put all the problems into perspective. Not incidentally, it reveals some of the results of the American style of industry-government collaboration.[7]

Uranium 235 constitutes 0.7 of uranium ore, the rest of which consists of the fission-reaction-stopping uranium 238. The ore is mined and refined in several Western states, principally Colorado, Utah, New Mexico, and Texas. Most mines and mills are located on federal lands, but some are on Navajo Nation lands and others on private sites. Private companies do the mining and processing and then ship the ore to one of two plants in Illinois and Oklahoma. There it is prepared for "enrichment"—raising the U-235 content to about 3 percent so that the vital chain reaction can occur.

A recent problem in the mining process involved the radioactivity of the "tailings"—sandlike ore residues left behind as uranium mill wastes.[8] By 1978, there were twenty two abandoned mills in eight Western states where uranium had been processed for weapons and power plants between the 1940s and the early 1970s, with about 25 million tons of unattended tailings. The tailings had not originally been recognized as radioactive. Some had even been used in construction in Colorado and Utah. But in 1978, Environmental Protection Agency (EPA) officials said that about 85 percent of the radioactivity occurring naturally in uranium remained in the

tailings. Therefore, tailings were among the most severe radiation problems in the nation. Including the tailings from the sixteen operating plants,
about 140 million tons had accumulated. Although cleanup technology had
not been perfected, Congress authorized 90 percent federal funding for the
task in 1978.

From the conversion plants the uranium is shipped in gaseous form to
one of three government-owned enrichment plants in Oak Ridge, Tennessee, Paducah, Kentucky, and Portsmouth, Ohio. After enrichment, it is
shipped to one of about a dozen fuel-rod fabrication plants scattered
around the country. The uranium is made into long thin rods that can be
embedded in water, which enables simultaneous slowing of the reaction
process, cooling, and heating of the water to occur. From the fabrication
plants, the fuel rods are shipped to the nation's roughly seventy operating
nuclear reactors. (The number remains approximate because a very small
number of new plants will be placed in operation in the early 1980s, while
older plants are frequently out of service—sometimes for extended periods.) Together, these reactors generated 11.5 percent of the 225 GWe of
electricity used in the United States in 1979.[9]

But the other product of nuclear power plants is highly radioactive
waste. It is at this stage that the nuclear power system has its greatest
problems. Originally, there were to be three reprocessing plants to which
spent fuel rods would be sent. There, the remaining uranium 235 was to
have been separated and returned to the fuel cycle again, thereby
stretching out the limited uranium supply and keeping costs down. The
other two results of reprocessing, however, are plutonium (the primary
ingredient of nuclear weapons) and useless (but still radioactive) waste.
The creation of deadly plutonium raises the level of risks to general public
safety and might necessitate elaborate security measures to guard against
terrorists acquiring nuclear weapons. Radioactive waste is very dangerous
to people and the environment for at least 200,000 years but has to be
disposed of somewhere. Neither the technical means nor an acceptable site
for nuclear waste disposal has been found.

Reprocessing was deemed too likely to lead to the spread of nuclear
weapons and simply abandoned in 1977. In the absence of permanent
waste disposal arrangements, however, the mounting tons of radioactive
waste must be stored in carefully shielded pools of water at the various
reactor sites. Because the storage capacity of several such sites was nearly
exhausted in 1980, the government sought to find "interim" storage
locations while still looking for acceptable procedures for "permanent"
disposal. The original reprocessing plants in Illinois, New York, and South
Carolina provide the most likely choices for government purchase and
expansion into such facilities. Eleven sites for possible permanent disposal
in Washington, Nevada, Mississippi, Texas, Louisiana, Utah, and New

Mexico are being studied. But estimates regarding the time needed to perfect the technology and prepare a burial site for permanent waste disposal *begin* at fifteen years. Political opposition to the choice of any specific site for either interim or permanent storage was quick and vigorous.[10] Some communities reacted against the possible presence of a nuclear dump and others against the prospect of frequent shipments of such materials on their railroads or highways. Meanwhile, industry sources estimated that seventeen reactors would be out of on-site storage space by 1984.

Why was the nuclear power production system allowed to develop in such an incomplete form? Part of the answer seems to lie in the fact that nuclear weapons development has always dominated government research and funding. By far the largest proportion of the ERDA budget (and before it the AEC) has been devoted to making bombs and building the appropriate support and service systems; disposal of military nuclear wastes has been accomplished in deep underground sites. Another reason is that nuclear power generation was turned over to private industry as soon as it proved practical and profitable. The government kept ownership only of the enrichment plants, in order to guard against the dangers involved in wide availability of fuel for potential nuclear weapons. Presumably, the private utility companies were expected to take care of finding the means of disposal of their wastes.

A final reason may be that as soon as the nuclear industry appeared to be on its feet, government research began to look toward a second generation of nuclear power plants, the so-called breeder reactors. These reactors actually produce more fuel than they use, thereby solving the problem of limited supply and mounting uranium costs confronting the light water reactors now in operation. The problem is that the fuel produced and used is plutonium, with all its attendant dangers. And many technical problems still remain unsolved. The combination of dangers and problems, plus steadily mounting cost estimates, led President Carter to seek to terminate the government's one prototype breeder reactor project at Clinch River, Tennessee. As noted earlier, Congress remained committed to the project and the issue stayed unresolved.

. . . that other White House, populated by no-growth, counter-culture activists [seeking to] convert the country into a drab, energyless, no-growth sleeping bag society. That is their goddamned transcendental notion of a great future for the USA.

Craig Hosmer, President, American Nuclear Energy Council, in a speech to the Atomic Industrial Forum, November 28, 1977.

The nuclear picture today is that of an industry—and, to some extent, a government—in paralysis. (See accompanying box material) No new orders for reactors were placed by utilities in 1979; many projects were deferred or canceled; and eight completed reactors were not granted licenses.[11] Waste disposal progress was very slight. In the wake of Three Mile Island investigations, the Nuclear Regulatory Commission (NRC) issued a list of more than 100 safety improvements that will be required of all reactors, with cost estimates beginning at $30 million per reactor. Although ninety new reactor projects have construction permits, there is no way of predicting when (or if) they will be placed in operation. The hope of having any substantial proportion of the nation's electricity demand met by nuclear power by 1990 seemed to be fading. Ironically, growth in electricity demand revived to 5 percent per year in the late 1970s, although the recession of 1980 cut into it again.

The problems and dilemmas of nuclear power center on safety, costs, and waste disposal. Safety problems include basic reactor design, multiple shutoff precautions, operating personnel and procedures, and all the shipments of radioactive materials (and, necessarily soon, wastes) that crisscross the country daily by rail and truck. Nuclear advocates argue that the risks of damaging radiation from a nuclear accident are less than those from automobile accidents or other life hazards. But the scope of death and destruction from a nuclear accident, should it ever occur, are such that the safety concerns of many people probably can never be satisfied. Opposition to nuclear power generation on this ground alone is strong and growing, not only in the United States but elsewhere as well. Only France and the Soviet bloc countries are free of opposition and continuing to expand their nuclear capacity.

The cost problems are connected closely to efforts to improve safety standards. Capital construction costs have risen sharply since the early 1970s, to the point where only the largest utilities can consider financing new reactor projects. Some have sought to pass current construction costs for work in progress on to their customers, but this also has provoked opposition. Delays in NRC licensing procedures have contributed somewhat to the impact of inflation on costs, and President Carter unsuccessfully sought to speed up the process of review and licensing in 1979 and 1980. But most of the upward pressure on costs was directly traceable to new safety features. Uranium was also rising in cost, although fuel costs as a proportion of total costs dropped as construction costs jumped. By 1980, there was no clear cost advantage between new nuclear plants and new coal-fired plants with all the required pollution controls, and no real difference in their daily operating costs.

The waste disposal problem is entirely separate from safety and cost, although both will be powerfully affected if and when waste disposal is solved. As analyzed above, the problem arises from the incompleteness of the nuclear power system, a product of the gap between government and private industry. It seems clear that the solution, if any, will be at government expense.

Another disposal problem surrounds another waste product of nuclear power generation—heat. The use of river water for cooling and ultimate return means that the temperature downstream will be raised several degrees, with possible impact on fish and plant life. Thermal pollution raises the temperature and changes the content of the atmosphere, with unknown but possibly damaging consequences. In both cases, costs cannot be assigned entirely to the private utility involved. Instead, at least some portion is shared more widely.

In the early 1980s, the nuclear industry's prospect of contributing significantly to solving the energy crisis appeared to depend on three factors. One is simply weathering the crisis of performance and public confidence symbolized by the Three Mile Island incident—and staying afloat as a profitable enterprise. Public utilities might suffer losses, but could always switch to coal and/or pass on costs to customers. Nuclear manufacturers, however, ultimately would be forced to shut down if orders were nonexistent and construction blocked. For the moment, they were doing well enough from ongoing construction and the expensive modifications of existing reactors required by the NRC. Exports also took up some of the slack, as all four manufacturers had several projects underway overseas.

The second factor is political support. The Reagan administration is clearly pronuclear, and may well seek to restore the industry through reduced regulations, speeded-up licensing, and financial aid. The industry has mounted an intensified public information campaign to allay fears about safety, and would have substantial support from the banking industry in any future lobbying effort. A new oil embargo or major price increases, however, might be the most important factor in regaining some of the momentum of the early 1970s.

The third factor is the speed with which power from nuclear *fusion*, rather than *fission*, can be developed on a commercial scale. Fusion power is produced not by splitting but by the combination of atomic particles (in this case, hydrogen) under conditions of intense heat and pressure; the sun's energy is produced in this way. The advantages to fusion power are its plentiful fuel supply (chiefly water, consumed at infinitesimal rates) and comparatively much lower safety risks. But as yet no known substance can withstand the high temperatures involved in the fusion process. If and when the current much-expanded research program develops a means of controlling nuclear fusion, the capital costs of building commercial plants are likely to be tremendous. Nevertheless, given the problems of the light water and breeder reactor fission systems, fusion power may be the key to the nuclear future—if there is one.

Oil and Gas

The dilemmas involved in developing greater supplies of crude oil and natural gas from domestic sources center on two highly controversial issues.[12] The first is the question of how much oil and gas actually is available. The answer cannot be given for two reasons: (1) exploration was not intensive in the 1960s and early 1970s; and (2) improvement of recovery techniques might well change *both* the proportion derived from known sources *and* the kinds of sources from which oil can be derived.

Moreover, how much oil and gas actually will be produced depends on the second issue—what will be the price of oil and gas to consumers in any given period. At high prices, producers will find it economical to employ costly recovery techniques. An included issue is whether prices should be based on actual costs of production plus a normal profit margin, or on the value of the oil or gas in a market where control over supply has forced prices far beyond such levels. For decades, the United States government employed elaborate systems of price controls on both oil and gas in an effort to keep prices on domestic production somewhere near the costs-plus-normal-profit level. But with the success of OPEC in driving up the world "market" price, such controls inhibited domestic production. They are now being removed in stages.

Available Domestic Supplies   "Proved" reserves of oil and gas are those already identified in specific fields, discounted by how much can actually be produced using standard recovery procedures. About 35 percent of the oil in an average well is now recovered, and a higher but varying proportion of gas. In 1980, proven domestic reserves of oil were less than 30 billion barrels, while domestic production amounted to about 3.5 billion barrels per year and total consumption to about 6.5 billion barrels per year. Proven gas reserves were slightly less than 200 trillion cubic feet (tcf), while production was about 19 tcf and total consumption about 20 tcf. These numbers give rise to the impression that we are "running out" of these resources.

But these data do not reflect the sharp drop in exploratory effort from 1957 to the mid-1970s and the potential reserves in unexplored areas. Oil company and government geologists differ sharply over the extent of potential reserves, averaging less than 100 billion barrels and 300 billion or more respectively. Undoubtedly, however, exploratory efforts (measured by wells drilled or hours of effort invested) dropped by more than half after 1957. Greater profitability from foreign oil mandated a shift in oil company activities from the United States to the Middle East and Africa. About half of the oil companies' exploratory efforts were still directed overseas in 1979.[13]

The most authoritative assessment of United States petroleum reserves is a study published in 1970 by the National Petroleum Council (a body made up of oil company officers and leading geologists). The Council's report linked the drop in exploratory effort to the low price of oil and greater profitability of foreign oil. The study went on to estimate possible United State oil reserves, including the outer continental shelf, as "enormous," perhaps as high as 320 billion barrels.[14] Because gas is usually found with oil, a proportionate expansion of gas reserves might also be anticipated. But other estimates of available gas supply vary dramatically, ranging from 15 to 100 years' supply.[15]

With steadily rising world market prices and the decontrol of domestic prices, there should be greater inducement for the oil companies to resume exploration in the United States. As if in proof, by 1980 new records were being set for drilling and exploration; domestic production was beginning to climb.[16] New legislation in 1978 made the outer continental shelf much more available for competitive bidding and leasing rights, while establishing certain environmental protections. The shelf begins at the 3-mile limit and extends seaward for 200 miles. Most exploration so far had been in the Gulf of Mexico near Louisiana and around Santa Barbara in California, but the new areas were to run along the entire East and West Coasts. Estimates of recoverable resources of 10 billion to 49 billion barrels of oil and 42 to 81 tcf of gas were made by the U.S. Geological Survey.[17]

The steady improvement in recovery techniques also seems likely to add to the total of "recoverable resources." From 1930 to 1974, efficiency of recovery doubled (from 15 percent to 33 percent) and was continuing to rise in 1980. Moreover, rising prices led to the use of secondary and tertiary recovery techniques. In the former, water and gas is injected into wells in one part of a field in order to force the oil or gas toward other wells. Tertiary procedures involve more sophisticated ways of applying pressure to the oil or gas in its underground formations. Funds to support such "enhanced recovery" developments are to be provided through the new Synthetic Fuels Corporation. Possibilities also exist, also to be developed by the Synthetic Fuels Corporation, for deriving "heavy oil" from tar sands; as further inducement, such production was taxed at significantly lower rates.

For all these reasons, it is simply not possible to put a firm figure on the remaining United States reserves of oil and gas. Some still believe that the era of oil is over; others argue that there is an adequate supply of oil for fifty years, or until alternatives can be developed.[18] It does seem clear, however, that how much oil will be produced depends very much on the price for which it can be sold.

The Retail Price of Oil and Gas The struggle over government price controls on domestic production of oil and gas has been a long and bitter one, particularly with regard to gas. The producing companies and the states in which they are located (in which they pay taxes and provide jobs) are regularly pitted against consumers and their representatives. Regional and economic interests thus combine with the ideological issue: should prices reflect costs of production, or actual value in a marketplace where supplies are tightly controlled and deliberately manipulated upwards? For very practical reasons, the answer given has increasingly been the latter.

The price of domestic oil production was controlled by legislation that was regularly renewed throughout the postwar period. Certain exceptions were made for smaller producers and to encourage production from newly discovered wells. The effect was to keep the price per barrel of domestic oil trailing several dollars behind that of OPEC oil, once the price rises of the 1970s began. Although President Carter had pledged to retain controls, he reversed himself in 1979 and began staged decontrol intended to eliminate all price controls by 1981. One of the strongest voices urging such action was OECD, which argued that American oil production would continue to decline otherwise.[19]

The price of domestic gas production has also been controlled since World War II. However, as a result of Supreme Court decisions and regulatory agency interpretations, here two separate markets developed. One was the interstate market, where gas produced in one state was shipped through pipelines and sold to consumers in distant states. The other was the intrastate market, about a third of total sales, where gas was produced and sold to consumers in the same state. Only the interstate market was held to be subject to federal regulation; the intrastate market remained subject to the workings of supply-and-demand forces.

In the early 1970s, intrastate prices began to rise much faster than the interstate prices were allowed to. By 1976, intrastate prices were more than double the average of interstate prices. As a result, some gas was held off the market entirely in hopes of higher interstate prices, and some was simply reserved for intrastate sale. For interstate consumers, there were severe shortages, with school and industrial plant closings. The emergency led to new federal allocations of supplies and ultimately to a new price control policy.

The Natural Gas Policy Act of 1978 provides for decontrolling newly discovered natural gas in stages, allowing prices to rise in steps, and ending all price controls in ten years. It also allows the price of gas from older wells to rise more slowly as existing sales contracts expire and are replaced. Perhaps most important, it imposes temporary controls over intrastate gas, so that sharp price differences and curtailments are less likely. Ironically, reduced industrial and utility use of gas led to a surplus at about the same time. The long-term likelihood, however, was for continued price increases in both markets, with possibly greater exploration and production and certainly continued conflict over the billions of dollars in costs and profits involved.

Thus we end as we began, with uncertainty in regard to the remaining supplies of domestic gas and oil. With much higher prices, there will be more oil and gas produced. But there *are* limits to how much can be expected from domestic sources. The dilemma for public policy is what balance to strike between producers' profits and consumers' costs, and whether the time that oil and gas reserves might provide will be long enough to develop viable alternatives.

II FUTURE POLICY ALTERNATIVES

The moral and practical dilemmas just reviewed involve profound problems of choice and direction in United States public policy. Current policy seeks to overcome these problems in order to develop each alternative energy source to the fullest. As we have seen, this may be impossible and/or undesirable, and surely will be very expensive. Recent experience also teaches that choosing directions in each area and bringing new development programs into reality are sure to be difficult and time-consuming.

The costs involved in constructing the massive new plants and sophisticated technological equipment required in each of these areas carry some important implications. Not even the oil industry, the wealthiest of all American industries, can generate the capital required for these investments. Private bankers are understandably reluctant to risk major proportions of their assets on unproven projects.[20] Mobilization of this amount of capital requires the vigorous support of the national government. Private investment can be encouraged by tax incentives, loan guarantees, subsidies, guarantees of future prices, and other assurances of profitability. A good share of the capital involved will have to be provided directly from federal appropriations or borrowing. Together, these measures imply a vast new national government presence in the financing of American industry and profound dependence of the new industries upon central authority (and taxpayers' money).

Two sets of alternatives have been raised against the current trend of United States policy and the premises on which it is based. One is the conservation-solar alternative, a special version of which is the "soft paths" argument. Conservation and solar energy can be advocated on purely pragmatic grounds as the most workable of available solutions. Solar energy, and associated wind and wave alternatives, employ *renewable*, ever-present sources; all the other alternative energy sources (except the breeder reactor) are nonrenewable and ultimately will be exhausted. The soft paths position sees conservation and solar energy alternatives as part of a program for social change that would not only solve the energy problem but free people from the threat of nuclear destruction, help decentralize power and authority in the society, and replace personal alienation and dependence with self-confidence and independence. It stands in sharp contrast to the high-technology, centralized, costly, and allegedly dangerous, unworkable, and unnecessary programs involved in what it terms the "hard path" solutions of current policy.

The other set of alternatives, while not challenging the importance of conservation and solar energy, proposes deeper and more structural alternatives. At this level, neither the oil industry as it stands nor even the principle of private profit itself is taken as a given. Breaking up the oil industry, nationalizing the energy industries generally, and/or forming public corporations are among the solutions proposed. An examination of each set of alternatives follows.

The Conservation-Solar Alternative

The first premise of this position is widely shared: conservation offers the greatest and most immediate opportunity for major steps to alleviate the energy crisis. Some estimates hold that the United States could consume 30 percent to 40 percent less energy, with the same or a higher standard of living, if a serious commitment to energy efficiency were made.[21] Little in the way of new technology is needed. The costs of conservation are lower than the costs of today's energy, not to mention the costs of providing new energy sources. What *is* required is cooperation by millions of individuals, at least in certain actions and in some minimal behavior changes.

To be sure, conservation has been stressed in all national energy programs. Tax incentives have been provided for insulating homes and businesses and installing various energy-supplementing devices. But much of the emphasis on conservation has remained rhetorical exhortation, occurring in the context of massive programs for capital-intensive, high-technology development of alternative energy sources. The main thrust of government policy has assumed steadily rising demand for energy, in part because such increasing demand is thought to be necessary for economic growth. And in some respects, conservation has been presented as implying severe hardship or drastic changes in lifestyle. What conservation has been achieved is attributable primarily to dramatic rises in price for every form of energy.

By contrast, conservation—in the form of a number of relatively minor adjustments by many people—is one of two central themes of its more serious advocates (the other theme being solar energy). The only major centralized action necessary is the shift to producing cars with much greater fuel efficiency, thus reducing the distinctively high American energy consumption for transportation purposes. This seems well under-way, forced less by government policy than by the need of manufacturers to respond to the sales successes of high-mileage imported cars. If it is accompanied by behavioral changes—such as car pooling, reduced usage, and conservation-oriented driving—very significant reductions in energy usage are possible.

Conservation in industry has been underway for some time, as the data on declining energy usage per dollar of GNP demonstrate. Much more can be done by better maintenance of furnaces and heating systems, reduced lighting, reclaiming wastes, etc. A major area for development is that of *cogeneration*—the use for heating purposes of steam generated in the process of making electricity. In West Germany, 29 percent of total energy comes from cogeneration, compared to 4 percent in the United States.[22] One 1975 study done for the National Science Foundation reported that cogeneration could save billions of dollars in investment and enable American industry to provide half its own electricity needs by 1985.[23]

Much conservation is possible in the construction of new buildings and modification of old ones, without added costs. Sealed buildings with extensive glass areas require massive plants for heating, cooling, and circulating air. They are the product of cheap-energy days, and can be replaced by better-insulated, less brilliantly lighted, double-windowed structures using a fifth the energy. The American Institute of Architects projects vast savings—perhaps a third of all energy usage by 1990—from improved design and materials in new and old buildings.[24] Because the active supply of buildings changes much more slowly than automobiles, a major campaign to "retrofit" existing buildings with energy-saving devices will be necessary. With very small investments in insulation, for example, fuel consumption in residences can be sharply reduced and a return on investment of about 25 percent realized.[25]

These technical changes must be accompanied by usage changes on the part of employees and residents to reach their full effectiveness. The cost-reduction motivations are strong, but the measures (turning off lights, drawing curtains, using less hot water, etc.) are so undramatic that they can be forgotten once an emergency is past. Other obstacles to serious and widespread conservation are the lack of a strong constituency with economic interest in promoting it, building codes and construction practices that promote energy-using designs and equipment, and utility rate schedules that encourage extensive and wasteful usage. Government policy has yet to systematically educate people about and provide incentives for many of the forms of conservation just described.

Some of those who stress conservation introduce two related elements into the energy debate. One is a challenge to the growing use of electricity. They argue that electricity is extremely wasteful of primary energy (about two-thirds is lost in the process) and often unsuited to the uses made of it. The other is the more generally applicable concept of "end use." This sets the nature of the task to be performed by the energy at the forefront; selection of the kind of energy to perform it is based on the minimum necessary and appropriate to do the job. The "end use" concept contrasts with first producing energy by any means possible and then looking for all possible ways of using it.

The challenge to electricity is sparked by the contrast between the intense heat and large amounts of fuel required to make electricity and the low-temperature uses to which it is often put. Space heating and water heating in residences and commercial or industrial buildings, for example, require temperatures less than the boiling point of water, not the 3000°F temperature of a coal-fired utility or the much higher temperatures of a nuclear reactor. Nearly all uses of electricity necessarily involve a "thermodynamic overkill" between the energy used to produce it and the work it actually does. Only lighting, electronics, and electric motors are really efficient and appropriate uses of electricity, and they represent a small fraction of the total energy uses.

The end-use approach seeks to find the lowest quality of energy capable of performing (or being upgraded to perform) needed tasks. It not only deemphasizes electricity, which must so often be downgraded to do work, but also the need for nuclear power and much of the energy loss involved in generating electricity. It leads to a vertical continuum, in which the tasks requiring low levels of energy (such as space heating and then water heating) are ranked at the bottom, and more demanding tasks, requiring higher temperatures or qualities, at ascending levels. As the matching process begins, solar energy quickly emerges as the most available and appropriate at the lowest levels and the most readily upgraded to perform higher-energy tasks by means of concentration (as through a lens or other collector).

We come then to the other half of the conservation-solar alternative. The sun is the ultimate renewable energy source: it provides the earth with vast amounts of pure energy every day and will continue to do so for billions of years. Each day, the sun offers the United States energy equivalent to our entire annual usage. For years, conventional wisdom held that, because the sun's energy is so diffused and intermittent when it reaches the earth, there was no practical way to collect it, store it, and make it available when needed. Solar energy was viewed as a faintly ridiculous idea whose time would probably never come.

But solar advocates now see such conventional wisdom as a result of the narrow vision of government and industry supporters of oil, coal, and nuclear power, and their commitment to centralized production ·and distribution of energy. Instead, solar advocates argue, the very diffuseness of solar energy permits its use for low-quality tasks by everybody at affordable costs that can provide independence from the energy industries. Devices made with available minimal technologies (glass, piping, storage tanks) could account for all national space heating, water heating, and (if expanded to large mirror assemblies) all electric power generation. This would amount to 38 percent of all energy usage, according to one authority.[26] A more modest estimate from the Harvard Business School's Energy Project still set the proportion at 20 percent to 25 percent of all energy usage.[27]

Beyond that, solar energy might be converted into liquid fuel (hydrogen) or electricity (by means of photovoltaic cells) and have far wider uses. Only a grudging research program, an enduring prejudice in favor of the existing energy industries, and a fascination with the high-technology "quick solutions" (such as solar-collecting satellites or "power towers") seem to stand in the way. Solar advocates also note the difference between the standards of proven performance required of solar development and blithe assumptions about the success of far-less-tested coal, nuclear, or synthetic fuels alternatives.

Like conservation, utilization of solar energy in any substantial proportions will require individual actions by millions of homeowners and businesspeople. Solar collectors and minimal storage facilities will have to be installed in residences, apartment houses, and businesses all across the country to make hot water and space heating possible. The basic method is ancient, although modern means are more efficient; no technological breakthrough is involved. A "passive" system has no moving parts; it is simply the design and location of a building to take advantage of sunshine, perhaps with an associated greenhouse to maximize the sun's effects. An "active" system typically has a set of panels bolted onto the roof which collect or multiply the sun's warmth and transmit it to water or air which is then piped into the building's heating system or stored for the future.

Opposition to solar development comes from utilities and their rate structures, which penalize small users, such as those who require electricity only for backup purposes. Lack of familiarity with design and installation procedures, and outmoded building codes, also inhibit the infant solar industries. But probably the greatest obstacle is the initial investment required and the lack of substantial tax incentives or loan guarantees to make it seem economically feasible to the majority of hard-pressed middle- and low-income citizens.

The advocates of conservation and the solar energy alternative thus have a persuasive case, but one which faces serious obstacles because it requires widespread public implementation. Unfortunately, that is not likely to be forthcoming without substantial government encouragement in the form of tax or loan policies and consistent leadership. Moreover, like the antinuclear and environmental groups, conservation-solar advocates must face the widely held assumption that only rising energy consumption can assure economic growth and expansion of job opportunities.

There are two major points in what appears to be a winning argument that no necessary or even likely link exists between energy usage and *either* economic growth *or* jobs. One is that, while both growth and energy usage expanded together in the postwar decades, there was no causal relationship between the two. Indeed, the relationship was exactly the opposite: the more energy-intensive machinery, the fewer the employees. In industry after industry where large increases in energy usage were identifiable, the number of employees dropped or held essentially steady. What made for an apparent relationship between growth and energy usage was a combination of population increase, expansion of jobs in the low-energy service-producing fields, and general increased energy consumption. This conclusion, i.e., that there is no necessary link between energy usage and growth/jobs, is supported by some twenty major studies, from the Ford Foundation to the Harvard Business School to the National Academy of Sciences.[28]

The second major point is that capital investment in nonrenewable-energy fields produces far fewer jobs than much more modest investments in conservation or solar and associated alternatives. Once stated, the argument seems self-evident. Of course there are some jobs, mostly for highly skilled people, in the construction of nuclear reactors or development of synthetic fuel recovery systems. But conservation requires many more workers at varying skill levels, from plumbers to sheet-metal mechanics to carpenters and roofers and all their respective helpers.[29] The retrofit of existing buildings alone, with modest capital investment, offers a potential for jobs in the millions. A Senate Commerce Committee staff report in 1976 held that $1.6 billion in subsidies and loan guarantees for conservation retrofits would produce 400,000 jobs.[30] In the same year, the government's Bonneville Power Administration acknowledged that "High impact conservation programs create more jobs than would be created by building new power plants to generate an equivalent amount of energy."[31] The same is true of solar installations and wind power devices. The skills required are known and can be communicated to others readily. Millions of hours of work would be required to convert to solar usage.[32] Added up, there is just no comparison between the number of jobs involved in the high-technology nuclear and other projects and those produced by serious conservation-solar commitments. And still government agencies and other opinion leaders insist that the issue is really one of producing new energy or submitting to declining growth and fewer jobs.

Much of the foregoing conservation-solar alternative argument is shared by sober establishment studies and activist environmental or antinuclear groups. What distinguishes the "soft paths" version of this position is: (a) its rigorous avoidance of *all* high-technology, high-cost, centralized solutions; (b) its insistence on small-scale, diverse energy provision that can be managed directly by individuals and small groups; and (c) its overall purpose of enabling people to live healthy, satisfying lives in sustainable ecological balance with nature.

The leading voice of soft paths solutions is Amory Lovins, whose several books have had major impact in the alternative energy field. In *Soft Energy Paths*, for example, he presents the case for soft technologies (solar, wind, wave, vegetation—all the renewable sources) with a wealth of scientific data as to their practicality. He argues that the hard paths are not only undesirable and unworkable, but also foreclose the soft path possibilities. Hard paths are unsafe, costly, wasteful, require vast mobilization under central authority, and will still not provide the energy needed by the year 2000. The two paths are mutually exclusive because the hard paths direction will create an economic and social system that cannot be reversed except by the nuclear catastrophe to which it may lead. Lovins appeals for popular insistence upon reversal of current hard paths policies so much preferred by conventional experts before it is too late: "Perhaps our salvation will yet be that the basic issues in energy strategy, far from being too complex and technical for ordinary people to understand, are on the contrary too simple and political for experts to understand."[33]

The Structural Alternatives

While Lovins' and other major studies recognize that the chief obstacles to the conservation-solar alternative are institutional and political, they do little in the way of analysis of these factors. Soft paths prescriptions barely begin to take political realities into account. The Harvard Business School Energy Project report, for example, identifies many of the enduring conflicts that have snarled energy policy making for years. But prescriptions go no further than basic reliance on the marketplace, government assistance to the necessary new energy industries and incentives for conservation and solar development, and a "balanced energy program." The report argues that the contending interest groups in "the bitter American energy debate" are really "secret allies" who must be brought to recognize their mutual interest in higher prices.[34]

Similarly, although Lovins' proposals imply significant change in social values and practices, they are presented in a context of acquiescence to present structures and power relationships. Lovins appears to assume that the soft path and its goals can be achieved without altering the present energy industries or the basic profit motive. He says, for example, that the soft path "goes with, not against, our political grain. . . . It does not try to wipe the slate clean, but rather to redirect our future efforts, taking advantage of the big energy systems we already have without multiplying them further."[35] And he expects, with respect to the variety of small systems he proposes, that "Industrial resistance would presumably melt when . . . the scope for profit was perceived."[36]

Other analysts are far less optimistic about the willingness of the energy industries and utilities to accept the radical changes in their profitability, power, and prospects implied in the conservation-solar alternatives. To achieve the latter, they argue, advocates must be prepared at least for a major struggle with the oil companies and their political allies, and perhaps for reorganization of the basic nature of the economy itself.

The conclusion of Dr. John Blair's exhaustive *The Control of Oil*, for example, is that only divestiture and reinstitution of competition within the oil industry will make possible the necessary balanced energy program (including alternative sources, conservation, and solar usage). Divestiture has both vertical and horizontal meanings. Vertical divestiture means ending the oil companies' integrated character and separating their production, transportation, refining, and marketing functions into separate companies. Horizontal divestiture means forcing the oil companies to give up their holdings in other energy fields, such as coal, uranium, shale, synthetics, and solar. In both cases, greatly increased competition between much smaller companies would be the result and existing antitrust laws the means. Blair, endorsing the characterization of the oil industry as "the greatest aggregation of effective economic and political industrial power which the world and nations have ever known,"[37] sees no alternative to an effort to break its concentrated power. Citing an extended series of national government giveaways, subsidies, and supports to the oil industry, he argues that expecting any form of regulation to be successful would "fly in the face of all recorded history."[38] Although not overly optimistic about the outcome, Blair argues that the antitrust route has not really been tried since 1911.

With much the same analysis, although a different prescription, the president of the million-member International Association of Machinists and Aerospace Workers, William W. Winpisinger, argued for formation of public corporations in the energy field:

> It is time to realize that what we are really talking about, in terms of control, is economic and political power. To put it bluntly, the multinational energy corporations have control, have the power, and the governments and people do not. . . . Structural challenge to and changes in private control of energy investment are probably preconditions to any political possiblity of solving the

energy crisis in an equitable and just manner. [This is] why we must look toward public, as opposed to private, development of alternative energy sources.[39]

Winpisinger's goals were several: introduction of competition into the area of alternative energy development; creation of the many new jobs inherent in conservation and solar alternatives; and keeping solar power as "the people's power." Not least, he sought through public corporations in the energy field to break the energy industries' monopoly of information about actual costs and performance which had for years impeded government regulation and control.

Two other important energy studies with quite different approaches and foci nevertheless end up with overlapping calls for basic reconstruction of the economic system in order to solve the energy crisis. Robert Engler's *The Brotherhood of Oil* focuses on the "private government" of oil and tries to find a way to restore popular democracy. Barry Commoner's *The Poverty of Power* starts from the science of thermodynamics and examines the entire range of energy problems and possible solutions. Each is worth a brief summary.

Engler provides a detailed analysis of the political power and practice of the oil industry over time in support of his "private government" characterization. He argues that this private government has merged with the United States government to the point where the two are virtually indistinguishable. Only an independent new committee with investigatory powers can adequately assess the energy problem, particularly the oil industry component, and produce solutions in the public interest. He envisions an array of public corporations competing with the oil companies and developing alternative energy sources. Most important, he calls for democratic national and local planning bodies with the power to implement social goals in place of profit-seeking private choices.[40]

Commoner's work surveys the possibilities of various alternative energy sources, concluding that all but solar are costly, dangerous, and/or unworkable. Nevertheless, he sees their development likely, with the vast capital investments necessary being generated from reduced consumption and standards of living on the part of people generally. He locates the cause of this unwelcome prospect in the basic character of the economic system itself: its profit-maximizing imperative; replacement of people with energy-absorbing machines; exhaustion of resources and destruction of the environment; and failure to provide for social needs. The capital shortage is traced to shrinking rates of profit, caused by declining productivity per unit of capital invested. Only greatly increased profit margins, necessarily at the expense of the people's share of national income, can produce the new capital needed to produce more energy and energy-intensive machines, to replace more workers to make more profit, and so on. After analyzing oil as an energy source and the oil industry, he concludes: "It would appear, then, that the oil companies are not a reliable vehicle for the production of U.S. oil, for they seem to be interested less in producing oil than in producing profit."[41]

Commoner's analysis leads him to urge explicitly the consideration of a democratic socialist alternative, so that new energy developments "can be governed by social values rather than by private profit."[42] Energy problems are only symptoms of deeper, more fundamental contradictions between people's needs and profit imperatives. "The basic fault that has spawned the environmental crisis and the energy crisis, and that threatens —if no remedy is found—to engulf us in the wreckage of a crumbling economic system" is the capitalist system itself. Having "loudly proclaimed itself the best means of assuring a rising standard of living for the people of the United States, [it] can now survive if at all, only by reducing that standard. The powerful have confessed to the poverty of their power."[43]

Each of these alternatives prescribes structural change as the only way in which the energy problem can ultimately be solved. Each expects a major confrontation with the entrenched energy industries. Some see the necessity of a deeper reconstruction of at least this sector and perhaps the entire economy. All depend on an aroused public as the means of change. In the end, at least for this set of analysts, the energy problem becomes coherent: it is not a number of isolated issues to be resolved separately and on the basis of scientific information, but a fundamental question of social organization and purpose. If the energy crisis is to be solved in a manner that serves people's needs for a safe and satisfying future, they argue, the economic and political system known as capitalism must be replaced.

NOTES

1 *World Energy Outlook, December 1979* (New York: Exxon, 1980), p. 8.

2 All data in this paragraph are drawn from the *New York Times*, August 4, 1980.

3 Robert Stobaugh and Daniel Yergin, eds., *Energy Future: Report of the Energy Project at Harvard Business School* (New York: Random House, 1979), p. 105.

4 The term is used to distinguish the American systems from the Canadian "heavy water" system and the early British and French efforts to develop gas-graphite systems (since replaced by the American version, which then dominated the international market).

5 Stobaugh and Yergin, *Energy Future*, p. 115.

6 Leon Lindberg, ed., *The Energy Syndrome* (Lexington, Mass.: Lexington Books, 1977), pp. 298 ff., and *New York Times*, March 16, 1980, are the data base for this paragraph.

7 The next paragraphs are based on Barry Commoner, *The Poverty of Power* (New York: Knopf, 1976), chap. 5, and Lindberg, *Energy Syndrome*, pp. 297–320, unless otherwise indicated.

8 *Congressional Quarterly, Energy Policy*, pp. 123–126.

9 *New York Times*, March 16, 1980.

10 *Parade Magazine*, July 20, 1980.

11 *New York Times*, March 16, 1980.

12 Because they are normally found together, oil and natural gas will be considered together in this section.

13 *New York Times*, November 26, 1979.

14 *Future Petroleum Provinces of the United States* (Washington, D.C.: National Petroleum Council, 1970), p. 113.

15 Stobaugh and Yergin, *Energy Future*, summarizes these contrasts on p. 67.

16 *New York Times*, August 10, 1980.

17 Congressional Quarterly, *Energy Policy*, p. 73.

18 Commoner, *Poverty of Power*, p. 52.

19 OECD, *World Energy Outlook*, p. 40.

20 Commoner, *Poverty of Power*, summarizes both of the last points, from oil industry sources on pp. 58–59 and with regard to nuclear projects on p. 111.

21 Stobaugh and Yergin, *Energy Future*, p. 136.

22 Douglas Evans, *Western Energy Policy* (London: Macmillan, 1978), p. 138.

23 P. W. McCracken et al., *International Energy Center Study*, Dow Chemical Co. report to the National Science Foundation, June 1975.

24 Amory B. Lovins, *Soft Energy Paths* (New York: Harper & Row, 1979), p. 34.

25 Stobaugh and Yergin, *Energy Future*, p. 170.

26 Commoner, *Poverty of Power*, p. 127.

27 Ibid., p. 183.

28 The studies prior to 1978 are summarized in Richard Grossman and Gail Daneken, *Energy Jobs and the Economy* (Boston: Alyson, 1979), pp. 27 ff. The Harvard study is Stobaugh and Yergin, *Energy Future*, and the National Academy of Sciences report is summarized in *New York Times*, January 20, 1980.

29 *Council on Economic Priorities Newsletter: Jobs and Energy*, November 14, 1979, contains an excellent summary.

30 Grossman and Daneken, *Energy Jobs and the Economy*, p. 54.

31 Ibid., p. 118, n. 41.

32 Ibid., p. 70, citing Federal Energy Administration sources.

33 Lovins, *Soft Energy Paths*, pp. 23–24.

34 Stobaugh and Yergin, *Energy Future*, p. 231.

35 Lovins, *Soft Energy Paths*, pp. 23, 25.

36 Ibid., p. 41.

37 John M. Blair, *The Control of Oil* (New York: Pantheon, 1976), p. 398.

38 Ibid.

39 William W. Winpisinger, speech in Boston, March 1978, cited in Grossman and Daneken, *Energy Jobs and the Economy*, p. 84.

40 Engler, *Brotherhood of Oil*, Chap. 8.

41 Commoner, *Poverty of Power*, p. 58.

42 Ibid., p. 245.

43 Ibid., p. 249.

Chapter 8

Policy Making for Health Care

In sharp contrast to the sudden arrival of the energy crisis, problems concerning provision of adequate health care have existed since colonial days. Today, the leading problems are high and rising costs without equivalent improvement in health, gross inequalities of access to medical treatment, and marked contrasts in health and mortality between races, income levels, and regions within the United States *and* between the United States and other countries.[1] Americans spend more on health care, both in absolute dollars and in proportion of Gross National Product, than the people of any other country; but the United States trails several other countries in a variety of health and mortality indicators. Because medical treatment is so vital to curing serious illness or preserving life itself, many people see such problems as matters of deep personal importance. Scholars, professionals in the field, and other observers have characterized the American system as being in "crisis" ever since the early 1970s.[2]

Even among that great majority which agrees that the health care system is in crisis, however, there is wide variation in analysis of what is wrong and what can be done about it. At the heart of these differences is an often-unrecognized but crucial distinction between basic approaches to or definitions of the health care problem. All agree that "medical treatment" should be sharply distinguished from "health care," and that the best medical treatment cannot assure good health or long life. But the differences in definition go much deeper, and shape both understanding and solutions. The basic *medical treatment* definition of the problem of health in the United States emphasizes acute illnesses or life-threatening conditions and what doctors and hospitals can do about them, often with very sophisticated (and expensive) technology. The newer *health care system* definition looks at the causes of disease or illness, emphasizing preventive care as well as treatment by the major components of a far-flung "system" (doctors, hospitals, insurance and drug companies, government agencies, *and* the patient). A still more recent definition starts with the individual and asserts a *right to a healthy life* as a vital part of a democratic social system. These contrasting approaches will be evident from time to time as we proceed, and form the background for our consideration of alternative policies.

It should be obvious that these three definitions are not distinguished only by narrowness or breadth of scope. They also have political implications, whether consciously or not. But that is just the point: to think about health is to think about the organization and dynamics of a major component of the social order. This is inescapably a political act involving values and preferences, and carrying implications for the distribution of wealth *and* health in the society. The medical treatment definition has been clearly dominant throughout most of our history, but the health-care-system approach has risen recently to the point of nearly equal status. As yet, only a relative few approach the problem of health from the democratic-social-system perspective. In each view, of course, medical treatment and its life-determining effects remain at the core.

I CURRENT POLICIES

Health care policy (a) assumes a predominantly private system dispensing medical and related services, (b) provides financial support for people who use that system, along with support for medical research and certain inducements toward planning and cost control in the private system, and (c) undertakes comprehensive medical care directly for veterans, members of the armed forces and their dependents, and the top officials of government. By assuming the existing private system and adapting financing and other policies to it, policy makers have effectively embraced and made that system an important part of national health care policy. We shall therefore briefly describe that system first, and then explore the financing and other explicit policies that characterize our health care policy. Finally, we look at the consequences of those policies—the patterns of illness and mortality that characterize the American health care situation.

We should note at the outset that the problem of high and rising costs looms over the whole structure of the health care system and current public policy. Costs have shot up so dramatically since the 1960s that characteristics of the system and policy gain their principal meaning today from their relationship to the cost problem—whether as cause or cure. Health expenditures rose much faster than economic growth or costs in other industries over the decades of the 1960s and 1970s; they doubled as a share of GNP in this period. Average costs per person per year have increased more than 500 percent in the same period. Even with federal government and private insurance support, most people faced the prospect of simply not being able to pay for needed health services.

The Medical Treatment System

The dominant factor in the American medical system is the *physician*, sometimes called the "captain of the team."[3] This is true even though physicians number only about 325,000 persons out of a total of 4,400,000 in the system, or about one of every twelve health workers.[4] Physicians are the only ones who can prescribe drugs or perform treatments. Everything depends on their judgment and recommendations, which are very rarely questioned by patients, other doctors, or anyone else. They control their own fees, and also affect total costs by the number of laboratory tests, specialist consultations, hospital stays, surgical procedures, etc., that they prescribe. Although the proportion has declined somewhat recently, 62 percent of all physicians are still in private office practice. Another 29 percent work directly for hospitals in some capacity, and 9 percent are engaged in teaching or private industry. The occupation of physician is regularly ranked at or near the top in public prestige, as well as in income received.

Although the United States has more doctors per 100,000 of population than any other country except the Soviet Union, there are two forms of maldistribution that lead to impressions of a "doctor shortage." One is the high degree of specialization that now leaves only about 20 percent of all physicians in general practice or "primary care" (the first contact with a patient seeking care). The largest area of specialization is surgery, which draws 32 percent of all doctors, and is generally viewed as the "surgeon surplus."[5] Next are the medical specialties, chiefly internal medicine, pediatrics, and heart diseases, with 27 percent of all doctors, and then psychiatry and radiology, with 7 percent and 5 percent respectively.[6]

The other form of maldistribution is regional. The northeastern states and California have well above the national physician-population ratio, while the South and most rural states are equally far below the national average. Center-city minority populations are about on a par with the nation's most rural areas in regard to lack of available physicians.[7] Problems of access to medical treatment are thus real for many people, particularly those of lower income and of rural or center-city residence. General practitioners may be overworked and busy, while specialists are underutilized or engaged in nonessential operations.

But physicians as a profession remain in charge of the health care system. Hospitals are run by doctors, and merely provide facilities and equipment with which doctors treat their patients. The profession is well represented nationally by its organized voice, the American Medical Association, and locally by city or county medical societies. Threats to the personal autonomy of physicians, whether from government regulation or conditions on financing, normally call forth a vigorous and effective response.

Hospitals are usually classified by ownership, function, and length of stay, as in Table 8-1. There are almost 7,200 hospitals in the United States. About half of these are "voluntary," or not-for-profit, hospitals, owned by

Table 8-1   American Hospitals: A Composite Picture

	Short-Term		Long-Term	
	Number	Beds (thousands)	Number	Beds (thousands)
General				
Voluntary (nonprofit)	3,304	643	4	0.4
Proprietary (for profit)	743	68	2	0.4
Local gov't.	1,656	179	4	1.1
State gov't.	150	30	11	2.5
Federal gov't.	334	88	23	16.6
Total	6,187	1,009	44	21.0
Specialized				
Voluntary (nonprofit)	122	10.1	147	19.8
Proprietary (for profit)	98	5.0	57	5.4
Local gov't.	12	1.5	80	33.0
State gov't.	30	5.1	367	371.6
Federal gov't.	1	0.5	29	30.1
Total	263	21.2	680	460.0
Overall Total	6,450	1,031	724	481

Source: Hospital Statistics, 1975 ed. Published by the American Hospital Association, Chicago, Ill., annually as part of the "Guide Issue" (August) of *Hospitals: Journal of the American Hospital Association.*

religious groups or local corporations. About 12 percent are "proprie-tary," or for-profit, hospitals, owned by physicians or other investors either individually or in corporations. The remaining hospitals are owned by the federal (6 percent), state (8 percent), or local (22 percent) governments.

The largest proportion is made up of short-term, general hospitals; more than half of these are voluntary, and more than a quarter are owned by some form of local government. Federal hospitals in this category are Veterans' Administration or Defense Department installations. The spe-cialized hospitals are principally state mental institutions, voluntary and proprietary psychiatric hospitals, and other voluntary facilities.

The term "community hospital" refers to short-term, general hospi-tals exclusive of those owned by the federal government. More than two-thirds of the country's 1.5 million hospital beds are in these hospitals, but because of relatively rapid turnover they account for 98 percent of all the 38 million annual admissions and 78 percent of all hospital expenses.[8] In general, they are relatively smaller hospitals (averaging 160 beds), except for a few large city hospitals. The larger hospitals tend to be the long-term government-owned facilities or the nearly 700 leading hospitals associated with medical schools as "teaching hospitals."

The problem of rising hospital costs focuses upon the roughly 3,300 voluntary general hospitals. It is often argued that their nonprofit character enables them to use the income they generate to purchase costly new equipment, which is then used so seldom as to be both wasteful and dangerous to patients because of lack of experience.[9] There has been little effort to coordinate the services provided by hospitals in a given geograph-ic area, and no effective control of costs through competition or other means. Administrators are in no position to question physicians' judg-ments about length of stay in their hospitals or the need for hospitalization in the first place; if beds are available, they are likely to be used.[10]

But perhaps the greatest spur to costs has come from the manner in which hospital and physician charges have been paid. The *private insurance companies* are major components of the health care system because they now pay nearly 27 percent of all health care costs directly and also serve as fiscal intermediaries for Medicare and Medicaid. (The latter, to be discussed shortly, together make up the bulk of government's 42 percent share of health care costs.) What makes these insurance companies so important is that they essentially accept whatever hospitals and doctors charge for various services, and pass rising costs on to consumers in the form of higher premiums. Little is (or perhaps, can be) done to check actual costs of services or the propriety of charges.

Well over two-thirds of Americans are now covered by private insurance for at least some major share of their hospitalization and medical liabilities. Another perhaps 60 million persons are covered by Medicare or Medicaid, whose payments are made in the same manner by the same companies. Without some way in which their costs have to be justified, neither hospitals nor physicians face significant barriers if they choose to raise prices. Indeed, since the terms of some policies specify that payment depends on the patient's being hospitalized, doctors may order patients into the hospital for relatively routine procedures that could be performed elsewhere less expensively. All of this means that many aspects of rising costs are concealed in relatively invisible insurance premiums or higher Medicare/Medicaid demand for tax revenues. They are therefore less likely to encounter consumer resistance.

Other components of the health care system could be identified readily, such as the drug industry, pharmacists, nurses, dentists, etc. But the basic character of the system is set by the three leading components just described. It is indeed a nonmarket system. At its lifesaving core, unlimited utilization occurs without regard to cost, and often as a "right." Suppliers (physicians) decide how much will be consumed, and consumers accept their decisions, in part because about 70 percent of the costs are paid by third parties. All of these costs are passed back to consumers in premiums or taxes, and no effective challenge to hospitals' or physicians' charges can be mounted. Whether it should be made *more* of a market system by means of greater competition, fuller knowledge about products, etc., or acknowledged as inevitably nonmarket and therefore *regulated* by government, remains a matter of continuing controversy.

This overview of the key components of the health system is only preliminary, intended to sketch a background for understanding current policies. The problem of rising costs has been emphasized because it dominates and shapes much current policy. Many other problems and allegations remain to be analyzed. Nor does the focus on the medical treatment core of the health system imply a choice among the contrasting definitions of the health care problem discussed earlier. All of these issues must be deferred until we have a full grasp of current policies.

Direct Government Policies

United States government policies address the medical treatment system in three distinct ways. First, they provide financial support for patients who use the system. Second, they seek to improve that system by providing funds for medical research and construction of hospitals, and by encouraging cost controls, planning, and better distribution of physicians. Third, they supplement that system by providing comprehensive treatment for several million people and public health services for the nation as a whole. (Policy objects and costs are summarized in Tables 8-2 and 8-3.)

1   Financial Support for Patients   The total sum expended by Americans for health care has risen steadily, as has the proportion of the GNP that this total represents. By 1980, the nation was spending more than 9 percent of GNP, or nearly $240 billion, on health care.[11] As these costs escalated in the early 1960s, Congress enacted two programs, Medicare and Medicaid, to assist the elderly and the poor with their health care bills—and both programs in turn contributed to rising costs and greater total spending on health care. Together, Medicare and Medicaid represent the great bulk of national health expenditures; in 1980, these programs provided more than $55 billion in support of patients' health payments.

Medicare became effective in 1966. It provides limited coverage for persons 65 and over covered by Social Security and certain others. Part A is financed by Social Security payroll taxes and covers care rendered in hospitals and extended-care facilities. Part B is a voluntary supplemental program covering certain doctors' services, financed in part by general tax revenues and in part by payments from the elderly who join the program. Both parts contain deductibles (amounts the patient must pay each year before coverage becomes effective), copayment requirements (percentages of costs that must be paid by the patient), and coverage limitations (limits beyond which coverage ceases—in most cases, 90 days).

Because of these limitations, Medicare normally covers less than 40 percent of the total health care bills of the elderly. After all other government programs and private health insurance are taken into account, the elderly pay on the average about 35 percent of their bills from their own funds. When it is noted that more than half of all elderly individuals are in families with less than $5,000 in income, and only about 25 percent have family incomes over $10,000—and many of these represent fixed incomes—the financial part of the medical care problem of the elderly begins to become clear.

Medicaid was enacted at the same time as Medicare, and consists of federal cost-sharing for state assistance to welfare recipients for medical services. The federal share is based on the state's per capita income average, providing relatively more per recipient to the states with lower income levels. States are required to provide payment in full to the aged poor, the blind, the disabled, and families with dependent children for hospital care, laboratory and physicians' services, and skilled nursing care. A variety of optional coverages are authorized if states wish to provide them, and states are free to impose limits on coverage, deductibles, and copayments. The result is wide diversity in the kinds of coverage and conditions imposed in various states.

Roughly 23 million persons are covered in some way under Medicaid, although another 10 million persons officially designated as "poor" are estimated to remain excluded. Most working poor, childless couples, the medically indigent (those able to support themselves except for medical bills) in twenty seven states, and low-income families with an unemployed father present in twenty six states, are not covered.[12] Federal Medicaid expenses nevertheless climbed above $12 billion in 1980, with another $10 billion paid by the states.

Both Medicare and Medicaid are implemented in many respects by the private health insurance companies acting as fiscal intermediaries. That is, these companies (when selected for the purpose by the national and state governments) receive, process, and pay claims in a given area and are compensated for this work by the relevant government. Medicaid is much the more variable of the two programs, reflecting the diversity of state preferences and practices. It is also subject to continued changes in eligibility and funding levels as state legislatures change in makeup and attitude toward the poor. Medicare is generally rated more effective in reaching its intended population with reliable assistance.

2 Research, Construction, Cost-control, and Planning　The national government supported modest medical research programs under the Public Health Service for decades, but began much more ambitious research support after the medical advances of the 1940s. The National Institutes of Health now comprise eleven Institutes with research responsibilities in specific areas and a 1980 budget of $2 billion. The great bulk of these funds go to the support of research in the nation's medical schools. One source estimates that federal funds contribute some part of the salaries of half the faculty members in medical schools.[13]

Support for construction of hospital facilities dates from the passage of the Hill-Burton Act in 1946. The intent of this program was to spur construction of modern hospitals, particularly in rural areas or other state-selected areas of need, partly as a means of attracting physicians and easing the maldistribution problem. Federal support was provided at ratios of up to one-third, and about one-third of the nation's hospital-bed capacity came into being in this manner. Construction support is also provided now for research facilities; a total of between $1 billion and $2 billion per year is spent by the federal government for all construction purposes.

Cost-control and planning efforts have usually been undertaken together because of their close relationship. Several major efforts to contain costs, in part through greater planning and coordination, were made in the face of the rapidly rising costs of the 1970s. In 1972 amendments to the Social Security Act, Congress required that (effective in 1976) increases in physicians' fees for Medicare patients be limited to percentages equal to the increases in costs and earnings in the same area.

Enforcement is difficult, however, and the effects of this limitation are hard to identify.

Also in 1972, as part of the same package of amendments, a new mechanism for monitoring the quality of health care services was created. Called Professional Standards Review Organizations (PSRO), these bodies are intended to raise the quality and contain the costs of medical care rendered to recipients of federal financial supports. They are a form of "peer review" in which physicians establish local-area norms for the necessity and duration of hospital stays and the character and quality of treatment. Local physicians who do not conform to such standards are urged to do so, but their fees are not subject to review; and enforcement mechanisms governing other practices are, as a practical matter, limited to exclusion from participation in Medicare and Medicaid.

PSROs are formed when 25 percent of the physicians in active practice within the "service area" (on average, an area including thirty-five hospitals and a total population of 1 million) support the principle. Objection by 10 percent of practicing physicians requires a poll of all physicians in the area. The PSRO must go through a planning phase (enrolling physicians, setting up procedures and structure) and a two-year conditional stage (testing and refining its standards and practices) before it gains final federal approval. Cooperation from physicians has been spurred by government authority to designate other qualified organizations, such as local health departments, as PSROs. But the system necessarily requires a lengthy period for development, and will become fully operational only in the early 1980s.

In 1973, Congress authorized federal grants and loans to support the development of Health Maintenance Organizations (HMO). These are organizations formed for the purpose of providing, or contracting for

Table 8-2   Public Programs and Health Care Objects, 1979 (in percents)

	Hospital services	Physicians' services	Nursing homes	% of all care
Medicare	45	60	4	39
Medicaid	17	21	87	29
Veterans Administration	9	1	3	7
Department of Defense	6	1	—	5
Workers' compensation	4	13	—	4
State and local hospitals	14	—	—	10
All other	4	4	6	6
	100	100	100	100

Source: *Health Care Financing Review*, Summer 1980, Table D, p. 7.

provision of physicians' services, hospital care, emergency services, and preventive health services on a continuing basis to a defined population which pays fixed amounts on a regular basis. The idea behind HMOs is to combine the merits of prepaid group insurance with cost reductions through preventive measures. A small number of prepaid group insurance programs had developed previously and established that consumers' costs could be reduced when physicians accepted fixed salaries plus shares of surplus income generated by prescribing shorter hospital stays and less costly procedures. Preventive measures were thought likely to reduce the need for costly hospitalization and medical treatment still further, and thus to result in additional savings to consumers. Other intended advantages were greater assumption of collective responsibility by the medical team for the health of the population served and greater involvement of that population in preventive self-help and control over treatments rendered to them.

The concept of the HMO and prepaid group insurance has attracted major employers and the larger private health insurance companies to experiment with a variety of forms. By the end of the 1970s, about 175 HMOs or similar organizations were serving about 6 million subscribers.[14] Development of such organizations was slower than anticipated, however, because of statutory requirements placed on those that sought to qualify for government assistance. A wide range of services and benefits was mandated, for example, and all HMOs were required to open their admission rolls for a period of thirty days each year. Experience suggested that such requirements might drive premiums for HMO membership well above the low-benefit plans offered by private health insurance companies, which could also exclude or charge higher rates for certain high-risk people.

Late in 1974, Congress made a major effort to consolidate previous programs and develop coordinated health facilities and services planning in the National Health Planning and Resources Development Act. Three previous programs were brought under the responsibility of a single state or area agency known as the Health Systems Agency (HSA). The first of these was the Hill-Burton hospital construction program, previously described. The second was the 1965-created Regional Medical Programs designed to plan and implement services aimed particularly at heart disease, cancer, and stroke—the three major causes of death (along with car and other accidents). This program provided full federal funding to link service provision to the research capabilities of major medical schools through a series of new institutions and personnel. The third program was the 1966 Comprehensive Health Planning, or "partnership for health," program. This program sought to break the practice of focusing on specific diseases, populations, or types of services by offering matching funds to promote cooperation and planning among all the various components of local health care systems (except physicians in private practice).

Despite these efforts, fragmentation and duplication continued to characterize health planning. The new HSAs were intended to be coordinating bodies, and were supported by full federal funding. State governors were to designate areas of from 500,000 to 3 million people with some natural and medical homogeneity, and identify an existing public or private nonprofit body as the HSA. Most of the more than 200 HSAs served as data-collecting agencies and arenas where the competing claims of various health care entities could be heard and perhaps accommodated to each other.

Other provisions of this statute contain potentially important implications for overall planning (as we shall see in Section II of Chapter 9), if the HSAs are able to use them effectively. For example, HSAs are to review and approve or disapprove requests for federal grants for health programs in their areas. They can also play an important part in determining whether proposed new facilities receive the state-granted "certificate of need" that they must have to proceed. These and other powers could conceivably be developed to the point where standards of quality and cost could be enforced on physicians and hospitals. This possibility has not been ignored by the AMA, whose spokesperson has described this statute as follows: "It is the single most dangerous piece of legislation ever enacted by a United States Congress . . . it will totally restructure the practice of medicine, make the HEW Secretary an absolute czar of the delivery of health care and give nonmedical people the power to decide whether or not a service to be rendered in a hospital is the appropriate one."[15] The AMA challenged the statute on constitutional grounds, as usurping powers of the states and interfering with the private practice of medicine, but the United States Supreme Court upheld a lower court's judgment that the law was within congressional powers.

Much subsequent impetus toward rationalization of services and planning has come in the form of guidelines issued by the Department of Health and Human Services under the authority of this same act. The guidelines are aimed at maximizing the efficiency with which facilities and equipment are used, to avoid oversupply and underutilization—both of which add to costs and risks. The Department has also centralized its health functions in a single new body, and sought in various ways to challenge cost increases.

3 Direct Provision of Comprehensive Medical Services The national government maintains a large number of hospitals and provides comprehensive services to a significant proportion of the population. The Veterans Administration invests more than $3 billion per year in the largest centrally directed hospital and clinic system in the United States. About 29 million veterans, or about 13 percent of the population, are eligible to receive at least a portion of their medical care from the VA. Another 10 million persons, almost 5 percent of the population, receive their health care under the auspices of the Department of Defense. Most of them (active and retired military personnel, their dependents and survivors) are served directly in the more than 130 military hospitals in the United States, but some are covered via prepaid insurance for care purchased in the private sector.

The Public Health Service has grown from its original mission of caring for itinerant seamen and preventing the spread of communicable diseases to its present wide range of research and preventive education responsibilities. It operates eight hospitals for merchant seamen and Coast Guard personnel and another fifty as part of the Indian Health Service program. Its most visible operations, however, are probably the National Center for Disease Control, which monitors all communicable diseases, and the Food and Drug Administration, which carries responsibility for protecting the public from hazardous products.

The Consequences: Patterns of Morbidity and Mortality

The health conditions of the population served by this system-and-policy combination—people's illnesses and the causes of death—are partly a

Table 8-3   U.S. Government Health Expenditures, 1979

	$ in billions	% of total
Medicare	$30.3	39.2
Medicaid	12.5	16.2
Veterans Administration	5.4	7.0
Department of Defense	4.0	5.2
Public Health Service	1.3	1.7
Various other programs	2.9	3.8
Subtotal	$56.4	
Tax revenue losses*		
Exclusion of health insurance benefits from income	15.2	19.7
Individual tax deduction for medical care and health insurance	4.1	5.3
Deduction for charitable contributions to hospital and medical research	1.6	2.1
Total	$77.3	100.0†

*Amounting to subsidies to health care industry; calculated from U.S. budget, FY 1981, by *Congressional Quarterly, Weekly Edition,* February 2, 1980, p. 260.
†Figures may not add due to rounding.
Source: Health Care Financing Review, Summer 1980, Table 7, p. 33.

product of, and therefore one measure of, the performance of that system/policy. Such patterns also stem from factors outside the health care system and form part of the problem to be dealt with by future policies.

Measures of health tend to focus on death and its causes, partly because of the human anxiety about death but primarily because it is easier to distinguish death from life than sickness from health. Moreover, morbidity (illness) data depend to a considerable extent on a patient's own judgment that care is needed, success in obtaining treatment, and the definitions and conscientiousness with which illnesses are reported. Nevertheless, some note should be taken of the changing nature of diseases and their implications before concentrating on the meanings of death-rate data.

Several of the major diseases of the past have been almost entirely eliminated, at least in the developed countries. These include smallpox, cholera, yellow fever, typhus fever, scarlet fever, polio, and measles. Most of these were eliminated by improvements in sanitation, housing, nutrition, and pure food and water, but some were ended by vaccines.

By 1900, the leading diseases were those brought about by microorganisms: pneumonia/influenza, tuberculosis, diarrhea and enteritis (particularly in infants), nephritis (kidney disease), and diphtheria. Pneumonia and influenza frequently occurred on top of other chronic (long-term and likely to be incurable) diseases, such as heart disease and cancer. People whose systems had been weakened by chronic diseases often died from these terminal infections. The development of sulfa drugs in the 1930s, followed by penicillin in the 1940s and then the mycins, effectively controlled all of these diseases. For the first time, physicians had available resources that could actually cure existing diseases. Before then, there were preventive vaccines in some cases, but little they could offer a patient who had already contracted a disease, except painkillers. It is often said that medicine came of age only in the 1920s, in that a patient's chances of being helped by a visit to the doctor did not rise above fifty-fifty until that time.

One important result of these advances in the development of drugs is that chronic illnesses have risen sharply in importance. Eliminating the terminal infectious diseases permitted people to live longer while suffering from chronic illnesses, with respect to which little progress in effecting cures has been made (the "failure of success" in some observers' eyes).[16] Chronic illnesses range from some that are modest in effect or subject to control (though not cure), such as epilepsy and diabetes, to serious and often prolonged diseases or conditions, such as mongolism and senile brain disease. The major killers among all diseases now are chronic in character: heart disease, cancer, and stroke. The contrast in fatal diseases between 1900 and 1980 is shown in Table 8-4.

A byproduct of the rising importance of chronic illness is its staggering economic impact. One authority estimates that 40 percent to 50 percent of

Table 8-4 Percent of All Deaths from Specific Diseases

Disease	1900	1980
Pneumonia and influenza	12%	3%
Tuberculosis, diarrhea and enteritis, nephritis, diptheria	27	—
Heart disease	8	40
Cancer	4	19
Stroke	6	12

Source: David L. Dodge and Walter T. Martin, *Social Stress and Chronic Illness* (Notre Dame, Ind.: University of Notre Dame Press, 1970), p. 6 (for 1900); 1980 data from *Health Care Financing Review,* Summer 1981, p. 44.

all Americans suffer from some form of chronic illness, and that a quarter of them lose days at work for that reason.[17] Medical and hospital expenses are often substantial when the disease is first discovered, and if or when the disease is stabilized lifelong costs at only somewhat lower levels are involved. Extended care in nursing homes now draws more than $10 billion of public and private funds per year; with the time limits for coverage that are contained in Medicare and most private health insurance policies, the alternative for many people sooner or later is welfare assistance. Some diseases, such as kidney failure or certain heart conditions, can involve costs of $50,000 or more for surgery or mechanical implants.

A second major result of the revolution in treatment capabilities through drugs is much longer average life expectancy. Since 1900, life expectancy in the United States has increased from 47 years to more than 72 years. Much of this change results from greater capacity to treat children's diseases. The death rate for children under 1 year of age has been reduced by about 80 percent. For those from 1 to 4 years old, it has been reduced by more than 90 percent. But for those 55 or older, only very slight reductions have been achieved. Rising standards of living, chlorination of water, and pasteurization of milk are credited with beginning sharp reduction of the "pneumonia/diarrhea complex" in small children, a process that was speeded by the drug developments of the 1930s. Most infant mortality is now concentrated in the first month of life; it is associated with premature birth and/or the physical and emotional condition of the mother.

These developments are not due to the medical treatment system alone, of course. They are products also of environmental conditions and behavioral patterns as they interact with medical capabilities and utilization. As such, they begin to sketch the outlines of the problems that confront and will help to shape future policies.

II THE ORIGINS OF CURRENT POLICIES

In seeking to explain the origins of current health care policies, we shall focus chiefly on how the major units of the private medical treatment system—doctors, hospitals, and private insurance companies—achieved their dominant roles, obliging public policy to accept and support them. To do this accurately, we must also consider the decisive part played by one of the most powerful professional organizations in American society, the American Medical Association. We shall also trace the slow but steady expansion of government public health services over nearly two centuries.

The occupation of physician (and later surgeon as well) always carried with it a sense of status and importance. Built partly from the greater education of doctors (often the result of higher-class origins) and partly from the human fear of illness and death, this status endured despite recurring epidemics and physicians' relative inability to do anything about them. As early as the eighteenth century, however, there were conflicts between physicians trained in European universities and those trained under apprenticeship in the colonies. The more elite physicians also had to contend with the faith healing of ministers and varieties of "folk medicine" developed by Native Americans.

Failure at enforcing legal distinctions between "regulars" and "irregulars" led to the founding of university-based medical schools (1765, University of Pennsylvania; 1768, Columbia; 1783, Harvard) and the formation of local and state medical societies. The medical schools served to legitimate and preserve the status of their founders and faculty, and the students whom they selected to perpetuate themselves. The societies were the means for setting standards of practice, licensing those who accepted them and preventing others from engaging in medical treatment. The basis on which all services were provided was that of all other entrepreneurs in the society: fee for service rendered, payable in money or in kind at the time of the transaction. Certain "charity" services were, of course, provided voluntarily to the poor by those physicians so inclined.

Although the regulars had by 1830 secured licensing laws in thirteen states, outlawing the practice of medicine by those not certified by the elite physicians, folk healing and popular health movements continued in many parts of the developing nation. The latter drew upon frontier democratization and early feminism to wage an antielitism campaign that succeeded in gaining the repeal of several licensing laws. This led to the formation in 1847 of the American Medical Association (AMA), one of whose early purposes was to eliminate such "quackery." The battle continued almost to the twentieth century, until the AMA and its state components finally gained control of licensing standards throughout the country. The consequences of this achievement included the virtual elimination of women from any form of medical practice and reduction in the volume of services available to poor people and rural residents.

The assumption of public responsibility for some kind of health care dates from 1798, when Congress established the Marine Hospital Service (later the United States Public Health Service) to provide treatment for merchant seamen. But the next step in this development did not occur until the middle of the nineteenth century, when repeated epidemics beginning in crowded, poverty-stricken immigrant tenements threatened all social classes in the major cities. Local governments began to institute preventive measures, such as sanitation, pure water supply, and housing standards. Partly because the recently initiated practice of recording the causes of death focused attention on preventable diseases, states began in 1870 to try to control such diseases through state-level boards of health. Nevertheless, illness and death from contaminated water and food continued to increase until the twentieth century. Public health reforms ran counter to prejudices against immigrants and the urban poor and the general laissez faire ethos of the times.

The decisive stage in the shaping of the current American medical treatment system occurred in the final decades of the nineteenth century. Most Americans, from the colonial period on, had felt a special fascination for science and its applications to economic development in the form of technology and machinery. In the field of medicine, this helped prepare the way for the "technological, cure-oriented, institution-based profession"[18] it was to become.

Each disease was thought to be brought about by a specific identifiable cause or agent, such as a particular germ or microbe, rather than by the interplay of environmental conditions (poverty, malnutrition, impure food and water, etc.) and such agents. Emphasis was therefore placed on scientific research that would identify these "single agents" and find the "cure" that would eliminate or control the spread of diseases. Relatively little effort was expended on trying to modify environmental conditions, and the practice of medicine became firmly linked to the provision of cures after illness had been contracted.

At about the same time, new developments in technology (particularly anesthesia, antiseptics, and surgical tools) raised the quality of treatment in hospitals and began to establish them as the locus for medical practice. Hospitals had been set up as early as a century before, but they were in part almshouses and often the center of infectious diseases. Hospitals were a place where poor patients were sent to die; the chances of death were greater among those sent to hospitals than for those who were able to receive treatment—or who merely remained—at home.[19]

With the development of scientific applications in research and hospitals came a new surge of expansion of medical schools. New knowledge was produced in laboratories, applied in clinical settings, and passed on in the classroom. The functions of research, teaching, and curative activity were united with the fusion of research institute, medical schools, and teaching hospital in a single entity.

The stature and influence of the major medical schools were greatly enhanced by two important developments of the early twentieth century. The first was the reinvigoration of the AMA by teaching faculties intent on raising the standards of the profession as a whole. One of their major causes, naturally, was the quality of medical education, and a committee was established to monitor and evaluate schools. But the AMA also began to take stands on social issues that brought it to public visibility and gained it support. One of these stands was endorsement in 1916 of a system of national health insurance.

The second major development of this period was an evaluation of American medical education sponsored by the Carnegie Commission. As many as 400 medical schools had been founded in the latter part of the nineteenth century, and about 150 were still operating at its end. The results of the celebrated Flexner Report of 1910, with its critical judgment of many schools, were the closing of many marginal schools, the ascendancy of the major schools, and a significant reduction in the number of doctors in succeeding generations. By 1922, the total number of graduates of medical schools had dropped to less than half the number graduated in 1904. The occasion also marked the entry of private foundations into a major role in shaping the research priorities and educational practices of the medical world.

From about the second decade of the twentieth century, the scientific and technological revolution in medicine took hold and began to accelerate. New drugs and techniques made treatments more effective, but made physicians more and more dependent on laboratory testing, expensive technologies and procedures, and (consequently) hospitals as the place where all but the simplest services would be rendered. The newest techniques, of course, were pioneered at the most elaborately equipped hospitals associated with the most advanced and best-funded medical schools.

Through this period, the AMA worked to raise the standards for admission to medical school, prolong the period of education, and stiffen the requirements for licensing to practice. The goal of assuring quality in medical services often translated into deliberate efforts to limit the supply of physicians. An AMA-financed study of educational principles initiated in 1925, for example, reported in 1932 that too many physicians had recently been produced, arguing: "An over-supply is likely to introduce excessive economic competition, the performance of unnecessary services, an elevated total cost of medical care, and conditions in the profession which will not encourage students of superior ability and character to enter the profession."[20] No doubt influenced by falling incomes in the depression decade of the 1930s, the AMA continued to serve the interests of private practitioners by vigorously pressing the medical schools to upgrade and reduce their output.

The 1930s were also the setting for the creation of a major new component of the medical treatment system. Hospitals found that their principally middle-class users were often unable to pay the costs of hospitalization from current income or savings. With the vigorous support of the American Hospital Association (AHA) and the cooperation of state lawmakers, a prepayment plan ultimately known as Blue Cross was established. Operating on insurance principles, a not-for-profit Blue Cross company offered AHA-approved specified coverages to those paying monthly premiums. Providers (hospitals) and insurers (the various Blue Cross companies in each state) worked in close partnership to assure that rising costs would be met and provider discretion preserved. The formal relationship between AHA and Blue Cross was not ended until 1972.[21]

The Blue Shield companies, which provide payments for physicians' services, were originated shortly after Blue Cross and along similar lines. State medical societies first initiated plans, and ultimately the AMA took over, formulating standards and approving state and local Blue Shield programs. Because both the "Blues" developed under provider sponsorship, and their control structures are still dominated by provider representatives, they often act in the interests of hospitals and doctors rather than as watchdogs for their premium-paying consumers. One of the factors that helped to gain passage of Medicare over determined AMA resistance, for example, was assurance that most of the administration would be in the hands of the Blues. More than 90 percent of hospital payments under Medicare Part A is handled by Blue Cross, and about 60 percent of physicians' payments under Part B by Blue Shield.

As other, profit-making health insurance companies entered the field in the 1940s, they tended to follow policies similar to those established by the Blues. Many of these companies developed as a result of the exemption of fringe benefits such as health insurance from the wage limitations on collective bargaining contracts during World War II. Businesses and unions eagerly sought health insurance plans, and a new industry was created. About 1,000 companies now provide this insurance on a commercial basis, and at significant profit levels. Roughly three out of four Americans have some form of coverage for hospital services and in-hospital physicians' care, and about 40 percent of each is paid through one or another form of private insurance. Much lower proportions of nursing home, dental, and drug bills are covered by private insurance.

The final development of the 1930s was the assumption of federal government responsibility for certain limited aspects of health care. The inadequacy and costs of medical care had been stressed by the report of the Committee on the Costs of Medical Care in 1932,[22] and made more visible by emergency federal medical care and supplies provided to supplement the states' relief efforts. The Social Security Act provided funds for state programs of medical assistance to mothers and children. Some research was initiated with federal funding, and direct care under the Public Health Service and Indian Health Service was expanded somewhat. There were several bills proposed to institute national health insurance, the principal result of which was to spur development of the voluntary programs under medical control that were just described.

The federal role began to expand more rapidly after World War II. Direct care under the Veterans Administration was a much larger responsibility, and the defense establishment was also much larger than before the war. The new availability of hospitalization insurance and the limited supply and poor distribution of hospital beds led to the Hill-Burton hospital construction program, which helped to solidify the role of hospitals as the locus of medical care. New medical knowledge and techniques gained during the war held out hope of even greater curative capabilities, so that research in a variety of areas was greatly spurred. Continued agitation for assistance that would expand the medical schools and for national health insurance kept the federal government on the apparent verge of even greater direct involvement in the health care system.

The greatest single bulwark against a larger federal role was the determined opposition mounted by the AMA. It became the largest spender among all political lobbyists during 1949 and 1950, when federal aid to medical schools and students was under consideration, despite the fact that the bill involved had been endorsed by all the deans of accredited public health schools and 75 percent of the deans of medical schools.[23] Similar programs, and increasingly more restricted ones providing assistance only for operating costs and then only for construction of new facilities, were also opposed throughout the 1950s on the grounds that there was no shortage of doctors. No federal assistance was provided for medical education until student loans and construction assistance were authorized in 1963 (over AMA opposition). At the same time, the AMA strongly supported federal support for medical research and hospital construction. One close observer concluded that the AMA simply supported whatever increased the *demand* for physicians' services and opposed whatever might increase the *supply* of physicians.[24]

The AMA was also the major opposition to Medicare in 1965. Its campaign set new records for lobbying expenditures: in the first quarter of 1965 alone it spent more than any other organization had spent for a full year's lobbying in the twenty previous years of financial disclosures and almost twenty times as much as the second-place spender.[25] A variety of state and national political action committees implement AMA preferences by selective funding of congressional candidates' campaigns. Although Medicare was ultimately passed, AMA political power remains a potent obstacle to efforts to gain control over rising costs or physicians' or hospitals' practices—and, of course, to the cause of national health insurance.

Much has been made of the question of internal democracy within AMA and whether the organization really represents the opinions of most practicing physicians in the United States today. The roots of AMA lie in state and local (usually county) medical societies. Physicians normally join their local medical society, and through it their state society and the AMA. Local societies select delegates to the governing bodies of their state societies, which in turn choose delegates (1 per 1,000 members) to the AMA House of Delegates. The latter meets semiannually to elect a president and the fifteen-member Board of Trustees that holds policy-making power between legislative sessions, and to decide various major issues. The Association publishes ten journals and enjoys substantial revenues from drug company and other advertising in them as well as from membership dues. To a considerable degree, therefore, the leadership is detached from the membership base and able to articulate positions which it endorses and/or believes to be in members' interests.

Moreover, although about 70 percent of all physicians belong to AMA, they are in some respects subject to its influence rather than the reverse. Considerable power over a physician's livelihood can be wielded by the local medical society, which effectively controls the vital access to local hospitals and the availability of lower group rates for the increasingly important malpractice insurance. A doctor in private practice who does not "go along" with AMA-initiated standards and practices could be seriously punished by the local medical society. Added to this enforcement capability is the control over state medical licensing exercised by state medical societies and the control over medical education generally exercised by a combination of state and AMA officials. Only those physicians who have tenured faculty, administrative, or other permanent salaried positions are really free to challenge AMA in its assertion of the right to speak for all practicing physicians in the country.

But in a way the issue of internal democracy and representativeness within AMA is beside the point. In prestige, resources, and political power, AMA is a major force on the policy-making scene and will continue to be for at least the immediate future. It therefore joins and implements the private system of doctors, hospitals, and insurance companies (not to mention drug companies, dentists, and other providers and producers) that public policy must assume and to which it must adapt. The dominant fact about the American medical system is that it is in private hands and conducted for private profit. Even that portion which is publicly financed is largely controlled by entrepreneurs and corporations in the private sector. In the words of one critic, "the stage was thus set, as funds became increasingly available, for uncontrolled, uncoordinated, chaotic technological and institutional growth."[26]

III COMPARATIVE HEALTH CARE POLICIES

Most of the major European nations spend less than the United States on health care but still outrank the United States in many health and mortality indicators. Part of the explanation seems to lie in relatively greater attention to the environmental sources of illness. Public health services are often more extensive and of much earlier origin than in the United States; record-keeping on such matters as the causes of death, for example, predates American practices by centuries. Another part of the explanation appears to be the generally free and comprehensive medical treatment programs provided by governments in those countries. Some of these have their origins in the nineteenth or early twentieth centuries. We shall look briefly at the basic contrasts in health and mortality indicators, and then in more detail at two different health care systems that have achieved greater success than ours, Great Britain and Sweden. In a summary section, we shall try to draw some lessons from these and other nations' experiences and currently changing directions.

Table 8-5 compares two key characteristics of health care systems and some traditional measures of health. Only Sweden compares with the United States in proportion of GNP spent on health care. All the other countries spend significantly lower shares. American expenditures are distinguished by sheer dollar amount and by the large share borne by private sources. What this investment buys seems, in this comparison, to show up best in the number of physicians per person and least in the health conditions of the people. In number of hospital beds per person, the United States ranks first. In infant mortality, however, the United States is only eighth among these nations, and also trails in age-specific death rates.

Great Britain

Although a relatively poor country by American standards, Great Britain has obtained relatively high levels of health quality. The roots of the British health care system go back to the sixteenth century, when the Royal College of Physicians of London was formed. This was an association made up of upper-class physicians who treated the royal family and the aristocracy; it dominated medical practice and eventually formed the top tier of a

Table 8-5 Ratio of Doctors and Hospital Beds to Population and Mortality Rates, Selected Industrial Countries

Country	Total (millions)	Population Per physician (hundreds)	Hospital beds (per 100,000 persons)	in first year	by age 10	by age 45
				Rank from lowest (1) to highest (9) in mortality per 100,000 live births		
1. United States	217	595	160	8	8	9
2. Britain	49	659	120	7	6	5
3. Canada	23	563	110	6	7	6
4. France	53	613	90	5	5	7
5. Germany	61	490	80	9	9	8
6. Sweden	8	563	70	1	1	3
7. Denmark	5	512	110	3	2	4
8. Netherlands	14	583	100	4	4	1
9. Japan	113	845	90	2	3	2

Note: Data pertain variously to years 1976, 1977, and 1978.

Source: World Health Statistics, 1980 (Geneva: World Health Organization, 1980), pp. 5–8, 380–381 (Tables 1, 4, and 11).

three-level system. Highly specialized elite physicians treated the wealthy, often in prestigious specialized private hospitals that also performed teaching functions.

The second level developed in the early nineteenth century and offered physicians only somewhat less prestigious hospital facilities for specialized practice. As a way of assuming responsibility for the "deserving poor," and sometimes of memorializing themselves, aristocrats took to founding hospitals at which the sons of other aristocrats would practice medicine. Much of this practice became specialized, and patients were admitted as much for the research and teaching opportunities their diseases offered as for general purposes of care.

The third level had its origins in the Elizabethan Poor Laws, in which paupers were to be cared for by their home parishes. These jurisdictions hired physicians for the purpose, and eventually built municipal hospitals to assume the burden.

With industrialization and the eventual rise of nonpauper working and lower-middle classes, however, there was a large bloc of people not served by any hospital-based medical system. Such needs greatly spurred the "apothecary," or general practitioner, movement. From the seventeenth century, those who dispensed drugs to fill physicians' prescriptions ("apothecaries") had begun to win the right to treat the sick as well. In the early nineteenth century, educational standards were raised and the

Society of Apothecaries given authority to license apothecaries to practice primary care medicine. Some had connections with hospitals, but their principal focus was private practice; a patient who required the services of a specialist or "consultant" physician or surgeon would be referred to a hospital. When the two types of practitioners were officially registered together in 1858, the general practitioners were recognized as being of lower status (and income), with the function of providing primary care to the paying working and middle classes, and generally denied access to hospitals.

As medicine became more and more scientific, the status of the elite, specialized, and hospital-based physicians became even greater. New hospitals developed to permit application of new techniques and to facilitate research and teaching. But the bulk of the population was by now connected to the general practitioners, and their association (the British Medical Association) was comparable in influence to the much older Royal Colleges. A subgroup of general practitioners began to provide salaried services to developing trade unions or "Friendly Societies," voluntary contributory associations formed to provide compensation for lost earnings and medical services to members.

In 1911, the Health Insurance Act was passed to compulsorily regularize medical care for manual workers. The act applied only to general practitioner services and covered only employed workers below a certain income level. General practitioners were paid a flat fee for each covered person on their list of patients, regardless of the amount of services actually provided. Administration was through insurance committees that included general practitioners and the established Friendly Societies and industrial insurance companies. Although not quite a third of the population was actually covered by this insurance program, the position of the general practitioners was significantly enhanced. They were able to maintain their autonomy, to resist being integrated with preventive health activities shortly thereafter, and ultimately to shape the modern form of British health care. By 1939, 90 percent of the general practitioners were participating in the insurance system and about 40 percent of the population was covered thereby for ambulatory services and sickness benefits.

The present British health care system, completed in 1948 with the National Health Service Act, institutionalizes the general practitioner's role. Each general practitioner has a list of specifically registered patients and provides primary care free of charge to every one of them; patients may shift to any general practitioner willing to accept them (although very few change for reasons other than change of residence). General practitioners have an average load of 2,300 patients and are paid a flat fee regardless of the amount of services rendered in any given year. Working singly or in groups and organizing their practices in any way they choose, the general practitioners provide a highly personalized form of primary care that regularly draws high rates of approval from the British public.

Hospital care and specialized medical services are also free, and available to all on referral from a general practitioner. The hospitals were integrated, and distinctions between them reduced, by the Act of 1948. After the Reorganization Act of 1974, fourteen regional health authorities and ninety area health authorities assumed responsibility for managing the hospital system, planning services, and undertaking preventive health activities. The National Health Service is almost entirely tax-supported, with fees for certain services producing less than 5 percent of its funds. Expenditures on privately provided medical services total only about 2 percent of all medical expenditures in Britain, although the consultants are still able to bring private patients into public hospitals.

British health care, essentially free to all, costs considerably less than health care in either the United States or Sweden and is of high quality. Vestiges of the elitist distinctions of the past remain, such as in the status and prerogatives of the consultants, but quality care is provided to all on a much more equitable basis than is the case in the United States. Rational planning is possible, and rising costs have been controlled more fully than elsewhere. The least satisfied constituency involved, however, is a key one—the specialists, whose incomes are less than desired.

Sweden

Although a very small country by contrast with the United States, Sweden is quite comparable in standard of living and level of technological development—and has perhaps the best overall health conditions in the world. Its medical care system developed around a core of state-owned or state-financed hospitals dating back to the eighteenth century. Physicians who worked in these hospitals were salaried and had very little outside practice; such appointments carried high prestige, and medical schools developed around teaching hospitals. Salaried physicians were also assigned public health functions in districts covering the country. Another early development that helped to generate comprehensive health care was the formation of "sickness funds," contributory voluntary funds sponsored by groups of craftsmen (later, employers and employee associations) that compensated members for lost income due to illness. In some cases, physicians were employed to provide care for members and/or provisions were made to reimburse members' medical costs.

In 1862, just before industrialization began in earnest, responsibility for financing and running the hospital system was transferred from the national government to counties and cities. Hospital care remained free, and the economic hardships of industrialization led to increased usage.

Even so, not all the doctors produced by state-run medical schools could find hospital positions, so that a system of private practice with fees for services also developed. The voluntary sickness funds continued to expand in the twentieth century, gaining support from government grants in 1931 and taking on health insurance responsibilities. By 1955, when about three-quarters of the population was covered, the government took over the financing and made the combined system of health insurance and sickness benefits a comprehensive and compulsory one for all citizens.

The present health care system in Sweden is a decentralized one in which ascending levels of care are provided in 274 districts, 26 counties, and 7 regions. Each of the several districts within a county has a district health center with several doctors and nurses attached. Chiefly general practitioners, these doctors provide both primary and preventive health care in conjunction with nurses and other health professionals. Each of the counties maintains a general hospital for every two or three districts and a larger central hospital providing more specialized care. Each region includes a highly specialized hospital which also serves as a teaching hospital with an associated medical school.

The purpose of such decentralization was to reduce costs by avoiding duplication of the more expensive services and making the most-often-needed services available locally at minimum cost. The counties are fully responsible for the management of the hospitals, district health centers, and salaried preventive health physicians within their jurisdictions, but public health functions are discharged at the district level. Although the distribution of power to local units is real and problems of coordination do exist, by and large this arrangement appears to have resulted in a rationalized system in which overall planning is possible.

The private component of the Swedish system is quite limited. Only about 10 percent of all physicians are in private practice, although they account for about a quarter of ambulatory visits to doctors. There are very few private hospital beds, and a private physician's patient would receive hospital care and/or a specialist's attention in the same way that any other patient would—by referral from the primary care physician to the salaried hospital specialist.

All hospital care (including medical, surgical, nursing, medicines, etc.) is entirely free to patients. Most of the costs are paid by the counties, with some help from the national government. The national health insurance plan pays a small part of hospital costs, but is responsible for most ambulatory visits to doctors and compensates people for earnings that are lost because of illness. Overall, the counties bear about 75 percent of total health care costs (some of it later reimbursed by the national government), the national government contributes about 14 percent directly for its hospitals, medical schools, and other functions, and the

Table 8-6   Total Public Expenditures as Percent of Gross Domestic Product, 1965–1977

Country	1965	1970	1977
Sweden	35	43	62
Britain	37	41	44
United States	27	32	33

Note: Gross Domestic Product (GDP) includes only goods and services produced within a country's territorial limits, while the more familiar GNP includes production overseas. GDP is the standard measure for most European countries having little or no external productive capacity.
Source: Theodore Geiger, Welfare and Efficiency (Washington, D.C.: National Planning Association, 1978), p. 17.

national health insurance plan accounts for another 10 percent. The remaining 1 percent is paid by patients in the form of fees for service.

Sweden has experienced rising health costs in recent years, not unlike the United States. One factor was a wave of technological innovation. Another and more permanent source of pressure on costs is the rising proportion of elderly persons. Hospital usage, length of stays, and doctor visits rise rapidly with age, and no country has yet found a way to change such patterns. Because the Swedish system is so hospital-focused (with 720 hospitals for a population of 8 million people, more than twice the number of beds per population than the United States), it is vulnerable to both of these types of cost pressure. All of these costs, of course, ultimately become part of the tax burden assumed by citizens.

Summary: Lessons and Directions

The two systems just examined are quite distinct in character. Great Britain's emphasizes the independent general practitioner, providing continuing primary care to a fixed list of persons whom the physician comes to know. Sweden's is based on decentralized hospital-based care and groups of salaried doctors in district primary-care centers. But they also have some important features in common. They both emphasize preventive health activities and education; they are both entirely free to patients (and therefore presumably provide services to more people and at an earlier stage of illnesses); and they both seek to rationally plan the allocation of resources and services. Table 8-6 compares the increasing scope of government activity (and hence revenue-raising needs) in all three countries. It helps explain mounting opposition to increased taxation.

The latter concern, shared among many nations, has led to reduced emphasis on new medical research and technology, an effort to provide services elsewhere than in hospitals, and general skepticism about the need for more doctors. Instead, it is argued that greater gains in general health levels are to be realized from increased emphasis on preventive health programs. Improvement in environmental and work conditions, and in the personal behavior of individuals, is coming to be the focus of national health programs. Enhanced primary care is almost the only strictly medical-treatment activity that is included in current planning documents.

NOTES

1 These problems are repeatedly identified in the literature on this field. For a particularly incisive presentation, see Victor R. Fuchs, *Who Shall Live? Health, Economics, and Social Choice* (New York: Basic Books, 1974), pp. 9–16.

2 Jordan Braverman, *Crisis in Health Care* (Washington, D.C.: Acropolis 1978) is a recent user of that characterization. For a full survey of the range of observers joining in the same characterization, see Steven Jonas, ed., *Health Care Delivery in the United States* (New York: Springer, 1977), pp. 1–3.

3 Fuchs, op. cit., p. 56.

4 Florence A. Wilson and Duncan Neuhausen, eds., *Health Services in the United States* (Cambridge, Mass.: Ballinger, 1976), pp. 72–73. This is a valuable summary of the basic facts and statutory provisions in the field. Other data in this paragraph are from the same source.

5 The characterization is widely used, but again see Fuchs, op. cit., p. 15, for documentation.

6 Wilson and Neuhauser, op. cit., p. 72.

7 Victor W. Sidel and Ruth Sidel, *A Healthy State* (New York: Pantheon, 1977), p. 63. This is one of the more sensitive portrayals of a universally observed condition.

8 Fuchs, op. cit., p. 82.

9 Ibid., p. 85.

10 Ibid., p. 96.

11 All data in this and the next paragraph are drawn from the *Social Security Bulletin*, February 1980.

12 Carol McCarthy, "Financing for Health Care," pp. 247–288, in Jonas, op. cit., at p. 257.

13 Ibid., p. 259.

14 Braverman, op. cit., p. 91

15 James H. Sammons, "That Blockbusting Health Planning Act: How Will Doctors Fit In?" *Medical World News*, April 5, 1976, p. 55. Sammons was executive vice-president of the American Medical Association at the time.

16 Ernest M. Gruenberg, "The Failures of Success," *Milbank Memorial Fund Quarterly*, Winter 1977, pp. 3–24.

17 Darryl D. Enos and Paul Sultan, *The Sociology of Health Care* (New York: Praeger, 1977), p. 127.

18 Sidel and Sidel, op. cit., p. 231.

19 Elton Rayack, *Professional Power and American Medicine* (New York: World Publishing, 1967), p. 25.

20 *Final Report of the Commission on Medical Education* (1932), cited in ibid., p. 73.

21 McCarthy, op. cit., p. 261. All data in this and the next paragraph are drawn from this source.

22 The same paragraph is quoted in nearly every work in this field, and may as well be cited here as edited by Sidel and Sidel, op. cit., p. 238:

The problem of providing satisfactory medical service to all the people of the United States at costs they can meet is a pressing one. At the present time many persons do not receive service which is adequate in either quantity or quality and the costs of service are inequitably distributed. . . . Furthermore, these conditions are . . . largely unnecessary. The United States has the economic resources, the organizing ability and the technical experience to solve this problem.

23 Rayack, op. cit., p. 89.
24 Ibid., p. 99.
25 Ibid., p. 11.
26 Sidel and Sidel, op. cit., p. 241.

Chapter 9

Health Care: Issues and Alternatives

The future of health care policy, and perhaps of the quality of health in the United States, revolves around two central facts and a major conceptual or definitional problem. The first fact is that of the private and independent nature of the key service providers—doctors, hospitals, and the insurance companies. Their independent and profit-seeking character shape all policy considerations. The second fact is that of high and rising costs—costs so high, and racing so far ahead of the inflation rate, that *something* will have to be done. In the context of the first fact, this probably means limiting the government's contributions and forcing patients to pay a larger share or forgo treatment, rather than an effort to effectively control fees and charges.

　　The conceptual or definitional problem is that described at the outset of the last chapter. Our understanding of health care has focused on *medical cures*, often with dramatic research breakthroughs and new technology focused on acute illnesses or life-threatening situations. Recently, however, people have begun to think in terms of a *health care system* whose concerns would reach to the causes of illness and disease and focus on prevention. A still newer approach is to think of a *right to a healthy life* as part of a democratic social system, with all that implies in the way of environmental improvements, work safety, nutrition, and availability of health services. Which definition of the problem of health care is accepted profoundly determines one's view of what should be done.

I CONTEMPORARY PROBLEMS

The problems that lead many close observers of the American health care system to view it as being in crisis have already been identified at various stages of this analysis, but will be explored in greater depth here. First is the problem of the health condition of Americans. Although the United States medical system has produced dramatic research findings and developed ingenious technological capabilities, the general level of health does not compare favorably with other industrialized nations—particularly when our massive financial investment in health care is considered. Moreover, levels of health are very different for different sectors of our population: the poor and racial minorities and both rural and center-city dwellers (these are, of course, overlapping categories) all have much higher morbidity and mortality rates than the white middle class.

The second problem, closely related to levels of health, is that of lack of access to medical services for many people. Because of inability to pay, the unavailability of physicians, and/or their special needs, many people do not receive the services they need. This lack shows up particularly in the way that health indicators differ by income, race, and residence, but it is also felt by a wide range of people of relative affluence. Its roots lie as much or more in characteristics of the medical treatment system as in characteristics of prospective patients.

The third problem is also linked to that of levels of health but goes beyond that to threaten the whole medical system itself. It is, of course, the problem of high and rising costs that continue to outstrip the rate of inflation and far exceed increases in real personal income. Without effective action to contain costs, most Americans face the prospect of economic catastrophe in the event of a serious illness to themselves or a family member and/or significantly lower levels of general health for themselves, their families, and the nation.

The fourth problem involves the quality of medical and hospital care rendered. The technical competence and professional judgment of physicians, particularly surgeons, is being increasingly called into question—often in the form of malpractice suits. Public dissatisfaction appears, on the basis of several indicators, to be rising. A major source of resentment against the medical establishment involves the psychological dimensions of "care" as well. American physicians and hospitals appear to be better at the technological and physical aspects of curing than at providing the human compassion, warmth, and encouragement that may be equally important to eventual rehabilitation. In particular, sexism and racism seem to continue to play a major role in the organization and application of medical services. And Americans appear to need caring as much as cures. In the words of John Knowles, then President of the Rockefeller Foundation:

> Beyond death and disease statistics, there exist a steadily expanding number of the "worried well" and those with minor illness. *Has life itself become a disease to be cured in the American culture?* Some 80 percent of the doctor's work consists of treating minor complaints and giving reassurance. Common colds, minor injuries, gastrointestinal upsets, back pain, arthritis, and psychoneurotic anxiety states account for the vast majority of visits to clinics and doctors' offices. One out of four people is "emotionally tense" and worried about insomnia, fatigue, too much or too little appetite and ability to cope with modern life. At least ten percent of the population suffers some form of mental illness, and one-seventh of these receive some form of psychiatric care. Meanwhile, the figures for longevity are the highest, and for infant mortality the lowest in U.S. history, and the gap continues to narrow. We are doing better, but feeling worse.[1]

Behind these highly visible problems lie some more general and fundamental premises, priorities, and practices that must also be examined. The basic fact is that the American medical system developed in a fragmented way. Individual doctors, hospitals, medical schools, insurance companies, drug companies, and professional associations each sought to serve their own interests and maximize their own rewards. The fee-for-service principle systematically pointed them toward those with the ability to pay, and the physicians' autonomy principle helped to keep doctors at the decision-making center for both medical and social issues.

The American system thus focuses on medical cures, with a heavy emphasis on high technology and specialization, instead of balancing curative capabilities with preventive health measures and expanded primary care. Because it is so principally a private system with profit and/or prestige as its imperatives, it has effectively resisted such planning and coordination as was attempted. Lack of planning shows up particularly in the training, functions, and distribution of the human resources involved in health care, but also in duplication of expensive equipment and services in hospitals and the lack of facilities for particularly needy groups in the population, such as our growing proportion of elderly persons. We shall take up each of the four highly visible problems, and then turn to the premises and practices behind them (with particular attention to the issue of planning and coordination) at the outset of the next section.

1 Health Status: General Levels and Specific Contrasts

In the concluding segment of Section II of Chapter 8, and again in Table 8-5, we surveyed major indicators of health levels in the United States. We saw that the elimination of infectious diseases had greatly reduced infant mortality, extended life expectancy, and made chronic illnesses much more significant medical problems. Heart disease, cancer, and stroke are now the major causes of death in the United States. A disquieting aspect of the American health picture was the fact that, in two widely accepted indicators of general health levels—infant mortality and age-specific death rates—the United States does not compare favorably with many other industrialized nations. Instead, the United States ranked only fifteenth among all countries in infant mortality and trailed several other countries in age-specific death rate categories.

Data on general health levels reflect only aggregate totals, moreover, and may conceal as much as they reveal. Table 9-1 is a comprehensive portrayal of both totals and some contrasts between subgroups of the population, and will be supplemented from other sources in the following discussion. Many of these contrasts, of course, are linked directly to sex, age, race, residence, and economic circumstances; some are due to lifestyle characteristics.

Females have much longer life expectancies than males at every age level. Ten percent more male babies die before birth, from one-third to one-half more during childhood, and three times as many during early adulthood. Around age 60, the probability of death for males is about double that for females, principally because of heart disease, where male rates are triple those of women.

Among males, there are basic differences—but changing ones—at every age level and between whites and nonwhites. The infant mortality rate for black babies is almost double that of white babies, for example, and remains significantly higher even at comparable levels of income and medical care.[2] Comparing white and nonwhite death rates per 100,000 of the male population at various age categories presents a discouraging picture of American life. Nonwhites die from all causes at from 50 percent to 300 percent greater proportions than whites at every stage of life. In the 15- to 24-year category, 50 percent of white male deaths are from automobile accidents; when other accidents, suicides, and homicides are taken into account, 80 percent of all deaths are from such violent causes. Nonwhites have fewer automobile deaths, and much lower suicide rates, but ten times the homicide rate and almost the same resulting total proportion of violent deaths. This self-destructiveness is a distinctively American characteristic with important economic and social implications.

By the time that men reach the ages of 35 through 44, the pattern has changed sharply (even though violent deaths of various kinds still account

Table 9-1 Death Rates by Age, Color, and Sex, U.S., 1973

Age in Years	Total			White			All other		
	Both sexes	Male	Female	Both sexes	Male	Female	Both Sexes	Male	Female
All ages*	9.4	10.7	8.2	9.5	10.7	8.3	9.2	10.9	7.6
Under 1	18.0	20.0	15.8	15.3	17.5	13.1	31.2	33.0	29.4
1–4	0.8	0.9	0.7	0.7	0.8	0.6	1.1	1.3	1.0
5–14	0.4	0.5	0.3	0.4	0.5	0.3	0.5	0.7	0.4
15–24	1.3	2.0	0.6	1.2	1.8	0.6	1.9	2.9	0.9
25–34	1.5	2.1	0.9	1.3	1.8	0.8	3.3	4.8	2.0
35–44	2.9	3.6	2.2	2.4	3.1	1.8	6.1	8.0	4.6
45–54	7.0	9.2	4.9	6.4	8.4	4.4	12.3	16.1	9.0
55–59	13.1	17.9	8.7	12.3	17.0	8.0	20.6	26.7	15.2
60–64	19.4	27.0	12.8	18.5	26.1	11.9	27.7	36.2	20.4
65–69	27.9	38.7	19.2	27.1	38.1	18.2	35.6	44.0	28.8
70–74	43.1	59.1	31.4	41.7	58.1	29.8	58.5	68.8	49.8
75–79	67.7	87.2	54.9	67.3	86.9	54.4	73.7	90.1	61.2
80–84	98.1	123.7	83.2	99.8	126.7	84.3	78.0	91.7	68.6
85 and over	174.5	199.4	162.0	179.2	205.1	166.4	124.1	141.9	112.0

Note: Table based on a 10% sample of deaths. Rates per 1,000 population in specified group. Due to rounding estimates of deaths, figures may not add to totals.
*Figures for age not stated included in "All ages" but not distributed among age groups.
Source: Annual Summary, *Vital Statistics of the United States; Monthly Vital Statistics Report,* June 27, 1974, Table 6. (See Appendix I, A4 and A5.)

for nearly 30 percent of all deaths). Heart disease and cancer lead for whites, and heart disease and homicide for nonwhites. Cirrhosis of the liver, linked to alcoholism, begins to claim significant numbers. Together with smoking's effect on lung cancer and heart disease, and alcohol's involvement with car accidents, the cumulative impact of cigarettes and liquor on health is substantial.

In late middle age, ages 55 to 64, death rates are higher in all categories. The greatest increases occur in heart attacks. For white males, the death rates from this cause *and* from lung cancer are both ten times what they were at ages 35–44; apparently, these figures are the cumulative result of decades of earlier behavior. White suicide rates are three times those of nonwhites, but nonwhite homicide rates are eight times those of whites. Overall, however, deaths from forms of violence are only tiny proportions of those from heart disease, cancer, and stroke at this age level.

Although the nonwhite category compared with whites here included more blacks than any other single race, it also covers Chicanos, Puerto Ricans, Asian-Americans, and Native Americans. Each group has certain distinctive health problems, and all but Asian-Americans trail far behind whites in health levels.[3] Chicanos have high early mortality and disease rates, and very low physician-contact rates; the same is true of Puerto Ricans. But Native Americans have the poorest health of all American minorities. Infant and maternal mortality rates are two to three times those of whites, and disease levels on reservations are from four to fifty-four times higher than for the rest of the nation. Poverty is one cause of these conditions, but minorities consistently have poorer health levels than whites of comparable incomes at all levels of income.

Residence too helps to determine health conditions. Rural and center-city dwellers have from 50 percent to 100 percent higher infant mortality rates than people of similar characteristics (sex and race) who live elsewhere.[4] The range of infant mortality in the United States in the mid-1970s (not including Native Americans) ran from 11.3 per thousand live births in a largely white middle-class area in Massachusetts to 27.1 in a rural and heavily black section of South Carolina.

Income level plays an important part in shaping mortality patterns, and is clearly reflected in the earlier racial contrasts. The incidence of chronic diseases, such as arthritis, heart conditions, diabetes, hypertension, and hearing and vision impairments, is from 30 percent to 50 percent higher in the lower-income strata than in the higher.[5] Similarly, the poor have many more hospitalizations, days lost from work, and more days of restricted activity than do the wealthy.[6] Malnutrition and poor physical condition are also prevalent among lower-income groups. Propensity to disease is thus highest among those who can least afford medical treatment (and are least likely to seek it). Racial, residence, and income factors often combine to make the health levels of the nearly 20 percent of Americans who fit in such categories very poor indeed. But more whites live in poverty than minorities, and their health is distinctively poor as well.

Although race, sex, age, and economic circumstances set the basic pattern of mortality, certain lifestyle characteristics are also relevant. Smoking and drinking have already been identified as important causes of disease and ultimate death. Stress is associated with heart illnesses, and perhaps also with some forms of cancer. Marital status is also closely related to health: at middle age, unmarried males have twice the death rate of married men and five times that of married women. Divorced and widowed men have death rates substantially higher than men who have been single all their lives. Unmarried or widowed women have only slightly higher death rates than their married counterparts, suggesting that they are better able to cope with single status.

One summary analysis of the effects of lifestyle on mortality compared death rates in the adjoining states of Utah and Nevada.[7] In income, climate, urbanization, number of physicians and hospital capacity, and other relevant factors, the two states are very similar. But in mortality rates at all ages, Utah is among the healthiest of all the states, and Nevada the unhealthiest. From infant mortality, which is 40 percent higher in Nevada, through the vulnerable middle-age period, where rates are 60 percent higher in Nevada, up to the highest age categories, the differences consistently favor Utah. The reasons seem to lie in Nevada's larger proportion of in-migrants and people who are divorced or widowed, and much greater consumption of alcohol and tobacco.

This profile of health conditions and problems should not be understood as an assessment of the American medical treatment system. Indeed, medical care might have very little to do with these conditions. Many problems of access and cost, shortly to be reviewed, are involved also; so are the interactions of medical treatment with environmental conditions and behavior patterns, as the survey indicates. But this is just the point: much that is relevant to health conditions lies well outside the scope of a system designed chiefly to provide medical cures. The more we examine current problems of health for Americans, the more we are directed toward the second (or perhaps even the third) of the definitions of the "health care problem" set forth at the outset of this chapter.

2 Access to Medical Care

The problem of access is actually two problems. One has to do with the special characteristics of the people who need care—their inability to pay or to withstand income loss, or other reasons (cultural, educational) for not seeking treatment; their residence; or their particular condition and medical needs. The other is more general and rooted in the characteristics of the medical system itself—the distribution and specialization of medical professionals, hospital facilities, and treatment capabilities.

The people who need care, as we have seen, are often those with the least ability to pay. Partly for the same reason, they are also the least likely to carry hospitalization and medical insurance. Visits to physicians, therefore, run far behind the levels appropriate to need.[8] Rates of visits for preventive care rise sharply with income; 35 percent of all low-income children did not see a doctor for any purpose during some years of the mid-1970s.[9] Nonwhites, among whom the incidence of disease and mortality is distinctly higher than whites, have *lower* rates of physician visits. And the doctors they do see are two to three times more likely to be those in hospital outpatient clinics or emergency rooms than in private offices.

Before the advent of Medicare and Medicaid, hospitalization rates for low- and high-income persons were roughly the same despite the greater health problems of the poor.[10] Since that time, hospitalization rates for the poor have increased by nearly 50 percent, although there is no way of telling whether this is yet appropriate to need. Medicare and Medicaid have also increased the incidence of physician visits by the poor.

Financial barriers are not the only factor standing in the way of people seeking medical care, however. Rural residents may simply be unwilling or unable to travel the necessary distances to see an appropriate doctor. Ghetto residents may be unwilling to consult a white doctor in an affluent section of the city. Less-educated persons may not recognize symptoms in a timely manner, or understand how to locate needed services. Drug addiction, alcoholism, and various forms of mental illness are rising steadily among all groups of the population, and may seem to be normal features of everyday life. Some persons have disabilities or chronic illnesses for which there are no corrective procedures or cures available. For all these reasons, but principally for reasons of inability to pay (as demonstrated by the sharp rises in both hospitalization and physician visits after Medicare and Medicaid), many people do not seek the care they need. Probably many more receive little or no preventive care or health education.

But only part of the access problem is related to characteristics of prospective patients. Rather than simply "blaming the victim," we should look carefully at some characteristics of the medical care system itself. Perhaps most important is the *distribution* of physicians, both geographically and in terms of specialties. (The sheer *number* of physicians is much less of a problem. The United States already has a relatively high and steadily increasing ratio of doctors to total population—one doctor for every 580 persons in 1980[11]—exceeded in the world only by Israel and the

Soviet Union. But this distinctly high ratio, as we have seen, does not translate into better health levels.)

Geographic maldistribution is brought about by the need of specialists to be near major hospitals and the affinity of most doctors for the cultural and other amenities of urban life. For example, New York has 205 doctors engaged in patient care for every 100,000 persons, while South Dakota has only 89.[12] This contrast of more than 100 percent is exceeded by differences between counties in many states. One out of every twenty counties in the United States has not a single doctor, and more than half lack a pediatrician.

Specialization is brought about by the greater status and prestige, control over time invested, and income that are involved, and perhaps also by the greater challenges and satisfactions that most doctors see in specialty medicine. The United States has a much higher ratio of specialists to generalists (or "primary care" physicians) than any other industrial country.[13] Although definitions of what amounts to "specialization" vary, the proportion of physicians engaged in general practice, or primary care, has dropped steadily in the twentieth century to about 21 percent in the late 1970s.[14] Many more doctors are engaged in surgery of some kind (32 percent of all doctors), so many that there has not only been widespread use of the term "surgeon surplus" but also talk of the need to limit admission to surgical specialties—all within the medical profession itself.[15] By contrast, 78 percent of doctors in Sweden, 70 percent in West Germany, and 58 percent in Britain are primary care physicians.[16]

The decline of general practice in the United States is probably the single most important factor in the access-to-services problem. Nearly 42 percent of all visits to office-based practitioners are to general or family doctors, 25 percent are to medical specialists, and 28 percent to surgical specialists.[17] Given the breakdown of the profession, the generalists have about double the workload of other doctors. At the turn of the century, the ratio of generalists to population was about 1:450; in the mid-1970s, it was about 1:3000.

Efforts recently have been made to expand the numbers of primary care physicians and to encourage them to practice in rural or center-city ghetto areas. The National Health Service Corps grants scholarships and stipends to medical students in exchange for commitments to work at least temporarily in such areas. "Health manpower shortage areas" are defined by the Federal Health Resources Administration as places with only one doctor for every 3,500 or more persons (3,000 in poverty areas) and are eligible to apply for doctors under the NHSC. But about 25 percent of Americans live in such shortage areas, and there is no way that the NHSC can force doctors into the most needy places or keep them permanently where they do agree to locate. The NHSC had 2,060 physicians located in 1980, but estimates were that 16,000 primary care physicians would be needed in underserved areas by 1990.[18]

The availability of physicians is complicated still further by the problem of foreign medical graduates (FMGs). Changes in the Immigration and Naturalization Act in 1965 permitted entry of professionals in areas "thought to be in short supply in the United States."[19] FMGs began to flow to the United States from Europe, India, and the Philippines, as well as from other Third World countries, chiefly in Asia. In the mid-1970s, about 20 percent of all doctors in the United States were FMGs, and FMGs entering the country each year outnumbered doctors graduated by American medical schools. Moreover, as admissions to medical schools became more and more difficult, thousands of American students chose to study in foreign schools, chiefly in Mexico and Italy. All of these FMGs faced serious difficulty in passing licensing examinations (either in command of English or in medical competency, or both), but substantial proportions ultimately did so.

The dilemmas involved in this development are several. On one hand, it would cost a great deal to build and equip medical schools to train such a significant number of new doctors. On the other, the FMGs do not help much in solving our major problem of distribution, for they engage in specialties and locate themselves in urban areas in about the same proportions as other doctors. There are also some important issues of quality involved. One-third of all interns and residents in American hospitals are FMGs. They are often concentrated in the most overcrowded and least desirable municipal hospitals, where language deficiencies and emergency cases may make for a dangerous mix. Finally, there is the moral question of furthering a "brain drain" in which prospective income levels lure doctors away from the desperate needs of their native countries to comfortable practices in an already well-supplied United States.

A final system characteristic that contributes to access problems is the disjunction between its technological curative capability and the growing proportion of patient needs that involve disability, chronic illness, or mental illness. Most health insurance policies cover hospital care but not ambulatory care or continuing or preventive care, and so the medical system has had added incentive to orient toward acute illness and away from chronic conditions. Mental health services are particularly underprovided; there is little interest or reward among professionals, and less political support, for major efforts in this direction.

3 The Costs of Health Care

We shall first describe the scope and character of the problem of rising costs, employing various comparisons to try to see just how serious it really is. Then we shall explore some of the reasons for these increases and the effectiveness of such remedies as have been tried.

The stark fact is that health care costs have been rising rapidly, faster than inflation and much faster than wages, ever since the mid-1960s. Table 9-2 summarizes some of the increases since 1950. By 1975, to use one measure, average annual health care costs per person amounted to $547. This means that the average family of four would pay $2,188, or nearly 10 percent of its income, for health care. As recently as 1940, the per capita expenditure had been only $25. In other terms, the country had spent only $12 billion on health care in 1950, only 4.6 percent of the total GNP. By 1979, it was spending $212 billion, nearly 10 percent of GNP.

Health expenses tripled between 1965 and 1975; they increased at a rate well in excess of those for food, automobiles, housing, and other consumer items, and were approached only by price rises in energy costs. The largest share of the burden of rising expenditures in this period was borne by the federal government, whose health expenses increased by 813 percent. But state and local government health spending rose 172 percent, private insurance benefits 200 percent, and patients' own direct payments 74 percent.

In dollar amounts, proportions of GNP and family income, and rate of increase, these are staggering totals. But they do not lead to a single conclusion. We do not know that we are "spending too much" until we assess the benefits derived from such spending, compare them with other ways of providing health care, and rank spending for health against other

Table 9-2   Health Expenditures, Selected Years

	1950	1965	1979
Total health expenditures			
In $ billions	$ 12.7	$ 42.0	$212.2
As % of GNP	4.4%	6.1%	9.0%
Per capita	$ 81.86	$212.32	$942.94
Annual % increase	12.2%	9.3%	12.5%
Public expenditures			
In $ billions	$ 3.4	$ 11.0	$ 91.4
Per capita	$ 22.24	$ 55.48	$406.12
Annual % increase	15.5%	10.6%	13.3%
Private expenditures			
In $ billions	$ 9.2	$ 31.0	$120.8
Per capita	$ 59.62	$158.84	$538.82
Annual % increase	11.2%	8.9%	11.9%
Total GNP (in $ billions)	$286.2	$688.1	$2,369
Total population (thousands)	154,675	197,784	216,823

Source: *Health Care Financing Review*, Summer 1980, Table 1, p. 16.

possible uses of the same funds. Most contemporary observers give only perfunctory notice to the latter question, apparently because of a deep cultural faith in medicine.[20] There is broad consensus, however, that cost increases have not been accompanied by corresponding increases in benefits, and that a better mix of spending on health services could bring better results.[21]

What costs have risen distinctively, and why? Table 9-3 may serve as a starting point for analysis. It shows both the shares of total expenses borne by the major funding sources and the shares received by major health care providers. Public payments, principally by the federal government, represent the single largest source. But direct payments by patients and payments by private health insurance companies are also substantial shares of the total. Among recipients, hospitals lead by a wide margin, followed by physicians, and then by several other types of providers. Much the same ratio applies where cost increases are concerned. In 1974-1975, for example, hospital charges rose by 13 percent, as compared to the inflation rate (less medical care) of 7 percent.[22] Physicians' fees rose by 11.8 percent, dentists' by 7.8 percent, and drug charges by 7.4 percent.

Hospital charges are not only nearly 40 percent of all health care costs and the area of greatest cost increase, but also the area of lowest direct patient payments. Ninety-two percent of all hospital costs are borne by third parties, about 36 percent by private insurance companies and 56 percent by governments. In contrast, 65 percent of physicians' fees are paid by third parties, 39 percent by private insurance, and 26 percent by governments. Direct patient payments, only 8 percent and 35 percent for hospitals and physicians, are 85 percent of dentists' fees and drug costs. Direct patient payments to hospitals in 1950 were four times larger, or 34 percent of the total; such payments to physicians were more than twice as large, or 85 percent of the total. Relatively little change occurred in ratios of payments to other providers. The shift to third-party payments was partly to governments, particularly the federal government in the area of physicians' services in recent years. But private insurance companies' share of total costs also increased sharply in this period, more than doubling in share of payments to hospitals and nearly quadrupling in payments to physicians.

The extent of third-party payment thus appears to be a factor in the degree of increase in costs. In reality, all costs are ultimately borne by consumers, whether directly, as insurance premiums (or lower wages because of employers' insurance contributions), or in higher prices or taxes. But out-of-pocket costs are more visible and personal than insurance premium or tax increases, and probably generate greater resistance; the less visible the costs, the freer a provider may be to raise charges.

Table 9-3 How the $212 Billion Health Care Cost Flowed, 1979

Sources of health care payments			Health care receipts		
Direct out-of-pocket			Hospitals		40%
payments by patients		31.8%	from patients	8%	
			from federal		
Public payments		40.2	government	41	
			from state		
Federal government	28.2		governments	15	
Medicare	15.6		from private		
Medicaid	6.2		insurance	35	
All other	6.5				
State and			Physicians		19
local governments	12.0		from patients	36.5	
Medicaid	5.3		from federal		
All other	6.7		government	20	
			from state		
Private insurance			governments	6.5	
companies		26.7	from private		
			insurance	37	
Philanthropy and other		1.3			
			Drugs		8
			from patients	84	
			from federal		
			government	4	
			from state		
			governments	4	
			from private		
			insurance	8	
			Nursing homes		8
			from patients	42	
			from federal		
			government	31	
			from state		
			governments	26	
			from private		
			insurance	1	
			Dentists		6
			Research and		
			construction		5
			All other		14

Source: *Health Care Financing Review*, Summer 1980, Tables 1, 2, and 6, pp. 16–32.

Other explanations for cost increases include increased population, increased utilization of services, higher real costs for increasingly sophisticated technological treatments, and proliferation of high-technology service capabilities (such as intensive-care units). The chances are good that all of these are to some extent correct.

Hospital costs that were increasing significantly included food and fuel, but not distinctively wages; moreover, wages as a share of total costs was dropping steadily.[23] The greatest single source of increased hospital costs has been rapid development of advanced technology in most hospitals.[24] Only 11 percent of voluntary hospitals had an intensive-care unit in 1960, but 68 percent did by 1972. Only 18 percent had an electroencephalograph in 1960, but 45 percent did by 1972. The same kind of increase is evident in several other areas where new forms of treatment utilizing expensive technologies have been developed. Hospitals have also added about a third to bed capacity, despite a growing bed vacancy rate that averaged about 25 percent in the late 1970s.

Physicians' costs have increased in part because of increasing technological capabilities in their offices, and in part because of the steady trend toward greater and greater specialization. Rapid increases in malpractice insurance premiums, and defensive use of additional diagnostic tests, are also a factor. But the biggest rise in physicians' costs seems to be traceable to the fee increases, greater utilization, and readier payments associated with Medicare and Medicaid. Physicians' incomes jumped 14 percent in 1967, the year after those programs went into effect, and continued to rise steadily in real terms thereafter. Perhaps some doctors began to be paid for services previously rendered free to the poor, but probably others simply opened their doors to a new constituency and/or increased their fees.

Medicare and Medicaid are probably responsible for some share of the increases of health care costs across the board. About 80 percent of the increase in federal spending is in these two programs; hospitals derived the largest share, and physicians the next largest. But Medicare still paid only about 60 percent of the elderly's hospital bills and about 52 percent of their physician charges; the out-of-pocket share of all health costs paid by the elderly remained about 34 percent.[25] And many doctors do not participate in Medicaid, apparently because of delays in payment and changing bureaucratic standards and procedures in the various states. Balanced against the increase in demand for services promoted by these two programs, therefore, are all the other factors making for cost increases throughout the health care system.

Efforts that have been made to contain costs include state limits on hospital charges. Six states had imposed such limits by 1980, and early results suggested that the rate of increases had been held below the national average (11.2 percent as opposed to 14.3 percent) for the three-year period 1977–1979.[26] But some hospitals argued that they were being pushed toward reduced standards of care and/or bankruptcy. Legislation to impose similar federal standards was urged by the Carter administration but rejected by the Congress. Nor have effective measures to contain physician costs been considered seriously. The only area in which major steps have been taken is in prescription drugs, where state laws frequently provide for the substitution of less-expensive generic drugs for high-priced brands.

4 The Quality of Care Rendered

As the utilization of medical services has increased (the number of doctor visits rose above 1 billion per year in the mid-1970s), the level of public satisfaction with the services rendered seems to have declined. Rising expectations about the efficacy of medical treatment may be partly to blame, but doctors' and hospitals' fees, impersonal procedures, and actual mistakes also seem to play a major part. In any event, the 1970s saw an unprecedented blossoming of media analyses and horror stories about poor-quality services. These were paralleled by equally unprecedented rises in the number of malpractice suits, staggering increases in dollar amounts of jury awards, and explosive leaps in malpractice insurance premiums. In some states, doctors went on strike demanding protective legislation; other doctors gave up parts of their practice, joined the military, or retired entirely. We shall survey the extent and possible causes of public dissatisfaction with the quality of medical services, and then take up the malpractice crisis.

The first fact is that the proportion of the public expressing "a great deal of confidence" in the leaders of medicine has declined from 73 percent in 1966 to 43 percent in 1977.[27] This may be understandable in view of the anxieties people often feel when forced to trust themselves to overworked medical personnel who have little time or inclination to explain what is happening or to reassure patients against recurring fears. But a number of studies by medical researchers themselves have painted a concrete picture of competence problems in medical care.

Several of these were collected and presented in a now-celegrated series in 1976 by the *New York Times*.[28] One study was cited as finding that American surgeons were performing nearly 2,400,000 unnecessary operations each year in which 11,900 patients died from complications. Others found that errors in judgment result in 260,000 needless hysterectomies and 500,000 unwarranted surgical removals of tonsils and adenoids each year. Doctors were found to be writing hundreds of thousands of prescriptions for powerful and dangerous drugs where safer alternatives were available and/or patients' diseases were known to be unaffected by antibiotics. Ten thousand people were estimated to die annually from the administration of antibiotics that were unneeded. About 2,200 hospitals, nearly one-third of the United States total, were found not to meet the minimum standards of patient care and safety set by the medical profession's commission on hospital accreditation; but there was no way to limit the medical or surgical activities carried on in such hospitals. Other media seized upon similar studies and dramatic individual cases of failure to respond properly to emergencies, or extremely bad judgment, to document the quality problem in great and often lurid detail.

Some of the sources of this problem lie in the area of greatest strength of the American medical system—its technological emphasis and capabilities. Diagnostic testing, drug applications, and surgery are most often cited for inflicting unnecessary danger, illness, or even death on patients. The most dangerous of the frequently ordered tests are x-rays, from which several thousand disabilities or deaths are thought to result.[29] In many cases, x-rays could be dispensed with, deferred, or administered under conditions of greater safety. Each year, about 300,000 people are hospitalized because of reactions to prescription drugs. The most widely prescribed drugs and those that produce the largest number of reactions are the antibiotics. The prescription of such drugs has risen six times faster than the population in recent years, although there has been no increase in the incidence of diseases for which they are appropriate.

Finally, of the 18 million surgical operations performed in an average year, about 14 million are "elective," or nonemergency, situations. Some of these are necessary even though not immediately critical, but many could be deferred or are unnecessary to continued well-being. Considering that approximately 1 out of every 200 such operations ends in the death of the patient in the operating room or from resulting complications, tens of thousands of deaths per year may be unnecessary from this cause alone. Moreover, data indicate that the number of surgical operations increases as the number of surgeons increases, at a rate of about 10 percent every five years, rather than as a result of patients' changing conditions. Many surgeons performing operations, however, apparently more than a third, have either never passed or never taken the examination for board certification of the American Board of Surgery.

Another source of public dissatisfaction and general concern about quality lies in the interpersonal dimensions of the transaction between the patient and the medical treatment system. Visits by doctors to patients' homes are now almost unknown. Instead, an increasing proportion of ambulatory care occurs in emergency rooms or outpatient clinics, where doctors "expect—or even hope—never to see the patient again, and behave accordingly."[30] Patients of minority races and lower social classes are treated more callously, given the rougher treatments (such as electric shock) more often, and attended by the lower-ranking personnel—

according to several studies in different settings.[31] Deliberate mystification may combine with busy schedules and technological impersonality to make the patient feel dehumanized, and utterly dependent in the hospital setting. Before this, the patient had been encouraged to believe in the curative capacities of modern medicine and to have complete faith in his or her doctor. The contrast may simply be too strong, and the result is frustration and resentment.

For some, this resentment may contribute to the initiation of malpractice suits against doctors or hospitals. Data on the incidence of malpractice claims suggest, however, that only a very small proportion of instances of probable negligence by doctors or hospitals ever result in malpractice claims. In one early-1970s study based on local hospital records, 7.5 percent of the patients discharged in a given period were found to have suffered some form of medical injury.[32] But only 29 percent of these were attributable to negligence, and only 6 percent actually filed claims. Overall, if these ratios held nationally, this would mean that 2.2 percent of all hospital admissions would result in legitimate negligence claims; but only 0.1 percent actually filed claims. The total of hospital admissions is 30 million per year, however, and the possible cases of negligence thus 660,000. If even a substantial proportion of such claims were filed, neither doctors, hospitals, nor insurance companies could stay in business. Instead, only one claim out of every fifty two that are plausible is actually filed.

But even this tiny proportion was enough to have created massive disruptions and threatened crisis within the medical care system in the late 1970s. The early 1970s saw a sharp increase in the amounts of jury awards in malpractice cases that went to trial. Verdicts in the millions began to occur where the past had known only occasional judgments in the tens of thousands. The number of suits began to rise sharply, as did the average dollar value of awards and settlements. Insurance companies offering malpractice insurance began to raise their rates, sometimes by as much as 200 percent or 300 percent per year. Some doctors in vulnerable specialties were asked to pay from $20,000 to $40,000 per year for malpractice insurance. In some cases, insurance companies simply found the malpractice field unprofitable and raised their rates in this manner so as to be able to abandon the field. In other cases, they sought to protect themselves against prospective losses from projected trends in claims and awards.

The result for doctors and hospitals, and then for their patients, was sharply higher bills, "defensive medicine" (many more diagnostic tests, more exclusively conventional treatment, etc.), and reluctance to provide emergency services. A sizable proportion of doctors simply let their insurance expire and took steps to make themselves "judgment-proof" by transferring their assets to spouses or relatives.[33] Some began to file countersuits for defamation or abuse of the legal system, or to form (with hospitals) private insurance companies. The best hope appeared to be efforts to have state legislatures require arbitration of claims, impose new conditions of proof for malpractice claims, or limit the amount of awards that could be made. Some progress in these directions was made in the late 1970s.

II ALTERNATIVE POLICIES

There is widespread recognition of these problems as components of the crisis in health care today. There is no dispute about the paramount importance of controlling costs, although there might be minor differences of opinion about the relative gravity or importance of the other three problems. Many differing proposals have been made to cope with them, singly or together. One contrasting set of solutions for the cost problem, for example, pits advocates of free market solutions squarely against those who stress the need for greater planning and coordination. In other words, some would *make* a market where none exists, while others deny that possibility and instead seek regulation to make a better *non*market system. A wide variety of proposals are also made for contrasting forms of national health insurance. We might easily describe each proposal under these major headings, but that could leave unexplored the real nature of the disagreements involved.

More important than the details of any particular proposal are the premises and assumptions that lie behind them. By and large, the policy debate today is between those who subscribe to the medical-treatment definition of the health problem and those who hold the health-care-system definition. The former are likely to be most concerned with rising costs and the problems that stem from the nonmarket character of the system. The latter are not unconcerned with costs, but their orientation is toward a different mix of policy (and funding) priorities that would emphasize preventive care, education, and individual self-help. Both underlying definitions call for significant reforms in health care policy, but not much change in the core of the structure—the private, fee- and cure-oriented medical treatment system. Hardened observers of the health care field, however, are likely to view even modest reform of the present system as beyond the range of possibility.[34]

We shall survey some leading proposals for reform, particularly the market versus planning/coordination debate and National Health Insurance, as they are formulated by adherents of each of the contrasting definitions. Following that, we shall take up more briefly the set of proposals that flow from the democratic social system definition of the health care problem. Such proposals call for more far-reaching reconstruction of health care in the United States. They have been heard with growing frequency, in part because of frustration with inability to achieve more modest reforms.

This simultaneous distinction between medical cure and health care and between reforming and reconstructing the basic medical structure has its origins as far back as the final report of the Committee on the Costs of Medical Care in 1932. The Committee, established with ample foundation support and research staff, was composed of forty two leading private physicians, lawyers, public health and hospital administrators, etc. Its research effort in the field is unequaled before or since. Its final report, however, was highly controversial. The majority report called for converting fee-for-service private practice to group practice on the prepayment (insurance) principle, thereby reawakening the cause of compulsory government-backed National Health Insurance (NHI), first urged in 1916. (Several bills for different types of NHI were filed in the next twenty years, but none ever passed either house of Congress.) It also called for comprehensive health planning and coordination within defined geographic areas, including broader preventive efforts. The minority denounced any changes in the fee-for-service system, but reluctantly backed an insurance plan run by doctors that would assure payment to providers. The AMA appraised the issues raised as follows:

> The alignment is clear—on the one side the forces representing the great foundations, public health officialdom, social theory—even socialism and communism—inciting to revolution; on the other side, the organized medical profession of this country urging an orderly evaluation guided by controlled experimentation which will observe the principles that have been found through the centuries to be necessary to the sound practice of medicine.[35]

Many of the ideas subsequently debated at the national level were first floated in this Committee's report, partly because its assessment of the problems of health levels, access, quality, and costs remains largely accurate today. Much less attention has been paid, however, to the important differences in underlying perspective on the nature of the health care problem that are evident in its two reports.

Reform Proposals

Proposals Based on the Medical Treatment Perspective   Sharp disagreements are possible even among those who share the *medical treatment definition* of the health care problem and effectively take as given the private, profit-seeking character of the various providers. The leading example is the debate between market enthusiasts and certain types of planners. All acknowledge that restrictions on entry into the field, consumer ignorance and anxiety, provider control over utilization of services, professional reluctance to criticize colleagues, third-party payments of most costs, and other factors create a uniquely nonmarket situation. Few if any economic incentives exist to limit demand, promote price-cutting, or make quality differentials known.

For the market enthusiast, the answer is clear: liberalize licensing requirements, permit advertising, make costs and quality records known in advance, and generally encourage competition between physicians and hospitals for patients. The AMA and local medical societies would be pushed back some, particularly from control over medical school entry standards, licensing, and physicians' hospital appointments. The supply of medical school graduates would be encouraged to increase, as would the supply of foreign medical graduates. Consumers would be given much more information about physicians and hospitals, and possibly some inducements (in the form of required copayments) to act to minimize their payments to providers.

Others who regret the lack of an operating market in the medical system are much less confident that one could be created. They cite the patient's utter dependence on physicians and tendency, particularly in life-threatening situations, to demand every possible effort at cure regardless of cost. They see no real prospect of reducing physicians' control over the amount of services consumed, or of preventing hospitals' use of expensive technology and procedures. In their eyes, the principle of the autonomy of the physician as the guarantee of quality helps to support the power of local medical societies and the AMA, and works against promotion of a competitive market.

Acceptance of the apparent inevitability of nonmarket features can lead to certain kinds of planning as a way of improving the quality and containing the costs of the system. Consistent with this definition's taking the existing medical treatment system for granted, however, such planning is essentially turned over to units of that system itself. Very little effort is made to modify the practices of providers from outside the system. Instead, professionals are encouraged to take responsibility for policing themselves, in hopes that their better standards and concerns will converge with public needs and hopes for improved quality and cost control. A good example is the Professional Standards Review Organization system (see above p. 167), in which committees of physicians (with a few laypersons) monitor the services provided by other physicians. The original goal was to scrutinize and limit fees and other costs, but AMA opposition reduced the priority given to such specific actions of individual physicians in favor of a more general concern for quality and effective use of health resources.[36] Nevertheless, PSROs have the potential to be a start on containing fees, if physicians are able to establish standards of what is appropriate medical treatment and are willing to apply them. The physicians' fear of being forced to practice standardized medicine under national guidelines, however, stands in the way of realization of that potential.

A second example of the sorts of disagreements that are possible within this definition of the problem is found in several proposals for forms of National Health Insurance. All of these, despite their differences, assume and make no effort to modify the entrepreneurial and technology-dominated medical cure system. The limited scope of such proposals may be due in part to the long struggle over NHI, in which the AMA and its allies succeeded in bottling up or defeating one proposal after another from 1939 through 1951. NHI's strongest supporters, the Truman administration and the AFL-CIO, finally abandoned the cause. A much more limited version for the aged only was achieved in 1965 (Medicare), again over AMA opposition. But the reasons for leaving the entrepreneurial system untouched are less important than the implications: all of these proposals provide for insurance-based contributions to enable new groups of people to pump new funds into the existing system.

Proposals in this category include those put forward by the American Medical Association, the American Hospital Association, and the Health Insurance Association of America (made up of commercial health insurance companies), and the various proposals offered by Senator Long (D., La.) and President Carter for "catastrophic insurance." Areas of disagreement include the scope of services to be covered, whether to separate certain populations (the employed, the poor, the elderly) in different plans with different financing schemes, the extent of cost-sharing to demand from participants, and the role of private insurance companies (including the part they would play in administration of the plans).

The major issues are in the last area. The United States is the only country in the world in which commercial insurance companies play a substantial role in the medical system. These are very large companies, closely linked to the biggest banks and other units of the financial system, and they are likely to try to retain or expand their roles if a substantial new source of profitable business becomes available through NHI. The AMA and HIAA propose multiple plans that are "voluntary," in that plans *may* be purchased by employers for their workers, by state or federal governments for the unemployed and poor, through Medicare for the elderly, or by individuals, all at their own choice. But they must be purchased *from* private insurance companies, which would also administer the plans under regulation by state insurance departments. The AHA calls for two voluntary plans, one paid by employers for workers and one by governments for everybody else (with Medicare abolished). But the AHA would place administrative responsibilities in the hands of newly created nonprofit bodies called Health Care Corporations. Under the regulation of new

State Health Commissions, the HCCs would gain broad control over the standards and practices of the medical system—thus avoiding both direct government control and a possible takeover of the whole system by the private insurance companies. The potential managers of this important new agency controlling all health care payments within a single area would be the same groups represented on the boards of voluntary hospitals.[37]

The question of the effect of NHI on total costs of health care is an open and controversial one. The amounts of money funneled through taxes or contributions to the insurance companies and then on to medical providers will be large, but if ambulatory care is expanded and hospitalization reduced, the *total* amount spent by all parties in the country might be the same or even lower. But without controls over physician charges, and hospital usage and charges, it could be much higher.

Catastrophic insurance is often viewed as an early and less expensive precursor of NHI. Plans introduced expand Medicare coverage for expensive or extended hospitalization; federalize Medicaid, extend it to the working poor, and similarly expand its coverage; and set standards for catastrophic coverage to be provided by private insurance companies for purchase by employers. In this way, a form of "major medical" insurance would be provided for practically all Americans and supported by tax revenues or employer/employee contributions.

Proposals Based on the Health Care System Perspective   The second major group of proposals in the reform category are those flowing from the *health care system definition* of the health care problem. Their principal concern is to shift the focus away from treatment and toward preventing illness or injury. But there is also a related major effort to contain costs through more comprehensive planning that implies some change in the organization and practices of the medical treatment core. In particular, guidance if not control is to be provided from outside that core system, at national, state, and local levels.

These principles are evident in the ongoing development of the HMOs and HSAs. HMOs have multiplied more slowly than originally expected, in part because of the federal standards still imposed on them despite some 1976 loosening (see above p. 167), but have begun to establish a record of lower costs to consumers than private insurance systems linked to fee-for-service practice.[38] How much of these reduced costs is traceable to preventive health efforts is unclear. More experience will be required before the HMO-generated focus on preventive health can be expected to show up in definite ways. The principal source of today's lower costs, however, is readily identifiable: much lower rates of hospitalization, and much less surgery.[39] This confirms the results of earlier analyses of experience of thousands of federal employees over an eight-year period.

Hospital admissions, according to these studies, ran at about half the rate under HMOs as they did under private insurance, while surgical operations averaged less than half the frequency. There were only half as many appendectomies, half as much "female surgery" (principally hysterectomies and mastectomies), and a third as many tonsillectomies.[40] It seems clear that HMOs are becoming economically viable, and with continuing acceptance may be able to turn increasingly toward preventive health activities. But they are still limited in scope, both because they require the voluntary participation of physicians and because they can reach only the individuals who are members—not the social or economic factors that may contribute to the health problems of such members.

HSAs (see above p. 168) represent a more comprehensive planning capability and potentially a much more far-reaching opportunity to change the medical treatment system. The local HSAs (currently 205 serving populations of from 500,000 to 3 million people) are made up of a majority of consumers and government officials and a minority of health care providers. They have legal power to approve or disapprove applications for federal grant funds, new construction of health facilities, and perhaps ultimately the reimbursement of providers under Medicare, Medicaid, and any future health insurance program. These are broad powers for a board dominated by nonproviders to wield over the medical system. While their powers are to be exercised in accordance with the area plan previously prepared and are subject to state-level approval, they offer the prospect of significant leverage. The federal guidelines under which they are to operate, moreover, include major commitments to preventive activities (nutritional and environmental studies as well as personal education).

Both HMOs and HSAs owe their origins principally to the urgent need to control costs, which continues to be a primary force in turning attention toward the health care system considered as a whole. The two principles are closely related, however, and expanding concern for preventive activities seems inevitable. Similarly, while consumer involvement in managing the medical system is partly intended to humanize that core system, it offers for the first time outside influence that is capable of turning its priorities toward broader responsibilities. With national guidelines and effective consumer control, the potential exists for the medical system to be viewed increasingly as a public utility properly subject to popular preferences.

Articulating with these trends is a much more ambitious view of what NHI might do and mean for health care. Proposals in this category are put forward by Senator Kennedy and the AFL-CIO, represented by the Committee for National Health Insurance (CNHI). Instead of voluntary coverage, for example, they call for one compulsory program for all persons paid for by general taxation and employer/employee contributions under Social Security. While nobody would be required to use the benefits of the program, everybody would be required to contribute so that the healthier upper-income groups would help to build the economic base for services to the less healthy lower-income people.

CNHI proposals assume the continuity of the fee-for-service system, but provide reimbursement inducements for physicians to shift to salary or "capitation" arrangements (annual fees per person registered on that physician's list of patients). The private insurance companies would be eliminated entirely, with the system financed and administered exclusively by the national government (as it is in all other capitalist countries). A Health Security Board within the Department of Human and Social Services would guide regional and local implementation through a newly created system, with a minimum of state involvement. Quality and cost control would be closely monitored, with national standards for licensing and annual budgeting for providers rather than ad hoc reimbursement. Consumer participation would be encouraged, as would the development of HMOs.

Most of the proposals within this definition also contemplate other kinds of reform, partly for cost-containment reasons and partly to help reorient the focus of the system toward preventive health care. They call for better use of paraprofessionals and increased functions for nurses, together with reduced roles for hospitals and physicians. Medical education will be reoriented, away from acute-illness and high-technology specialized treatments and toward broader public health problems. Finally, proposals seek much greater use of decentralized health centers with outreach capabilities for preventive education and early detection of illness.

Long-term observers of health care policy and politics react to these reform proposals with a kind of sympathetic skepticism. Health cannot be assured by access to the medical system, they argue, but neither will the powerful and strategically located units of that system allow significant change in their shares of national health care spending. Thus neither major direction of reform is likely to show much results. All major innovations are seen as flawed sources of unreasonable expectations and the costs of change as prohibitively high. Better to spend money indirectly on health, one analyst argues, such as through the food stamp program's impact on nutrition levels, than to try to alter the medical system.[41]

Reconstruction Proposals

Most of these proposals rest on the democratic social system definition of the health care problem, in which rights to a healthy life and to participation in all matters affecting one's life are seen as leading principles of a just and democratic society. Health levels of the population as a whole are important measures of the quality of life and achievements of the society, and might be improved significantly in advance of the ultimately necessary and desirable (for health and other reasons) redistribution of wealth and income within the society. Some proposals for basic reconstruction of the medical treatment system, however, emerge from people who have sought unsuccessfully to accomplish more modest reforms in the health care system's direction. Whatever the origins, the fundamental premise now is that healthy lives can only be assured through (1) replacing the profit-oriented medical cure system with a salaried national health service as concerned with preventive health as with sensitively caring for the many needs of the already ill, (2) developing and enforcing health-oriented standards of practice that reach to every source of danger to health, and (3) engaging people directly in the process of controlling all phases of health and medical treatment affecting them. We shall take up each of these imperatives in turn.

Table 9-4   President Reagan's Proposed Reductions in Health Care Funding, 1982 and 1984 (in millions of current dollars)

	1982			1984		
	Current base*	Cuts	Reagan budget	Current base*	Cuts	Reagan budget
Medicaid	18,213	1,013	17,200	22,259	2,930	19,599
Merchant seamen medical services (8 hospitals, 29 clinics)	171	110	61	194	194	—
Research: National Institutes of Health	3,731	145	3,586	4,251	468	3,783
Health training subsidies	359	126	233	400	260	140
Health Maintenance Organizations	43	18	25	55	50	5
National Health Service Corps	187	14	173	231	45	186
Health care regulation (PSRO and HSA)	171	62	109	179	159	20
Child nutrition	3,918	1,575	2,343	4,646	1,835	2,811

*"Current base" is the figure projected by the Reagan administration, using its estimates of growth, inflation, etc., in its initial proposal of February 18, 1981.
    Source: New York Times, February 20, 1981, pp. A11–A16.

National Health Service   The idea of a national health service (NHS) attacks the structure of the medical cure system directly, seeking to alter it as a first priority. Advocates include the Medical Committee for Human Rights, the Committee for a National Health Service, and the Community Health Alternatives Project of the Institute for Policy Studies.[42] All doctors would become salaried employees providing services free to all patients. Hospitals would be owned and operated directly by the NHS, or under contract to it, in which case they would be reimbursed on an annual basis for services rendered. Community-control mechanisms would assure that local needs would be served under general national guidelines. Medical education would be opened to minorities and women, the multiple dimensions of caring stressed, and preventive care emphasized. The NHS staff would include greater numbers of nurses, paraprofessionals, and other health workers, with hierarchical distinctions (and the worst of the salary differentials) between them and doctors eliminated. Private insurance companies would play no part at all, as tax revenues would support the entire government-backed system.

Health-Oriented Practice Standards   The scope of health-oriented standards to be enforced would imply substantial change in the priorities of our economic and social systems. Again, health would take precedence over profit. The Environmental Protection Agency would be given power to require reduction of pollutants in the air and water, cleanup of existing toxic waste dumps, and prohibition of further such disposal; and broad protections against carcinogens would be implemented by a team of appropriate agencies. Work safety would be promoted vigorously by the Occupational Safety and Health Administration, with worker participation through local plant committees. Nutritional standards would be required of food producers, and supplementary food programs for needy people instituted. Advertising and use of dangerous substances, such as alcohol and tobacco, would be inhibited, and government subsidies to the latter industry eliminated. These examples only begin to suggest the extent to which alteration of environmental conditions might be sought as a means of promoting health. But they suffice to make the point that changes in basic economic and social priorities and personal lifestyles are implied, and perhaps necessary, to significant improvement in health levels.

Direct Public Involvement in the Health and Medical Systems   Control by consumers of the character of the health system available to them, as well as informed participation in any particular treatment decision with respect to them, is a vital component of these proposals. So is extensive self-help and preventive activity, such as nutritious diets, exercise, avoidance of dangerous substances and overeating, etc. The latter assumes extensive educational programs, as well as value and lifestyle changes on the part of a population newly willing and able to undertake such changes. Proponents argue that the effort has never been made and pessimism about the extent of popular willingness is unwarranted. Under conditions of reduced stress, general concern for health in all areas of life, broad consumer control and taxpayer financing, greater public awareness, no powerful sales campaigns for dangerous products, etc., large numbers of Americans might well assume more responsibility for their own health.

Advocates of these sorts of changes in the health care system acknowledge that they are not on the immediate political agenda. But they insist that the felt need for better health at lower cost is a powerful motivator for everybody, and that there is vast potential in this area for action to bring about the changes necessary to achieve it. And they count on the reactionary self-interest of medical cure providers to add steadily to their supporting constituency.

In the early 1980s, however, national policy seemed to be headed in precisely the opposite direction. As shown in Table 9-4, one of the Reagan administration's first acts was to seek sharp reductions in national government support for a wide variety of current programs.

NOTES

1 Darryl D. Enos and Paul Sultan, *The Sociology of Health Care* (New York: Praeger, 1977), pp. 133–134.

2 Victor R. Fuchs, *Who Shall Live? Health, Economics, and Social Choice* (New York: Basic Books, 1974), p. 35. Data in the next two paragraphs are from this source unless otherwise noted.

3 Enos and Sultan, op. cit., pp. 144–149.

4 Victor W. Sidel and Ruth Sidel, *A Healthy State* (New York: Pantheon, 1977), p. 17.

5 Ibid., p. 25.

6 "Changes in the Environment Affecting the Health Care System," *Health Planning Information Series No. 1, Trends Affecting the U.S. Health Care System* (Washington, D.C.: U.S. Department of Health, Education and Welfare, 1976), Figure 5.4.

7 Fuchs, op. cit., pp. 52 ff.

8 Sidel and Sidel, op. cit., pp. 64–68.

9 "Changes in the Environment Affecting the Health Care System," Table 5.4.

10 Ibid.

11 *New York Times*, September 14, 1980, p. 22E.

12 Ibid.

13 Ruth Hanft, "Health Manpower," pp. 67–95 in Steven Jonas, ed., *Health Care Delivery in the United States* (New York: Springer, 1977), at p. 84.

14 Florence A. Wilson and Duncan Neuhausen, eds., *Health Services in the United States* (Cambridge, Mass.: Ballinger, 1976), p. 72.

15 American College of Surgeons and Surgical Association, *Surgery in the United States* (Chicago: American College of Surgeons, 1975), p. 77.

16 Hanft, op. cit., pp. 84–85.

17 *The Nation's Use of Health Resources* (Washington, D.C.: U.S. Department of Health, Education and Welfare, 1976), p. 9.

18 *New York Times*, September 14, 1980, p. 22E.

19 Enos and Sultan, op. cit., p. 78.

20 An exception is Fuchs, op. cit.

21 Roger M. Battistella and Thomas G. Rundall, "The Future of Primary Health Services," in Roger M. Battistella, ed., *Health Care Policy in a Changing Environment*, p. 296.

22 All data in this and the next paragraph are drawn from Council on Wage and Price Stability, *The Problem of Rising Health Care Costs* (Washington, D.C.: Executive Office of the President, 1976).

23 Carol McCarthy, "Financing for Health Care," pp. 247–288, in Jonas, op. cit., at p. 281.

24 Enos and Sultan, op. cit., pp. 45–49. Data in this and the next paragraph are drawn from this source.

25 McCarthy, op. cit., p. 253.

26 *New York Times*, September 18, 1980, p. 1.

27 Sidel and Sidel, op. cit., p. 6.

28 *New York Times*, January 26–30, 1976.

29 Sidel and Sidel, op. cit., pp. 71 ff.

30 Ibid., p. 91.

31 Ibid., p. 317.

32 Data in this and the next paragraph are drawn from Enos and Sultan, op. cit., pp. 341 ff.

33 Jordan Braverman, *Crisis in Health Care* (Washington, D.C.: Acropolis, 1978), p. 160.

34 A good example is Eli Ginzberg, "The Potentials and Limits of Health Reform," pp. 201–208 in Rick J. Carlson and Robert Cunningham, eds., *Future Directions in Health Care: A New Public Policy* (Cambridge, Mass.: Ballinger, 1978).

35 *Journal of the American Medical Association*, 1932, p. 1952.

36 Enos and Sultan, op. cit., p. 281.

37 Steven Jonas, "National Health Insurance," pp. 434–466 in Jonas, op. cit., at p. 450.

38 Braverman, op. cit., p. 106.

39 Ibid.

40 Enos and Sultan, op. cit., p. 296.

41 Ginzberg, op. cit., p. 204.

42 This case is well argued in Sidel and Sidel, op. cit., pp. 282 ff., on which the next paragraphs are based.

Chapter 10

Income Support: The Standard Practices

The American income support system is one of the most costly, most complex, most controversial, and least understood areas of public policy today. More than 80 million people receive more than $200 billion each year through some form of federal income support program.[1] Stated differently, well over one-quarter of all Americans derive some or all of their livelihoods from a transfer system that accounts for about a third of all federal budget expenditures. On top of this, the states annually spend tens of billions of additional dollars for assistance to people in need.

One basic part of the system ("social security") has been strongly supported by the general public on the grounds that people are now receiving the benefits for which they previously made regular contributions on the insurance principle. The other major part ("welfare") has been stigmatized and suspected of serving as support for numbers of people able but not willing to work. On the evidence, both sets of assumptions are for the most part false. Nor are these broad judgments the only kinds of confusion and controversy about the income support system. It seems safe to say that most people have little or no idea of the number of programs that exist, their beneficiaries, or their significance for the society.

An elaborate national-state-local apparatus dispenses money, imposes standards, and monitors eligibility. Policy makers and political candidates routinely criticize various parts of the system, often propose solutions, but rarely succeed in achieving reform. In short, income support is little understood and less coherently managed. Our first task, therefore, is a basic portrayal of the major components of the system and their scope. We need to justify our selection of, and set in context, the relatively few (but major) programs we shall explore in this chapter. Along the way, we need to clarify some of the key definitions used in analysis and program development in this area. Only then will we be able to take up the policy field of income support in our standard manner.

Table 10-1 identifies the leading federal income support programs in terms of the two basic types involved, and shows the amount of federal funds committed to each in fiscal 1981. Contributory programs, sometimes called "social insurance," are those to which recipients have made some amount of direct monetary contribution. This is normally the most important criterion of their eligibility to receive benefits. Contributions to social insurance programs are kept separate from other government revenues, as independent trust funds, to provide benefits when people become entitled to them. But the term "social insurance" does *not* mean that the amount of benefits is tied to contributions made under strict insurance principles, as we shall see later.

Social Security, or more specifically Old Age, Survivors, and Disability Insurance (OASDI), is by far the largest category of contributory programs. In recent years, with the addition of Medicare coverage for hospitalization, OASDI has become OASDHI; but our consideration of Medicare has been reserved for Chapters 8 and 9, and we shall focus in this chapter exclusively on OASDI. Unemployment insurance is the second leading social insurance program, and merits some limited examination here. We have excluded *federal civil service retirement* (members of Congress and other federal government employees have their retirement provided for outside of the OASDI that applies to almost everybody else) and *veterans' disability and retirement* because of their less general implications and less political character—not because the sums involved are insignificant.

Noncontributory programs, known as "public assistance" or "welfare," include many more types of transfers and services. In this category, the basic criterion of eligibility is *need*. But the criteria are often set, and always administered, by the fifty states—with resultant sometimes exotic diversity. Not the most costly program, but surely the most controversial, is Aid to Families with Dependent Children (AFDC). Expenditures in this category increased rapidly in the mid- and late 1960s, and were sometimes referred to as the "welfare explosion." By contrast, Supplementary

Table 10-1   Federal Income Support Programs, 1981 (Cash and In-Kind Transfers)

	Contributory ("social insurance")	Noncontributory ("Public assistance" or "welfare")
Major programs	Old Age, Survivors, and Disability Insurance (OASDI, "social security") ($140 billion)	Aid to families with dependent children (AFDC) ($8 billion)
	Unemployment insurance ($20 billion)	Old age assistance, Aid to the blind, aid to the permanently and totally disabled ("Supplementary Security Income," SSI) ($8 billion)
	Medicare* ($45 billion)	Food stamp program ($11 billion)
		Earned income credit ($1.5 billion)
		Medicaid* ($18 billion)
Minor programs	Federal civil service retirement ($14 billion)	Housing assistance ($6 billion)
	Veterans' disability and retirement ($13 billion)	School lunch program ($3.5 billion)
		Various educational, jobs, child care, family job training, etc. loans and services

Note: Dollar amounts are rounded to nearest hundred million for fiscal year 1981.
*Considered in Chapters 8 and 9.
Source: Derived from U.S. Budget in Brief, 1981.

Security Income (SSI), now provided as of right and constituting an effective guaranteed income for the needy aged, blind, and disabled, evokes little or no notice. The food stamp program, through which the eligible poor can purchase food at substantial discounts, was initiated in part to better dispose of agricultural surpluses and also has grown substantially. Particularly in times of recession, it has more recipients than any other public assistance program. Another recent innovation is the earned income credit, through which the tax system is used to grant aid to the working poor by refunding some share of what would otherwise be their tax obligations. Medicaid, a much larger federal-state shared program, is considered in Chapters 8 and 9. Many other programs and services too numerous to detail are of necessity excluded from consideration here in order to deal adequately with the major characterizing features of this side of the income support system.

The number of people receiving benefits from one or the other side of this system is not readily specified, for perhaps obvious reasons. There were in 1980 about 35 million persons receiving OASDI benefits. This total changes relatively slowly and predictably along demographic and acturial lines. But the number of unemployment insurance beneficiaries depends primarily on the state of the business cycle and whether or not benefits have been extended beyond normal limits because of the severity of conditions. Similarly, while the number of SSI recipients is fairly steady, food stamp and earned income credit beneficiaries fluctuate with the business cycle and AFDC varies upward from a basic core according to both the business cycle and recipient awareness of entitlement. In fiscal 1980, the total of people receiving some form of federal public assistance was about 45 million.

These figures suggest one vital way in which the health of the private economy affects the income support system: it fundamentally determines both the number of claimants and the level of their needs. But the stage of the business cycle also profoundly affects other aspects of income support. Recession limits government revenues and hence creates pressure for reduction of all forms of social services. Inflation forces all government expenditures up, squeezing all recipients, creating pressures for equivalent increases, and forcing choices between desired goals (e.g., defense versus income support). The combination of recession *and* inflation puts specially heavy pressure on income support policy, and even some previously legislated "entitlements" (legal rights to payments, and at certain levels) may not survive under sustained stagflation.

Some further distinctions are helpful to an understanding of income support policy. One often made is between "cash transfers" and "in-kind" payments. Cash transfers are payments made in cash to recipients, such as Social Security or unemployment compensation checks. The concept of "transfer" stems from the realization that the revenues used to make such payments are raised from other people, often people in higher income brackets, and are effectively redistributed to people of lower incomes. The earned income credit is another version of a cash transfer, for it leaves money in the hands of the working poor while others pay slightly higher taxes to maintain total revenues at desired levels. Payments "in-kind" are nonmonetary grants of commodities or services, such as the food obtained through the food stamp program or medical care or other social services rendered to people.

Another important distinction is often made in regard to criteria of eligibility for income support assistance. Some programs are limited to those who have contributed while working ("wage-related"), and have limits on how much income can be earned while receiving benefits ("wage-tested"). Another kind of eligibility is found in the "categorical" grants, where assistance is extended to all who fit within a certain category of intended beneficiaries, such as the blind or permanently disabled. Public assistance programs, on the other hand, are "means-tested," meaning that recipients must demonstrate that their income from all sources is below certain levels or actually zero. The first two sets of eligibility criteria are relatively easily demonstrated, and often involve only a single act of proving eligibility for benefits that have been earned and belong to the claimant as a matter of right. The second set, however, require continuous and often demeaning proof, and may be subject to constant suspicion and efforts at verification.

Both major components of national income support are today subject to criticism from both left and right. The contributory programs are seen on the left as too low in benefits and too closely tied to insurance principles—thereby limiting the number of people eligible and the level of benefits received. They are viewed on the right as providing excessive benefits and as having strayed so far from insurance principles that they are threatened with bankruptcy and/or dependency on general revenue contributions to bolster their trust funds. The noncontributory programs are criticized from the left as niggardly in the context of severe and worsening poverty, demeaning, and a combination of "blaming the victim," scapegoating, and social control. From the right, they are condemned as wasteful, destructive of families and the work ethic, and unnecessary in the context of a war against poverty that has already been won.[2] Only Social Security has a powerful supportive constituency; public assistance programs have relatively few politically potent friends except on rare occasions of popular mobilization.

In broad outline, these are the programs and problems that we shall analyze in detail below. In looking at income support in terms only of the major programs in its two component categories (OASDI and unemployment insurance among the contributory programs, and AFDC, SSI, food stamps, and earned income credit among the noncontributory), we are leaving out literally hundreds of federal programs costing tens of billions of dollars per year. But there seems no other way to show the basic features of the system in a single chapter, and we think its essentials can all be revealed in this manner.

I CURRENT POLICIES

We shall follow the contributory-noncontributory distinction throughout this analysis, partly because it is a traditional one within the income support world and partly because data are developed and reported in these categories. But it is possible to make too much of this rather formal difference. The Social Security program is much the largest of all, enjoys broad public support, and has been until recently under the nearly exclusive guidance of its own Washington bureaucracy. Thus, it has many more and perhaps more important distinguishing features besides the basis of its funding. Analogously, AFDC is a relatively small but highly controversial nation-state-local program serving a predominantly female, youthful, and disproportionately nonwhite population, with very little apparent general public support. Moreover, each is best understood in the context of its particular developmental history, and the arbitrary cutoff observed here between "current" policies (the 1970s and 1980s) and their "origins" (prehistory through the 1960s) may also be misleading.

Contributory Programs

Unemployment compensation is a national-state program in which most employers pay a tax based on their payrolls and the states individually fix standards of eligibility and payment levels. Employees of state and local governments are not covered, nor are most farm workers, domestics, and others who work for very small firms. Benefits, usually calculated as a proportion of previous earnings up to certain maximums, are paid for a period of twenty six weeks to those involuntarily unemployed who continue to seek work. When unemployment is low, the proportion of the unemployed receiving benefits from such insurance runs about 40 percent. When unemployment rises, so does the proportion of the unemployed receiving benefits: early in the 1974–1975 recession, 56 percent of the more than 6 million unemployed were receiving about $1 billion per month.[3]

When unemployment is sustained for a year or more, however, the proportion will drop again as the period of entitlement expires. Congress first extended the period an additional thirteen weeks in states with high and rising unemployment, and then contributed federal funds directly to extend aid still further. By March 1975, the maximum period had been extended to sixty-five weeks and an additional 12 million noncovered workers were brought into the system, all with federal funds rather than payroll taxes. A monthly average of nearly 6 million people were receiving $1.5 billion in benefits, far more than at any previous period in United States history.

Pressure from the number of unemployed thus converted the system from one based on insurance to outright cash transfer, or a form of public assistance. Because state funds built from payroll taxes were exhausted in many cases, federal support covered half of regular extended benefits and all of the benefits beyond that. But there was little or no opposition to this dramatic change; recipients were apparently considered "deserving" of such assistance. Nearly all were adults; three-quarters were male; and the vast majority were heads of households with dependents.

Part of the reason for the conversion and expansion of this program, of course, was to plug a major gap in the income maintenance system that was made visible by this major recession. The underlying premise of unemployment insurance had been that working males needed (and should have) only temporary coverage for "between jobs" periods; direct welfare assistance for able-bodied males remained tightly limited. Long-term unemployment without welfare support would have left millions of male-headed families without income, however, and their reduced purchasing power might lower consumer demand to the point where further layoffs would follow. Both workers and businesses therefore had reason to approve the extension of unemployment compensation. Welfare-in-fact was preferable to changing the welfare system in principle.

Social Security (OASDI) has had a similar recent history, in that its original insurance principle has shifted to a simple transfer system. Taxes paid by employers and younger workers are the basic source of benefits paid to retired or disabled workers or their survivors. But OASDI has not yet been funded directly from general federal revenues.

Social Security is financed by a compulsory payroll tax paid equally by employers and employees. The rate of taxation and the amount of income subject to the tax have both risen steeply in recent years. In 1980, the tax was 6.65 percent on all income through $29,700, and already enacted increases would raise the tax rate to 6.7 percent in 1982. The maximum tax payable by employees was $94.50 in 1957, $290.40 in 1967, $965.25 in 1978, and is scheduled to rise to $3,045.90 by 1987. The combined Social Security tax on employers and employees now represents about 4.5 percent of total Gross National Product (GNP). Social Security expenses account for most of the rise in government spending for domestic purposes in recent decades: between 1970 and 1975, Social Security expenditures more than doubled, from $32 billion to $67 billion, and in 1981 they were over $140 billion. These rates of increase far exceeded increases in number of beneficiaries and the rate of inflation.

Nine out of every ten persons over the age of 65 were receiving benefits under Social Security in 1980. Retirees or their dependents numbered 21 million persons, while 4.8 million received disability benefits and another 7.6 million received benefits as survivors of covered workers. A retired couple at the highest covered income level could have received $8,280 per year in 1980, but the average was about $4,800.

Social Security is redistributive rather than strictly insurance-based in several ways. No beneficiaries are limited to sums equivalent to the actuarial extension of their contributions. Instead, benefits are set separately by Congress and paid for out of current taxes on employers and employees.

Lower-income people receive much higher proportions of their previous earnings than higher-income people. Because the benefit/contribution ratio declines as income rises, recent increases in the maximum taxable income have had the effect of increasing this redistribution. These forms of redistribution have come about because of a continuing series of changes in the basic statute: coverage has been expanded to new groups of people (some of whom were nearing retirement), the number of years of required covered employment prior to entitlement was reduced, and the level of benefits has been repeatedly raised. But because it is mandatory and nearly universal, and administrative costs have remained very low, the Social Security System has economies of scale and benefit levels that enable it to continue to seem a sound investment. Certainly, its contributory principle takes a considerable burden off the public assistance side of the income support system.

The expansion of Social Security has been a continuing saga, but the years 1972 and 1977 mark important thresholds.[4] For example, 1972 was a year of concern about poverty, hunger, and welfare reform. Partly because the latter was such a difficult and controversial issue, expansion of Social Security was seen as a relatively practical and popular way of improving the lot of the otherwise needy. Without any serious consideration, Congress simply increased benefits by 20 percent and "indexed" them—connected benefit levels to rises in the cost of living so that automatic upward adjustments would regularly occur.

In the aftermath of these hasty, election-year increases, Social Security suddenly rose to public notice and concern. The new benefit levels, and the stubborn and unprecedented levels of inflation that now seemed permanent, made a deficit appear likely in the not-too-distant future. The specter of bankruptcy was raised (referring, of course, only to the independent trust funds and ignoring the readily available tactic of replenishing them from general revenues). In any calculus of future receipts and expenditures, Social Security planners must take into account the number of future wage-earners and beneficiaries, and their levels of earnings (partly dependent on estimates of productivity and growth) and benefits (partly dependent on estimates of congressional generosity). Tax rates and taxable-income amounts are then projected as needed in order to preserve the pay-as-you-go nature of the program. The Board of Trustees of the OASDI Trust Fund noted the reduced birth rate of recent years and its contrast with the World War II baby boom, as well as rapidly rising disability claims. The Board estimated only modest growth and productivity increases, with resulting slow expansion of earnings and continuing inflation. Its reports from 1973 on thus increasingly emphasized the prospect of sharply increased taxes and/or large deficits after the turn of the century.

Ironically, as a leading authority noted, by indexing benefits to the cost of living Congress had made the system depend directly on the performance of the economy just as the economy was entering its worst period since the Great Depression; and by the large expansion of benefits it had abandoned defenses against error just at the time it made a major error about future growth and revenues.[5] The result was a sharp rise in both tax rates and the amount of income subjected to the tax, enacted in 1977 to take effect cumulatively over the next several years. The share of the incomes of covered workers made subject to the tax was increased from 81 percent to 91 percent. The benefit formula for active workers was trimmed somewhat, so that it depended only on increases in their wages rather than on wage *and* price increases. The Carter administration proposed to remove all ceilings on the employers' share while keeping employees' fixed, and to introduce general revenues into the program whenever the unemployment rate rose beyond 6 percent. These measures would have held the rising, regressive, and increasingly unpopular employee payroll tax at current levels while expanding revenues, but Congress rejected them in favor of more familiar insurance-oriented funding. The Carter administration was left with the problem of finding ways to offset the inflationary and personal impact of the new tax levels.

Noncontributory Programs

Another part of the 1972 amendments to the basic Social Security statute was an effort to raise and standardize benefits in the three public assistance categories. *Old Age Assistance* (OAA), *Aid to the Blind* (AB), and *Aid to the Permanently and Totally Disabled* (APTD) had originally been conceived as means of providing for people who could not or did not work (or, not for periods long enough to qualify for benefits) in jobs covered by social insurance. While the states determined eligibility criteria and benefit levels, the federal government provided an increasing share of the funding in the 1960s. A total of about 3.2 million people were receiving $3.5 billion in benefits before the 1972 changes took effect. OAA and AB were declining in numbers of recipients, while APTD was rising sharply; all were increasing in total benefits, the first two modestly and the last sevenfold between 1960 and 1973.

The problems with these three programs involved low benefits and high variability between the states as well as lack of integration with other public assistance programs. OAA payments ranged from $54 to $118 per month in different states, and eligibility standards and formulas for counting other income and allowances varied even more chaotically among the fifty states. In some cases, OAA recipients lost benefits dollar for dollar when Social Security was increased, while only certain categories were eligible for food stamps or other in-kind programs.

In contrast with the high visibility and controversy of the Nixon Family Assistance Plan (discussed in Section II of Chapter 11), the changes in these programs received very little attention and less opposition. The three distinct programs were merged into one, known as *Supplemental Security Income* SSI). Higher monthly benefits were established and made uniform throughout the country, although the states previously paying higher benefits were required to maintain such levels for current recipients and allowed to supplement the federally funded minimums for new recipients, if they wished. Uniform eligibility criteria and income exemption formulae more generous than those of many states were also established, and the federal government either absorbed or funded much of the administrative cost.

SSI went into effect in 1974. In effect, it provided a guaranteed annual income (though a very low one, initially $1,740 per year for an individual and $2,520 for a couple) for people in the three eligible categories. In the first year, recipients increased by 26 percent and benefits paid by 63 percent. By 1980, total expenditures were double what they had been before the changes. One lesson seemed to be that federalization and uniformity of standards and practices could only be purchased through increasing benefits. Another was that welfare reform was complicated, difficult, and costly, particularly because efforts at reform sought to avoid *reducing* benefits to any group of recipients.

Food stamps became a federal program in 1970 as a result of growing concern about the problem of hunger and malnutrition among millions of low-income families. Prior to that time, federal funds had helped the states run a very modest version of the program. Many states had tight eligibility standards and low benefits, and some refused to participate in the program at all, so that only a little more than 3 million people received such aid. Federalization in this instance meant establishing national standards of eligibility based on the cost of a nutritionally adequate diet. Families with little or no income, including welfare recipients, could receive their entire monthly allocation (initially $116 per month) free. As income rose (after taxes and certain other deductions), the federal subsidy decreased; but it is estimated by supporters of the program that between a sixth and a fifth of the entire United States population could conceivably qualify for at least some aid under these standards.[6]

The immediate consequence of federalizing and expanding the food stamp program was to nearly quadruple the participants and set costs at about $2 billion by 1973. As the recession of 1974–1975 worsened, participants rose to about 20 million and the costs to nearly $6 billion. As a flexible supplement to the income support system, however, the food stamp program drew relatively little criticism until 1980. By that time, its costs had reached $9 billion per year.

The *earned income credit* was added to federal income tax provisions in 1975, in an effort to increase the financial incentive for low-income family heads to go to work. A number of analysts had stressed the "poverty wall" of combined taxes and loss of benefits that took away nearly all income earned by low-income families as they sought to rise past the official poverty thresholds.[7] The earned income credit applies to earnings up to $8,000 per year, granting credits at the rate of 10 percent of income earned up to $4,000 and at declining rates thereafter.

At these levels, most families are not obligated for federal income taxes, and they thus receive checks for amounts equal to 10 percent of their earned income from the federal government up to $4,000 per year. In effect, the government is paying poor families a bonus of 10% of their earned income up to $4,000, in a new form of public assistance program currently involving more than 6 million taxpaying units and about $1.5 billion per year. Beyond $4,000, the earned income credit is applied at declining rates, and it is eliminated at the $8,000 level. Because federal taxes become applicable for a family of four at $6,000, the rise in taxes is still very steep for welfare and low-income nonwelfare families alike.

These three forms of public assistance—SSI, food stamps, and earned income credit—together total about twice the number of recipients and more than twice the amount of money spent on *Aid to Families with Dependent Children* (AFDC). But the latter program is the one that draws attention, creates controversy, and is generally synonymous with "welfare" in the public mind. AFDC provides assistance to needy families with children under 18. Federal funds are distributed by the states in accordance with their varying eligibility standards and benefit levels. About 11 million persons in slightly more than 3 million families were receiving just under $7 billion in such aid at the end of the 1970s. Although the federal government authorizes aid to families headed by unemployed fathers, in fact nearly all recipients are in families headed by women. This is because an increasing proportion of poor families are headed by women, and because many states refuse to make employable males eligible for assistance.

AFDC has generated controversy in part because the number of recipients more than tripled during the 1960s and continued to rise (though more slowly) despite restrictive measures throughout the 1970s. But its controversial character may really be owed to the way in which it touches some of the most sensitive areas of American life: race, sex, family, and work. When the program chiefly supported widows with children to raise, it did not draw attention. When its constituency changed to include divorced, deserted, and unmarried mothers, many of them nonwhite, AFDC became the most visible component of the entire income support system. Suspicions were often voiced about the program's role in causing or encouraging divorce, illegitimate births, the breakup of families (without a man in the house, eligibility for assistance is much greater), and/or avoidance of work. Elaborate and demeaning personal investigations and extensive work training and inducement programs became enduring appendages of the program. But neither succeeded in accomplishing any significant reduction in the number of recipients. Nevertheless, calls for reform continue to target AFDC as the primary example of the "welfare mess."

Combining Contributory and Noncontributory Programs: The Income Support Network

Many needy persons receive some form of income support from two or more different programs. For example, four-fifths of SSI recipients also have benefits from OASDI, as do three-fourths of all veterans receiving pensions. Most such persons also receive health care from the Medicare, Medicaid, or veterans' programs.[8] Similarly, food stamps supplement both assistance and insurance programs, as do housing, school lunches, and government retirement. Table 10-2 is drawn from one of the few studies that have tried to map the overlap and multiple utilization of federal income support programs. Of the low-income-area households sampled in this survey, two-thirds took part in two or more programs, and nearly 20 percent drew benefits from five or more. The total of their benefits, including those from the in-kind programs, is difficult to calculate; but it is often enough to raise families in some areas of the country up close to (in some cases, even beyond) the official poverty thresholds. Although surely much improved, the lives of these families are not rendered affluent by multiple income support programs.

One consequence of this extensive overlap of programs is that, given all their highly divergent standards, benefits, and formulae for deductions or exemptions, it is very difficult to understand the variety of ways in which they actually combine to produce particular results for differently situated people. Purposeful modification of the system's effects thus becomes very difficult, even without considering questions of political feasibility. People in similar situations receive very different benefits in different parts of the country, in part because the states' differing eligibility standards control how many programs they can qualify for, and partly because of starkly contrasting state-set benefit levels within the same program. In short, it is a very complicated system with some clear basic values but many inconsistencies, idiosyncrasies, and contradictions. Criticism is frequent and fervid, but reform is technically and politically frustrating.

II THE ORIGINS OF CURRENT POLICIES

Except in minor ways, the national government played no part in income support in the United States before the Great Depression of the 1930s. Public assistance, such as it was, had its origins and much of its character

Table 10-2 Overlap of Social Welfare Programs in Low-Income Areas, 1972 (percent)

Program	Households also receiving benefits from—								
	Public assistance programs	Social Security cash programs	Veterans' cash programs	Other cash programs	Food programs	Health care programs	Housing programs	Education and Workforce programs	Other aid in kind
Cash benefits:									
Public assistance	100	28	4	4	64	82	26	18	14
Social Security	25	100	10	7	23	53	14	4	6
Veterans' programs	22	22	100	11	19	44	15	3	42
Other programs	12	12	6	100	24	27	6	12	2
In-kind aid:									
Food programs	62	25	3	8	100	67	24	21	16
Health care	54	39	5	5	46	100	21	14	11
Housing	55	33	6	48	52	65	100	23	13
Education and workforce	100	13	1	11	63	58	30	100	14
Other	68	21	5	3	55	59	21	18	100

Source: James R. Storey, Alair A. Townsend, and Irene Cox, How Public Welfare Benefits Are Distributed in Low-Income Areas, Joint Economic Committee, 93d Cong., 1st Sess. (Washington: Government Printing Office, March 1973), pp. 70–75.

from the Elizabethan Poor Laws; i.e., local communities were obligated to care for those absolutely incapable of providing for themselves. Social insurance advocates, necessarily focusing on the state governments, had achieved success only in regard to workmen's compensation. They had been soundly defeated in efforts to institute health and unemployment insurance despite (or perhaps in part because of) decades of experience with it in Europe, and had made only ambiguous progress toward "mothers' pensions" and retirement provisions for the aged.

The passage of the Social Security Act in 1935, with its combination of social insurance and direct assistance to certain categories of needy people, thus marks a dramatic change in American public policy. But it can only be understood against the background of earlier inaction and the reasons for it. Income support policy was profoundly affected by the Social Darwinist ideology of the nineteenth century, particularly its emphases on individual responsibility and the work ethic. Other factors included religious principles of charity and salvation, the power of the private insurance companies, the federal structure of the country and the dominant constitutional interpretations of the times, and the power (both pro and con) of the models set by the European countries, particularly Germany. We shall summarize these and other contextual factors before returning to the Social Security Act and its later expansion into the comprehensive income support system now in place.

It would be hard to overestimate the importance of the dominant belief in individualism, personal responsibility, and hard work for the development of American society and public policy. A person's moral character and worth, not to mention social status and advancement, depended on sustained hard work and self-denial. Such discipline was also the basis of social progress. Those who were dependent or in need were morally unfit, and should be forced to learn the virtues of work and thrift. Public assistance, except in cases of obvious invalidism or utter destitution, was destructive of a person's character and dangerous as an example to others. Social Darwinism went one step further, applying the Darwinian notion of survival of the fittest to justify little or no aid to the weakest and least fit of the human species.

Within these principles, there was an appropriate role for charity. Just as Protestant beliefs helped to make responsibility for adversity a personal matter, perhaps even a test of character, so did Protestantism welcome the opportunity for fortunate others to contribute to their own prospects for salvation through appropriate acts of charity. This led to a network of private associations and institutions that provided assistance and rehabilitation to various types of people in need. Under the general head of "voluntarism," wealthy patrons helped themselves toward salavation and immortality, and the "dependent, defective, and delinquent" were granted aid and taught how to better care for themselves. The profession of social work arose in the latter part of the nineteenth century to administer both aid and instruction.

Public assistance ran counter to these neatly integrated beliefs and practices. If the state were to provide help, it would damage, if not destroy, the vital self-help impulse of beneficiaries and impinge upon the opportunities of benefactors to do good works. The principles of the Poor Laws of 1601, adopted by the early colonies, seemed appropriate: where a person was destitute or incapable of self-care, and no relatives could provide, the local township or county in which the person was truly resident had the residual obligation of support—in exchange for whatever work the person was able to do. Some larger towns erected almshouses or poor farms to house the indigent, while others granted minimal allowances or relief in kind to people in their homes. In both cases, standards of living provided were very marginal and aid was administered grudgingly as a gift to the undeserving.

Social insurance was not much more favorably perceived, for it seemed at best a form of paternalism likely to undermine personal character and thus the foundations of free society itself. State insurance and pension programs would divert wealth from the thrifty and industrious to the idle and incompetent; if people looked to the state for support, they would no longer fear dependency and lose the "chief discipline . . . of wholesome living."[9] Moreover, social insurance was seen by some as a German device integrated with imperialism and militarism, whose compulsory character was inconsistent with American traditions of voluntarism. A variety of benefit funds was established from the 1890s on, some by companies and some by private associations, frequently in conjunction with private insurance companies. These were urged as the American alternative to compulsory and state-supported insurance.

This was the context in which the social insurance movement sought to generate support for establishing an income-maintenance system that would transfer responsibility from voluntary to public hands and from local to more centralized authorities. Studies of the workings of the European systems began to be published in the 1890s, but the movement really dates from the founding of the American Association for Labor Legislation (AALL) in 1906. The AALL was composed chiefly of university economists and political scientists whose interests focused on reducing the causes of labor-management friction through application of the newly developing social sciences. Labor leaders in general, and Samuel Gompers of the AFL in particular, were not supportive; they distrusted "scientific labor legislation" and preferred direct union controls over workers' benefits. Some of the more "progressive" leaders of the business world, however, such as the National Civic Federation, lent enthusiastic backing to the initial proposals.

The focus of the movement had to be on state governments, because constitutional interpretations of the times held that the act of earning a living was strictly local and therefore not subject to congressional power. But any state considering an insurance plan would have to be concerned lest, by taxing its employers more than did other states, it placed such employers at a competitive disadvantage and effectively drove them out of state. Thus any campaign for a social insurance program had to be national in scope and targeted on all major industrial states simultaneously.

The first campaign mounted, and the most successful, was that for workmen's compensation. This is an insurance system in which employers are required to pay a proportion of their total payroll into a fund for the benefit of employees who may become injured on the job at some time in the future. Dangerous working conditions had been characteristic of many occupations for some time; literally thousands of workers were killed, permanently disabled, or injured on the job each year, and several "muckraking" studies documented these facts in detail. The only remedy for death or injury because of an employer's unsafe or speeded-up working conditions was a lawsuit, but a number of legal defenses against liability and inevitable difficulties and delay in proving a case through trial made this route impractical for workers. Nevertheless, occasional heavy judgments and the burden of defending lawsuits made employers open to the idea of an alternative.

The AALL and its allies emphasized the preventive effects of workmen's compensation insurance as a means of mobilizing support. Just as the costs of fire insurance, when based on actual experience of fires and fire-safety precautions, induced greater efforts to prevent fires, so might the costs of compensation insurance promote attention to job-safety provisions. The campaign was so successful that results began to appear in 1910. By 1913, twenty-one states had enacted compensation legislation. By 1917, the number rose to thirty-nine, and to forty-three by 1920.

But this rapid spread of insurance-based legislation was far from the opening wedge for which the movement had hoped. Instead, its success depended on factors quite unique to the compensation field. Most statutes provided for employer payments based on actual accident or injury experience, and thus did emphasize preventive efforts. But the insurance carriers were private, profit-oriented insurance companies rather than state funds. Their obligations were limited to the employer's legal liability, as determined by their claims adjusters, and compensation levels were set at decidedly low dollar amounts. And most statutes substituted such insurance benefits for employees' rights to sue in court for damages for injuries

suffered, thus relieving employers of all liability. Injured workers continued to bear most of the costs, and one leading social insurance expert
asked, "what wonder that a few years of experience created a greater
enthusiasm for the compensation systems among the employers than
among employees?"[10] Low benefits and limited liabilities continue to
characterize this system today.

The second major campaign of the social insurance movement was for
compulsory health insurance. The issue was widely debated between 1915
and 1920, and model statutes were drafted and introduced in several states.
The AALL sought to promote a compulsory program that would provide
universal coverage, make medical care and preventive measures available
to all classes, and rest on contributions from employers, employees, and
the states. But physicans generally opposed the idea of any interference
with the direct fee-for-service basis of medical treatment, and the private
insurance companies objected to being left out of the program. During
World War I the similarity of the AALL proposal to the German system in
effect since 1884 provided another basis for rallying the opposition.
Together with many employers, some labor leaders, and organized Chris-
tian Scientists, the physican–insurance company coalition was able to
decisively defeat health insurance legislation in the key states of California
and New York in 1918 and 1919. With that failure, health insurance faded
as a serious possibility.

Not actually insurance programs, but nevertheless supported vigorously as related matters by the social insurance movement, were "mothers'
pensions" and old age pensions or other assistance. In the case of mothers'
pensions, however, advocates had to overcome the resistance of the
voluntary charity network and the organized social work profession, both
of which insisted that individualized attention (and grants conditioned
upon desired behavior) were preferable. Advocates argued for a system
which would allow widowed mothers (in some cases, other "deserving"
mothers, such as those deserted or left without a breadwinner through no
fault of their own) to bring up their young children at home. By 1919,
thirty nine states had enacted some form of such legislation, but assistance
was minimal and locally administered in essentially the same manner as
other poor relief. Even so, spirited opposition continued from voluntary
organizations, particularly those combined into various local Charity
Organizations Societies (COS), on the grounds that mothers' pensions
were the "entering wedge to state socialism" and a host of other forms of
public assistance to the needy.

In a way, the COS opposition was correct. The mothers' pension
experience helped to establish the principle that public assistance could be
in some cases both justified and efficiently administered. It helped to shift
the emphasis in assistance to the needy away from the instruction-

rehabilitation emphasis of social workers toward the provision of basic financial aid with which beneficiaries could help themselves. But public agencies also soon assumed responsibility for educating the poor in the virtues of hard work and self-denial, and abandoned the idea of economic assistance as an individual right and/or independently justifiable. Limited state benefits and grudging local administration contributed to making mothers' pensions a quite ambiguous success for the social insurance movement.

With the precedent of mothers' pensions and the slowly expanding provisions for aid to the blind, support began to develop for some form of pensions for the aged. Two much larger old age assistance programs were already in effect at the federal level: veterans' pensions and federal employees' pensions. The defenses were familiar. One was that lifelong work discipline, thrift, and self-denial would be lost if workers did not have to provide for their own old age. The other was that whatever need for collective measures there was could be met by privately provided (employer- or individual-paid) insurance or the voluntary charity network.

Old age pensions became the leading issue of the 1920s, and states began to enact such legislation in 1923. Vetoes by governors and voiding by state courts slowed progress, and by 1929 only six states had such laws in effect; these were optional rather than compulsory, and as likely to be ignored or rejected by local authorities as were mothers' pensions. But eighteen states enacted compulsory laws between 1929 and 1933, and bills were introduced in Congress to provide federal grants-in-aid to assist state programs. In short, the way was prepared for later, more comprehensive federal action.

Unemployment insurance was the last in the series of social insurance programs to be urged by the AALL and its allies. Central to the campaign that began in 1914 and continued (without legislative results) throughout the 1920s was the claim that employers' payment obligations could result in prevention of unemployment. Relatively few supporters gave priority to the economic security principle in open fashion. Again, advocates undertook studies that showed conclusively the inadequacy of voluntary programs sponsored by companies and unions. But only Wisconsin passed a statute requiring employers to institute such insurance, and then a very limited one, in 1932. Not until the federal Social Security Act became law in 1935 did unemployment insurance become a reality in other states.

The Social Security Act

The Depression that began in 1929 was the first additional factor that, combining with nearly three decades of effort by the social insurance movement, ultimately resulted in this single most decisive act of the entire income support field.[11] Although President Franklin Roosevelt had cam-

paigned on pledges of balancing the budget and retrenchment, his administration immediately sought ways to provide assistance to the millions of
unemployed and destitute persons who were overwhelming local resources
in 1933. Congress created and funded the Federal Emergency Relief
Administration, which promptly opted for distribution of funds through
public agencies only. With this one stroke, the status of the voluntary
system was decisively undercut; soon reluctant or nonexistent local administrators were circumvented by new state delivery systems responsive to
federal guidelines. A variety of job programs followed, with the effect of
making the federal government even more directly responsible for income
support.

As the Depression continued, some other factors began to build
momentum toward dramatic new federal action. One was the Townsend
movement of 1934, which called for giving everyone over 60 a pension of
$200 a month. Very popular in California, this movement helped to
generate heavy pressure on Congress from the aged and their supporters
all across the country. Another source of pressure was the Share Our
Wealth movement started by Senator Huey Long of Louisiana. Although
he was assassinated in 1935, he succeeded in stirring up poor people's
aspirations in ways perceived by many as very dangerous. Finally, the
Roosevelt administration sought not only to blunt these movements but to
put public assistance efforts on a more regularized, long-term basis. A
coherent public works program (the Works Progress Administration, or
WPA) was one part of this design. The other was the substitution of social
insurance for the ad hoc package of relief programs then in existence.

One irony of the momentous Social Security Act of 1935 is that there
was no well-organized movement targeted on this goal—despite all the
efforts of the previous three decades. Roosevelt appointed a cabinet-level
committee to produce a plan for permanent economic security, and made
clear that the insurance principle should predominate. Just as the AALL
had been composed of labor economists, so was the drafting of the Social
Security Act dominated by a concern for reducing labor-management
conflict through providing for unemployment and retirement in strictly
insurance ways. In any event, Roosevelt's committee promptly produced a
draft bill which served simultaneously as the framework for legislation and
an agenda for future development.

As enacted, the statute provided for both immediate public assistance
(to defined categories: the aged, the blind, dependent children) and two
types of social insurance (unemployment and old age). It also included
federal aid for state public health activities, such as maternal and child
health and various children's services. The public assistance grants provided 50 percent of state-set benefits and effectively required the development
of state and local departments of public welfare, to replace the haphazard

and sharply varying local discretionary arrangements of the past. Unemployment insurance was also created in the form of separate state programs. A national tax was placed on all payrolls, with the revenues returned to the states if they enacted appropriate legislation. This method was used in part to meet constitutional limits on national power but also in part to allow states to vary levels of benefits as they saw fit. In many cases, tax rates were linked to the employer's record of avoiding unemployment —in a kind of carryover of the view that such insurance was really a preventive rather than a basic economic security measure.

But the old age insurance component, the heart of the act, was a national program administered entirely by a new federal agency. Constitutional objections were met by imposing a tax equally on employers and employees and drawing the money into the national treasury, from which it was then transferred to the Social Security Trust Fund. Taxes at the rate of 1 percent on all income up to $3,000 became effective in 1937, benefits in 1942. Relatively few workers were covered, chiefly those in the largest commercial and industrial companies. They were to receive benefits if they had worked enough "quarters" (of years) in covered employment, and at levels based on their total taxed wages. In other words, as enacted the law strongly stressed the insurance principle, offering low benefits to a limited number of people (but making those benefits a matter of *right*), and avoiding the areas of health and disability insurance entirely. It was presented to the Congress and prospective opponents in the most conservative terms possible. In the words of its principal drafter:

> Only to a very minor degree does it modify the distribution of wealth and it does not alter at all the fundamentals of our capitalistic and individualistic economy. Nor does it relieve the individual of primary responsibility for his own support and that of his dependents. . . . Social Security does not dampen initiative or render thrift outmoded.[12]

By 1939, however, the act had gained both general public approval and the Supreme Court's certification of constitutionality. Congress then began what has become a steady process of shifting the emphasis of Social Security away from insurance and toward the principle of need. The start of benefits was advanced to 1940, benefits were based on average monthly wages rather than the total actually taxed, dependents of beneficiaries were made eligible for supplementary benefits, and Survivor's Insurance (SI) was added to provide benefits to survivors of deceased beneficiaries. The relationship between taxes paid and benefits received thus became much weaker. In 1950 amendments made it even more tenuous: benefits were raised in proportion to the increase in the cost of living, and 10 million additional workers were added and given the opportunity to qualify for benefits after only one and one-half years of covered employment.

The high initial ratio of taxpayers to beneficiaries meant that the tax rate could be kept low. It did not rise above 1 percent until 1950. Presumably this also contributed to public acceptance of the program. From 1.5 percent in 1950, the rate was increased to 2.5 percent in 1959. The taxable base was raised to $3,600 in 1951 and $4,800 in 1959. Full reserves for all future beneficiaries were no longer required after 1959, and the program began to use both reserves and current contributions to pay the growing number of beneficiaries. As the ratio of beneficiaries to taxpayers rose, the system has become more and more of a pay-as-you-go operation, thus eroding the insurance principle still further.

As it took shape, however, Social Security had the appearance of insurance and of a design that permitted workers to receive benefits as a right they had earned. But it also provided benefits in many ways in accordance with needs that existed, and even redistributed income somewhat from wealthier to poorer people. The bureaucracies that administered various parts of the program did so in alliance with their clientele and in recognition of their rights, rather than in the challenging, denigrating, adversary relationship that often characterized public assistance.

In 1956, Disability Insurance (DI) was added to provide benefits to covered workers who became unable to work before retirement age. This first version included limits on the definition of disability, on recipients' ages, benefit levels, waiting periods, and coverage requirements, all of which were progressively liberalized or abandoned in the 1960s. Medicare was added in 1965, after a protracted campaign. In 1965, and again in 1967, benefits and earnings exemptions were increased and requirements for benefits were lowered. As inflation took hold, benefits were increased by 15 percent in 1969, 10 percent in 1971, 20 percent in 1972, and 11 percent in 1973; effective in 1975, benefits were linked directly to rises in the cost of living.

The public assistance categories of Social Security were also expanded in these decades. A new categorical program, Aid to the Permanently and Totally Disabled (APTD), was created in 1950 to pay half the costs of state assistance to people who were severely handicapped or otherwise unable to work. Federal guidelines steadily improved the quality of state administration, removing it from its early spoils-system connection with local politics. Old age assistance, often promoted vigorously by organizations of elderly people, enjoyed financial support and general public acceptance.

But ADC, originally conceived as a federal version of mothers' pensions (i.e., widows and the "deserving" deserted), grew both in caseload and controversiality. Divorce, illegitimacy, and family breakups were increasing in the society and showing up in growing numbers of ADC recipients and rising costs. Efforts were made from time to time to add requirements to track down missing fathers and otherwise tighten up eligibility and work requirements. Nevertheless, recipients and costs tripled in the 1960s, in part because of organized efforts to get eligible people to claim their benefits. One analysis holds that both federal and certain state governments deliberately increased benefits and loosened eligibility requirements in the mid- and late 1960s in order to cool down racial protest in the cities.[13] Whatever the various causes, AFDC (as it became after 1961, when families with unemployed fathers were made eligible) began to serve as a lightning rod for the entire public assistance system.

Finally, we should note again that social insurance and public assistance are only two of several ways in which a government provides income support. Full employment greatly reduces the need for public assistance or unemployment benefits, and lightens the burden of taxes and contributions for programs that serve the aged and needy. Consistent with the expansion of a federal role in income support, therefore, is the expansion of federal responsibility for managing the economy, maintaining price stability and maximum employment, and providing jobs as the employer of last resort when necessary. Tax policy, minimum wage laws, equal employment opportunity regulations, etc., all play a part in the overall process of income maintenance.

NOTES

1 Basic data about the number of income support recipients, and the amount and sources of their income, are available from the *Social Security Bulletin Annual Statistical Supplement*, the *Budget of the United States*, and the *Statistical Abstract of the United States* (all Washington, D.C.: Government Printing Office, annually).

2 This particular argument is made by Martin Anderson in *Welfare: The Political Economy of Welfare Reform in the United States* (Palo Alto, Calif.: Hoover Institution, 1978).

3 All data in this paragraph are drawn from Sar A. Levitan and Robert Taggart, *The Promise of Greatness* (Cambridge, Mass.: Harvard, 1976), pp. 65ff.

4 This account draws from the best work on how Social Security policy is made, Martha Derthicks's *Policymaking for Social Security*, (Washington, D.C.: Brookings, 1979).

5 Ibid., pp. 384–385.

6 Levitan and Taggart, op. cit., p. 67.

7 The most articulate of these is Anderson op. cit., chap. 2, on which these paragraphs are based.

8 Levitan and Taggart, op. cit., p. 70.

9 Cited in Roy Lubove, *The Struggle for Social Security, 1900–1935* (Cambridge, Mass.: Harvard, 1968), p. 5. This excellent source informs the next several paragraphs.

10 Ibid., p. 57.

11 This account rests also on Derthick, op. cit.

12 Edwin Witte, "Social Security: A Wild Dream or a Practical Plan?" in Robert J. Lampman, ed., *Social Security Perspectives: Essays by Edwin Witte* (Madison: University of Wisconsin Press, 1962), p. 11.

13 Frances Piven and Richard Cloward, *Regulating the Poor* (New York: Vintage Books, 1971).

Chapter 11

The Grim Alternatives: Social Insurance and Public Assistance in the 1980s

The American income support system is in deep trouble. Inflation and unemployment, sustained over a period of years, have pushed both social insurance programs and public assistance to the financial breaking point. Social Security taxes have been raised sharply, but bankruptcy still seems indicated unless general revenues are committed. Unemployment insurance is in much the same condition, putting further strain on general revenues just when demands are highest. Moderate remedies have been proposed for the problems in public assistance, but proved to be politically unfeasible. Only drastic remedies remain. But *something* must be done in regard to both systems, and soon. In the context of continued stagflation, the strongest pressures would seem to be in the direction of cutting back an already comparatively modest income support program.

In this chapter, we shall examine the nature of other countries' programs in a way that points up the significance of cultural values in shaping income support policy. Then we shall explore our current problems and why moderate remedies have failed before taking up the possible alternatives that remain.

I COMPARATIVE INCOME SUPPORT POLICIES

Perhaps the most striking fact about the income support policies of the European countries is the similarities that they bear to each other and to those of the United States.[1] These similarities include program components, order of introduction, subsequent expansion characteristics, and current substance. In almost every case, the drift has been from more or less insurance-based benefits toward more general public assistance–oriented distribution.

But the United States has in every case lagged from two to five decades behind some European countries in instituting its component programs. In terms of the proportion of GNP committed to social insurance spending, the United States trails all the industrialized European countries; it regularly spends less than half the proportion that is spent by West Germany, Belgium, France, the Netherlands, Sweden, and Italy, and less than two-thirds that of Britain, Denmark, and Norway. And the United States still has no general national health insurance or family allowance or earnings-replacement system.

This raises some absorbing questions that cut to the core of our social system and its underlying values. Why such delays in establishing income support programs, particularly when the United States is generally conceded to have had a longer tradition of democratic participation in politics? What is so distinctive about the United States that this pattern should apply in every area? Though starting late, is the United States still likely to (and/or should it) follow the European experience in major ways? We shall briefly survey the similarities and contrasts between European and American practice before returning to these questions.

Some general patterns should be noted at the outset.

Germany is clearly the leader in initiating social insurance programs. Chancellor Bismarck instituted early forms of sickness insurance for certain industrial employees (1883), workmen's compensation (1884), and old age and invalid insurance (1889) as frank ways of drawing working-class support to the state and away from socialism. France was usually second, although Great Britain was competitive in this regard. For Americans, however, the British model was always most persuasive, to the extent that any foreign experience served as an affirmative support. French practice was usually ignored, and the German served publicly (though not privately, for it was much studied by technicians) as an antimodel, one whose alleged regimentation and centralization made it the favorite of opponents of social insurance.

Workmen's compensation was normally the first form of social insurance to be enacted. Five European countries had statutes requiring accident insurance and compensation for lost earnings on the books before

1900. Most American states, and all the other European countries, had followed suit by the start of World War I. The extent of coverage today differs rather sharply, however. Most European countries include all employees, spouses of employees, the self-employed, those engaged in civic duties, and specific categories of other people (e.g., students and those helping the police in Germany). The American states cover employees only. In about half the states, employers can choose whether or not to provide coverage (but must remain liable for lawsuits if they do not), and small employers are exempted entirely. Most states have exclusions for agricultural workers, domestic servants, casual employees, and employees in nonhazardous occupations, so that many employees remain without protection. Benefits are also much more limited in the United States, covering only portions of medical costs and lost earnings and lasting only for fixed periods of time.

Old age and invalidism insurance was usually the second form of social insurance. The German lead was followed by Denmark in 1891, France in 1905, and Britain in 1908, and all major European countries had some form of such insurance in place by the early 1920s. The German and French systems were compulsory, contributory (by employers, employees, and the state), and combined both old age and invalid insurance. In Britain, opposition from the Friendly Societies (voluntary organizations providing sickness, age, and death benefits to members) was only slowly overcome, and old age assistance initially took the form of small pensions. These were steadily increased, and then the system was converted to a contributory basis (employers, employees, and the state) in 1950. In general, the level of old age benefits is considerably higher in the European countries than in the United States, where the assumption is that Social Security will be supplemented by savings or other insurance.

Unemployment is the third major category of social insurance. In this case, France and Britain led the way in 1905 and 1911, and Germany did not follow until 1927. For many years, the fact of unemployment was attributed to moral failings of the unemployed worker and dealt with only as the most reluctant form of public assistance, if at all. Finally, the sustained efforts of reformers, notably Sir William Beveridge in England, managed to shift the focus to systemic causes inherent in industry itself. Britain enacted the first national compulsory insurance program with the support of its trade unions in 1911; ironically, its coverage and benefits were then expanded so rapidly that even Beveridge, its original sponsor, denounced it for failure to maintain the insurance principle. The British model was followed by most European countries, although the German benefits were considerably more generous. Only the United States conducts its unemployment system on a subnational basis, and thus is unique in its fifty-state diversity of coverage, standards, and benefits. Because the cost to employers is often based on their experience with unemployment, employers have a motive to deny employees' entitlement to benefits; the United States is unique in this respect also.

Health insurance was the only area where American social insurance advocates favored the German model over the British. Developing from its inception in 1883, the compulsory German system had come to involve employer and employee contributions, local administration of both medical services and cash benefits for lost wages, and hospital and death benefits. British health insurance, instituted in 1911, was also a compulsory system, but medical and cash benefits were administered separately, there was a large role for the private insurance companies, and physicians seemed to have gained even greater autonomy. When the American health insurance movement failed, it was at least arguably because it did not yield to physicians and insurance companies in the manner of the British compromise.

The European development of social insurance programs, and their steady expansion, helped to take much of the burden from public assistance. To compare precisely how overlapping social insurance programs nevertheless leave openings to be filled by public assistance, and how that need is filled in various countries, would be prohibitively complicated. But two types of case studies may be summarized briefly as a way of getting some basic idea of the distinguishing trends and practices in Europe and the United States.

One of the leading students of comparative public policy, Hugh Heclo of the Brookings Institution, developed a case study on aid to one-parent families in Britain, West Germany, Sweden, and the United States.[2] He argued that a focus on such recipients would provide a revealing comparison because they are "potential clients for a great many income support programs, as well as being a group facing relatively severe income problems in the raising of children."[3] His analysis excluded the widowed, because they are usually singled out for relatively generous benefits in social insurance programs. The cagetory is thus made up of unmarried, divorced, separated, or deserted adults (usually females) with young children. In most industrialized nations, including those analyzed in this study, roughly one family out of ten with children under 18 is headed by a single adult, and the proportion is steadily increasing.

Using data from the late 1960s and early 1970s, Heclo found that the proportion of all one-parent families that were receiving welfare assistance was more than half in the United States, while it was around 40 percent in Britain and below 20 percent in Sweden.[4] In other words, other forms of income support and/or employment opportunities were more available elsewhere; American single parents had to turn to public assistance more often than their counterparts in Europe. This finding was borne out by the fact that single parents and their children represented 60 percent of all welfare recipients in the United States, but only 25 percent in Sweden and 16 percent in Britain.

Why do American single-parent families have to depend so much on welfare assistance? Heclo identified seven contributing public policy reasons. One is that family allowances are paid in each of the other countries. Sweden pays uniform taxfree allowances for all children up to 16 years of age; these yield about 12 percent of average female earnings (i.e., 12 percent of what the mother might have earned if she had been able to work at paid employment). Britain pays family allowances yielding about 6 percent of average female earnings where there are two or more children. West Germany pays such allowances only to low-income families, at a rate of about 2.5 percent. But the United States has no family allowance program.

Second, Sweden has public maintenance grants to provide certain levels of maintenance for any child when an absent parent cannot or will not fulfill his/her financial obligations of support. These grants are considered to be the child's right, and thus are paid regardless of the custodial parent's income. Consistently, they are generous, averaging about twice the value of family allowances, and are updated for inflation regularly. Britain and West Germany have studied but not enacted such programs, while the United States merely seeks to enforce parental obligations on behalf of certain welfare-recipient families.

Third, all three of the other countries provide maternity benefits and replacement of some portion of an employed mother's lost earnings for a considerable period of time. The first is of particular value to unmarried mothers, and the latter to all employed women. If medical bills do not cumulate, and lost wages are in part made up, it may be possible to avoid public assistance. Sweden pays relatively generous uniform grants to all women having children, and replaces about half of lost earnings for twenty-six weeks. Britain pays modest grants to all childbearing women with some record of social insurance, and replaces about a quarter of lost income for eighteen weeks. West Germany pays small maternity grants to women who belong to the state-supported sickness funds, but replaces 100 percent of lost earnings for fourteen weeks. The United States has no maternity benefit program, although Medicaid will cover doctors' and hospital bills for those with incomes low enough to qualify. There are no provisions regarding replacement of earnings.

Fourth, housing allowances are paid in cash in all three of the other countries, in accordance with formulae that are generous to begin with and advantage one-parent families besides. In Sweden, benefits are based on the presence of children, and single parents receive the same support that a married couple would. Germany has an income test set so high that even a single parent earning around the median male earnings would qualify for a cash grant. Britain provides allowances (or rent rebates in the case of public housing) for those whose rent is high in proportion to income and family size. The United States experimented briefly with rent subsidies for low-income people, but the basic direction of housing policy has been to build federally supported apartments that concentrate the poor in specific geographic areas.

Fifth, job training and placement are more vigorous and effective in Sweden and Germany. As part of general labor market development policy, these countries provide training grants and expense allowances (and day care centers) to enable people generally to acquire or improve vocational skills. About half the trainees are women. Britain does not have a similar program in this instance. The United States focuses training efforts on single parents already on welfare, but has had very little success in long-term job placement. This is due at least in part to the very low basic educational and skill levels of the population involved.

Sixth, tax policy in Britain and Sweden is more responsive to single-parent responsibilities than is the case in Germany or the United States. Extra allowances and/or rates at the same levels as for working couples make for a better tax situation than in the latter countries, where single parents start paying taxes at lower incomes than married couples and pay higher rates all along the income scale. The United States in particular has a number of tax "disincentives" that put a heavy burden on the earning of the initial several thousands of dollars by a person seeking to get off public assistance.

Finally, public assistance policies also differ. In Sweden and Germany local governments finance and provide short-term aid to all with income problems, but the assumption is that the total of public programs will enable recipients to return to work (or to find higher-paying work in the case of those employed). Britain provides nationally administered subsistence-level public assistance and income supplements to low-income working families, with less emphasis on encouraging full-time work. The United States has a more fragmented program (with aid directed at specific categories of people, one of which is single-parent families) and widely divergent local eligibility standards and benefit levels. Long-term job placement has been a continuing problem in the United States, and the public assistance population is both larger and more permanent as a result.

Summarizing his case study, Heclo compared the combined effects of all forms of income support on single-parent families (with no income and with modest earnings) in the four countries. The Swedish families emerged with relatively high levels of support, less provided by stigmatizing public assistance. The German and British families were next in level of support, and had more coming from public assistance. In all three countries, working single-parent families (and working two-parent families) still qualified for considerable income support programs. In the United States, nearly all policy assistance applied to welfare families only under AFDC provisions, and net income was well below the Swedish and German (but not the British) levels.

A second and much briefer case study can be built by comparing the basic assumptions and patterns of practice in the income support systems of Sweden and the United States.[5] In addition to the much-longer-standing tradition of social welfare in Sweden (universal national old age pensions date from 1913, hospital services much earlier), Swedish policy has always stressed government responsibility for full employment and, more recently, greater equality of incomes. Although there is a higher share of private ownership of the means of production in Sweden than in most other European countries, Sweden absorbs more than half of its total GNP in taxation (compared to about 20 percent in the United States). These revenues support elaborate employment-generating subsidy and training programs and a comparatively vast income-redistributing system of social insurance.

Sweden promotes employment through all the standard fiscal and monetary measures, and also by providing incentives for companies to move into labor-surplus areas and subsidizing declining firms so as to preserve jobs. Job information, training, and financial support for relocation are extensively available. During recessions, government purchases are expanded, public works programs instituted, and grants given to train workers instead of laying them off. Employment has been kept high and rising, despite considerable immigration and a rapidly rising proportion of women seeking work; the proportion of adult women who were employed rose from 37 percent in 1965 to more than 60 percent in 1975. Many new jobs are in the health or other social service areas. Unemployment has regularly been below 2 percent during the years in which the United States has been between 6 percent and 8 percent.

The Swedish social welfare system involves about 24 percent of the GNP, and almost all of it is in the form of social insurance; only 1 percent is in the form of public assistance. In contrast, when all federal and state social welfare expenditures in the United States are added together (including Medicare, Medicaid, and public service jobs and training), they total about 14 percent of GNP. Of this total, more than a third is direct public assistance. The difference averages out to about 50 percent higher social welfare expenditures per person in the whole population in Sweden than in the United States. The comprehensiveness of Swedish social insurance means much less use of public assistance, and for much shorter periods. Despite very few limitations on the availability of public assistance to those in need, the average length of stay on public aid is about five months. In part, this is due to the fact that those with long-term problems normally become eligible for more general long-term provisions, such as early retirement.

The public assistance population in Sweden is much more likely to include childless single men and women, and married couples with or without children, than it is single parents with children. The reverse is true in the United States: female-headed households with children predominate, with the aged, disabled, and blind next; very little is done for any other groups of people. Benefit levels also show sharp contrasts. In Sweden, assistance in the mid-1970s ran at about 93 percent of aftertax wages. In the United States in the same period, and including food stamps, it averaged about 49 percent of aftertax wages.

What do these comparisons yield in the way of answers to the questions posed earlier in this section? In his analysis, Heclo attributes the earlier and more comprehensive nature of the European programs to stronger central governments and/or stronger trade unions, consensus-building processes, and political party competition. In the United States, vetoes were more likely to be cast by interest groups at some vulnerable point in the separated and fragmented American political system. He concludes that social insurance programs were therefore "relatively late in arriving, more imbued with an individualistic rationale, and—paradoxically—less politically adaptable after implementation."[6] The latter inflexibility occurs for one of the same reasons that delay in enactment did: so much energy and organization is required to, move the cumbersome separated components of federal, state, and local governments and their bureaucracies that it is much easier just to leave things as they are.

These are answers only at a very general level, however, and themselves require explanation. Perhaps our questions cannot be answered from comparative description alone, and in a single policy area. But the evidence surely points toward a special role for the widely accepted American belief in individual responsibility and the importance of work. It also suggests the power of voluntary and private enterprises, particularly the private insurance companies. The latter are deeply engaged in the provision of workers' compensation insurance, corporate and individual health insurance programs, and the vast corporate and union pension funds that supplement Social Security. The importance of these private programs to income support, and their tacit incorporation into public policy, is signaled by the extent to which tax policy encourages participation by providing deductions for health insurance premiums and deferred taxes on income from private pensions and annuities. Given these conditions, it seems unlikely that the United States will ever substantially close the gap between the American and the European income support systems.

II CURRENT PROBLEMS—AND FAILED POLICY ALTERNATIVES

In this section, we shall consider first the problems that lead to efforts to change the public assistance system, and then the financial troubles of OASDHI. The major policy debates of the past decade have focused on welfare reform. Moreover, these problems and policy-change efforts point directly to an important dilemma now dominating the income support field.

The dilemma so well illustrated by the failed policy-change efforts of the 1970s is simple: the kind of welfare reform that is politically feasible is not technically possible. Three factors are, by general agreement of policy makers and professional observers, politically essential to enactment of reform: (1) there must be an adequate level of support for needy persons with no reductions for any significant number of current beneficiaries; (2) there must be effective incentives for recipients to seek work and hence reaffirmation of the work principle; and (3) the total costs must be tolerable in the context of government resources and obligations. But, as we shall see, it has not been possible to fulfill all of these imperatives in any single program.

We shall start with a brief survey of the basic data about poverty and human need on the part of Americans today, and then turn promptly to the contrasting interpretations of what these data mean and *why* people are poor or in need. Contrasting understandings of the *extent* of poverty and need, and of the *reasons* for it, carry over directly to positions on *what is wrong* with the welfare system and *what should be done* about it. This will be seen clearly in our analysis of the two major efforts to reconstruct welfare in the 1970s—the Nixon Family Assistance Plan and the Carter Program for Better Jobs and Income. So will the dilemma between political feasibility and technical possibility. Finally, we shall turn to the financial troubles of the Social Security System, which are causing at least some observers to view it as being in crisis also.

Poverty and Need

The debates over public policy toward the poor start with disagreement over how many people are in fact poor and/or in need. Part of this disagreement stems from the issues involved in setting a satisfactory definition of poverty. Setting an absolute money standard requires some quite arbitrary decisions about what goods and services are basic to existence, and how the costs of these differ for families at different stages of life, in different places and circumstances, etc. Different government agencies set different standards. The first United States standards were set by the Council of Economic Advisers as a preliminary to the "War on Poverty." They were quickly refined by the Social Security Administration, whose work now forms the basis of continuing Census Bureau figures. But the Bureau of Labor Statistics also regularly publishes three levels of family budgets for different areas of the country; its "lower standard budget" is normally well ahead of the official poverty line and slightly behind the public opinion estimates to be discussed shortly. Nongovernmental bodies naturally differ even more widely in definitions.

The current Census Bureau definition focuses on the cash income of families of four in farm and nonfarm settings, with adjustments only for inflation over time and not for the rise in the general standard of living of nonpoor families since the first standards were set in 1963. The poverty line was $7,450 for a nonfarm family of four in 1980, a total which allowed about $1.71 per person per day for all meals, or $2.27 per meal for the whole family. Other costs are set at similarly minimal levels, and neither "frills" nor self-improvement expenses are included.

This "poverty line" contrasts sharply (and consistently) with what public opinion surveys find to be the amount of income necessary "to get along in this community." Table 11-1 shows the relationship between popular and official governmental views of the needs of a family of four in selected years from 1967 to 1978, and also compares American public attitudes and policy with those of Canada. In column 1, it is clear that the views of Canadian and American public opinion are quite consistent on

Table 11-1   Popular and Governmental Views of the Needs of a Family of Four

Year	1. Public's view of amount needed to "get along"*		2. Poverty line†		Ratio of columns 1 and 2	
	Canada	United States	Canada	United States	Canada	United States
1967	$5,200	$5,252	$4,060	$3,410	0.78	0.65
1969	6,500	6,250	4,420	3,743	0.68	0.60
1973	7,600	7,750	5,295	4,540	0.78	0.57
1976	10,400	9,200	8,478	5,659	0.82	0.62
1978	10,400	10,452	9,976	6,367	0.96	0.61

*Canadian Institute of Public Opinion, "Family of Four Needs Minimum Two Hundred Dollars per Week," *Gallup Report* (April 12, 1978). Question: "What is the smallest amount of money a family of four needs to get along in this community?" Canadian figures include both nonfarm and farm families, while U.S. figures include only nonfarm families.

†Statistics Canada, *Revised Low Income Series and Updated Low Income Series* (January 20, 1978); low-income cutoff is for a family of four residing at a city of population 100,000–500,000; Bureau of Census Official Poverty Threshold; 1967–1973, reported in "The Low Income Population: What We Know about it," in HEW, *1977 Welfare Reform Study,* paper no. 3 (April 6, 1977), Table 3; 1976–1978, reported in Congressional Budget Office, *Welfare Reform; Issues, Objectives, and Approaches* (July 1977), Table C-2, Figure 6 for nonfarm family, average of levels for male-headed and female-headed.

Source: Christopher Leman *The Collapse of Welfare Reform* (Cambridge Ma.: MIT Press, 1980), p. 44.

what it takes to "get along." There is consistency also in the fact that both publics feel higher sums are necessary than do their governments (column 2). But in the case of the United States, the gap is substantial. Starting with a lower poverty line than Canada, the United States government definition steadily fell further behind both American public opinion and Canadian practice until by 1978 the official definition of poverty was only 61 percent of what the American people thought was necessary and barely two-thirds of Canada's official definition.

It is important to realize that these are only official *definitions* of poverty. They do not imply anything about assistance. For example, in 1977 the poverty line was $6,191, but the typical poor family had a cash income (including welfare benefits but not in-kind income, to be discussed shortly) of $3,292.[7] Nor do such definitions take into account how people *feel* about their income status. Many persons may be kept above the poverty line only through a combination of several forms of government assistance, by which they may feel stigmatized. Many working families above the poverty line may feel overwhelming financial pressure; a breadwinner's illness or unemployment, or a family member's sickness, could drop many families below the poverty line in a week or so. In short, official poverty definitions are inherently and inevitably arbitrary; we can employ them only with such recognition.

But even the minimal official United States government poverty definition has placed about 25 million people in poverty for the last ten years. To be sure, this is a reduction from the 34 million initially found to be in poverty at the outset of the "War on Poverty" in 1964. The decline is clearly due to the many government programs begun or expanded since that year, particularly Medicare and Medicaid, the increases in Social Security benefits, the growth of the food stamp program, and the expansion of AFDC and other public assistance programs. The decline continued into the very early 1970s, but then leveled off to the point where the official poverty population has remained roughly constant since 1971.

This total has been sharply challenged, however, perhaps most visibly by Martin Anderson, a conservative economist and former Nixon administration official who now serves as President Reagen's domestic policy adviser. Citing several studies, Anderson argues that the war on poverty has been essentially won through massive transfers of billions of dollars, and that only a negligible few millions now are actually poor.[8] The illusion of poverty for many millions, he says, results primarily from the Census Bureau's failure to include in-kind transfers (medical services, food stamps, and housing in particular, which were nonexistent or minimal in 1963) within its standard definition of poverty. Most observers accept this argument in principle, but as a cautionary discount to be applied to the official figures rather than as a basis for denying them. The amount of free medical services obtained, for example, cannot simply be added to income because at least that amount has been consumed by the illness suffered by family members. In other words, the Census Bureau figures are too high, but by how much is just not clear.

The makeup of the poverty population begins to frame the problem for public policy. Just below 12 percent of all Americans were poor in 1977, but this total included more than 31 percent of all blacks and 22 percent of all Spanish-origin persons.[9] Fourteen percent of all aged persons, and an equal proportion of children, lived in poverty. Stated differently, the poverty population included 3.2 million aged persons, about 20 per cent of whom were black; 4.5 million persons between 18 and 65 without children, less than 20 percent of whom were black; and 17 million persons in families with children. Of the latter, who represent 70 percent of all poor people, nearly half the families were headed by a male, 25 percent of whom were black; slightly more than half were headed by a woman, and more than half of these were black. The incidence of poverty was greater in rural areas and the South than in other parts of the country. Most of the poor worked at some point in the year; about three-quarters of the male heads of families with children worked, and nearly 40 percent of the female heads of such families.

The poverty population is thus slightly older, more Southern, blacker, and less able to find jobs than the general population. But poor people are much like other people, in that they are primarily white, younger families with children, urban, and working. Their distinctiveness, as we shall see shortly, stems from low education, large family size, poor health, and systematic cultural denigration and educational-occupational discrimination. And the poor are not the same people year after year. About half the poor population is almost always in this category. But the other half moves in and out of poverty year by year, which means that a considerably larger total number of people exist at the margins of poverty and may happen to be included among the "officially" poor in any given year.

The question of who is poor is also very much a product of government policies. Table 11-2 shows how certain categories of often-poor persons are aided by combined social insurance, cash, *and* in-kind welfare benefits, and medical services. The data are based on 150 percent of the United States poverty level to show the importance of such transfers for the near-poor. For example, nearly 70 percent of the aged are near-poor before government help is taken into account; but transfers have a dramatic effect, reducing this proportion by more than two-thirds.[10] Government policies have far less effect on the situation of mother-headed families or unattached individuals. Perhaps ironically, it is possible for people to be poor although working—and not be eligible for any benefit

Table 11-2   Incidence of Income Below 150 Percent of U.S. Poverty Level, 1976*

	Before transfers	After transfers, before medical benefits	After both transfers and medical benefits
Mother-headed Families	57%	41%	35%
Intact familes	20	11	10
Unattached individuals	56	42	32
Individuals over 65	68	35	20

*Calculated from Congressional Budget Office, *Welfare Reform: Issues Objectives, and Approaches* (July 1977), p. 121.

Note: Transfers include social insurance and cash and in-kind welfare benefits. Income is before taxes. One hundred and fifty percent of the poverty level amounted to $8,511 for an urban family of four in 1976.

Source: Christopher Leman, *The Collapse of Welfare Reform* (Cambridge, Mass.: MIT Press, 1980), p. 47.

program. Of all poor but intact families with a working head in 1971, for example, 51 percent received no benefits at all. Childless couples and unattached individuals who were poor fared even worse: 57 percent received no benefits at all.

Why Are People Poor?

It is often argued that people are poor for reasons of individual character: in effort, motivation, thrift, foresight, discipline, or some other feature of their individual makeup, they are just unable to make the grade. The assumption is that there are ample employment opportunities for those who want to take advantage of them. This is, of course, a rationale that appeals to middle-class people because it congratulates them for their diligence and resultant mobility. It also justifies a variety of restrictions on assistance and legitimates an equal number of ways of encouraging or forcing the unfortunate to improve themselves.

The converse of this is the argument that people are poor for systemic reasons—a lack of jobs, low wages, lack of education and skills, and behind all of these racial and sexual discrimination. Unemployment is tolerated at ever-increasing rates, and subemployment (part-time work when full-time is sought, or work at jobs below one's qualifications and appropriate level of pay) is often not even calculated. The legal minimum wage, if earned by one family member in 1980, would leave even a small family well within the poverty range. Year-round, full-time work thus leaves many people and families below or very near the poverty level. Education and skills are, of course, related to family income and status levels; the higher one's family's standing, the more likely are skills to be acquired and poverty to be avoided. Patterns of racial and sexual discrimination are too well established to require further comment. Their effects are visible in practically every occupational and educational category, and they reproduce themselves generation after generation.

On top of these systemic reasons are some special congruences of poverty-causing factors. Age and poor health go together, for example, so that the elderly are specially vulnerable. Larger families reduce opportunities sharply among the poor and near-poor.

But too much can be made of the fact that many of the poor are in families that are aged, female-headed, large, or undergoing sickness or disability. The largest single group among the poor consists of traditional male-headed families, most with the father working full-time all year. And, in the words of one leading analyst:

> Even those poor families who manifest distinctive demographic traits, such as broken homes, are not necessarily poor because of those traits. On the contrary, for the most part the aged poor were poor before they were aged, broken poor families were poor before they split up, large poor families were poor when they were smaller, and sick poor families were poor even when they were well.[11]

The basic determinant of income status, it is argued, is really one's relationship to the labor market—or, in short, whether there are jobs and who has the skills to qualify for them.

What Is Wrong with the Welfare System?

A short answer to the question of what is wrong with the welfare system can be derived from the contrasting judgments about why people are poor. From one perspective, the welfare system rewards indolence and failure at the cost of increasing burdens for hardworking taxpayers. From the other, it stigmatizes and starves people who are disadvantaged not through faults of their own, but by the basic workings of the economic and social order.

A more carefully balanced view might be that many separate and overlapping programs provide minimal benefits to particular populations, but there is little coherence or rationality evident in such fragmentation. Further, despite high and rising costs, many people remain in need, families are encouraged to break up in order that the children may receive assistance, and recipients are effectively discouraged from seeking work that might enable them to get off welfare. The latter point deserves elaboration. As a person begins to earn income, two things often happen: (1) welfare benefits are lost, sometimes gradually as earnings rise, and sometimes sharply when eligibility thresholds are crossed, as is the case with Medicaid; and (2) a variety of state, local, and national income taxes, as well as Social Security taxes, newly apply—some with the first dollars earned, others at later stages. The combined result of these losses may be so great that they amount to an effective tax ("marginal tax rate," in technical terms) of up to 70 percent (in some cases, 100 percent) on the first several thousand dollars earned. Martin Anderson aptly terms this the "poverty wall," in that such rates (the highest on any income-earner in the country) effectively discourage effort to rise out of poverty through work. Each of these three perspectives would lend support to the idea of welfare reform, though perhaps not to the specifics of any particular proposal.

Some idea of how the American public feels about welfare may help to sketch the political pressures and constraints that affect reform in this area. In the fifteen years between 1961 and 1976, public assistance expenditures nearly quadrupled as a proportion of GNP. AFDC in particular was much in the news, and various opinion-surveying organizations began to explore public reactions. In 1973, more than half the respondents in a national poll said welfare spending was too high, while only 21 percent said it was too little, and 25 percent, that it was about right.[12] Only 38 percent felt that it would be a serious loss if welfare spending were cut back by one-third.

Not only are costs felt to be too high, but recipients are seen as undeserving. In 1977, 54 percent of Americans agreed that "most people who receive money from welfare could get along without it if they tried." When the public is asked about the causes of poverty, as many people regularly cite lack of individual effort as blame circumstances. Work requirements for welfare recipients are strongly supported; and the suspicion endures that some recipients are getting benefits to which they are not entitled. In 1969, 71 percent of Americans agreed that many people getting welfare are not honest about their need and, in 1976, 85 percent said that too many people on welfare cheat by getting money they are not entitled to. Public estimates of the number of welfare recipients who lied about their finances in one Northern city averaged 41 percent. And yet, support remains steady for increasing Social Security benefits even when higher taxes are included.

The selectivity of public support for parts of the income support system implied in the last point is confirmed by a detailed survey undertaken in Chicago in 1976–1977.[13] This study found strong support for aid to the elderly and disabled, and next for aid to children. The lowest support was for aid to poor adults under 65—except that the latter group ranked highest of all for education and job training assistance. Evidence that the public discriminates precisely among recipients and programs was also provided by the finding that the next most strongly supported program was transportation for the disabled. These patterns of high and low support for various programs were consistent among all groups of the population, although blacks and poorer people were generally stronger in support of assistance. Further analysis showed that disabled persons were seen to be deserving because they are considered not responsible for their fate, and to a considerable extent this was also true of the elderly poor. But the nonelderly poor and even poor children were seen as less deserving, on the grounds that they bore responsibility for their circumstances. The overall conclusion was that the public was willing to support certain categories of programs and types of people quite strongly, but aid to the "underserving" hardly at all.

Summarizing the analysis so far, we find perhaps 20 million Americans living in poverty and perhaps twice that number close to the official poverty threshold. Some who are poor receive public income support of one kind or another, but many do not. Some of the near-poor are kept from poverty by public income support, while some receive no benefits at all. Observers disagree about why these people have such low or nonexistent incomes, and whether various categories deserve help or not. But there is a widespread feeling that the present system for helping costs too much, helps some who do not deserve it while denying adequate aid to some who do, and needs to be changed. Introducing his Family Assistance Plan (FAP) in 1969, President Nixon declared that "the present welfare system has to be judged a colossal failure. . . . It breaks up homes. It often penalizes work. It robs recipients of dignity. And it grows. . . . I propose that we abolish the present welfare system and that we adopt in its place a new family assistance system."[14] In introducing his Programs for Better Jobs and Income (PBJI) in 1977, President Carter declared, "The welfare system is too hopeless to be cured by minor modifications. We must make a complete and clean break with the past." But neither proposal was enacted. Instead, the system and all its problems continue to grow.

The Family Assistance Plan

The core of the Nixon proposal, which he acknowledged would cost more initially (but result in net savings later through correcting the causes of poverty), was a guaranteed income. This came as a surprise to most observers, because a guaranteed income (government assurance of a certain minimum income for all, whether they worked or not) had been advocated (with one or two major exceptions) only by some liberal and radical Democrats. The American public was clearly not in favor of a guaranteed income: several polls in the mid-1960s found opposition running at from 53 percent to 67 percent, with few strong advocates. The President denied that his plan involved a guaranteed income, arguing instead that it was a way to cure the problems of the welfare system and reinforce the work incentives within it.

One problem that the FAP sought to address was the unfairness involved in welfare families being better off than nonwelfare families who were working. Because of Social Security and income taxes, ineligibility and reduced eligibility for food stamps, a family with one or both parents employed might have substantially lower net income than a similar family on welfare. If the father in a family with young children were employed full-time but in relatively low-paying work, a 1972 study showed it would often be possible for him to increase his family's net income by one-third to one-half by simply deserting them.[15]

A related problem that the FAP sought to deal with was the work-discouraging effect of high marginal tax rates (the "poverty wall," discussed earlier). If a family sought to get off the welfare rolls by finding work, it would encounter the reduced eligibilities and various taxes with which a working family struggles. For its initial thousands of dollars in earnings, it would experience such high effective tax rates that full-time work would produce little or no net gain. Because these incentives to work are so limited, policy sometimes turns to simple forced work requirements. But this assumes that jobs are in fact available, and that the recipients subject to the requirement have the necessary skills. With high unemployment, and (for example) an AFDC population in which well over half the mothers have not completed high school, this may require both extensive training programs and the direct provision of jobs by government.

The vehicle chosen to clean up this "welfare mess" was the "negative income tax." This is an adjustment of the nation's income tax laws to provide for a two-way system: those with net income over a certain amount would pay the government in accordance with a progressive scale, as was previously the practice; but those with net incomes *under* that same amount would now receive checks from the government to bring them up to that amount. The negative income tax was attractive because it was a relatively simple program that applied to everyone and required no large and intrusive bureaucracy for implementation. Although the FAP contained a provision which financially penalized any family in which an employable person did not seek or accept work, the nature of a negative income tax is to set a specific (and guaranteed) floor under the incomes of all persons. The vital question for recipients and cost-conscious policy makers and taxpayers alike is at what dollar level the negative income tax or guaranteed income is set. The FAP as originally proposed in 1969 set this figure at $1,600 per year for a family of four. At this total, most welfare recipients would have suffered some decrease in benefits, but because of the extension of benefits to many other families not previously on welfare, the net cost to the government would have been higher.

The idea of a negative income tax had been broached before by Milton Friedman, the conservative economist, but its real constituency was a band of poverty-conscious liberal economists, Democratic politicians, and a number of lower-level technicians who identified with them. With the exception of the Office of Economic Opportunity, however, no Johnson administration support could be gained for the idea; it was an unwelcome additional expense in a time of rising Vietnam War costs. Recognizing that the extension of benefits to the working poor might be opposed as undermining their urge to work, OEO did fund large-scale experiments to develop evidence to the contrary and have it ready when and if the need ever arose. The major one was started in 1967 as the New Jersey Graduated Work Incentive Experiment (the term "negative income tax" being carefully avoided). As it turned out, results were needed long before any advocate had expected. Before the experiment had run its course, all sides of the FAP debate were using or attacking preliminary findings—and the experiment has become famous principally as a case study in the unsatisfactory relationship between social science research and public policy making.

The internal struggle within the Nixon administration over the proposals to be made to redeem the President's campaign pledge to "clean up the welfare mess" is a fascinating story of bureaucratic infighting and personality conflicts.[16] Over the objections of most of his Cabinet and nearly all of his economic advisers, Nixon endorsed the FAP and announced it on nationwide television in August 1969. Part of the reason may have been the vigorous campaign mounted by Health, Education and Welfare Secretary Robert Finch, then his most trusted adviser, and Daniel Patrick Moynihan, his urban affairs assistant and later head of his Domestic Policy Council. Part may also have been Nixon's immediately prior endorsement of a much-expanded and federalized food stamp program, which effectively granted a form of guaranteed income to all needy persons. Nixon had been pushed toward the latter move by the legislative intentions of the Democratic Congress, and it may have seemed to him an opportune moment to take initiative over social policy away from the Democrats on a broad front.

In any event, the FAP as proposed called for the $1,600 income floor, with supplementing food stamps and state benefits in the great majority of states where the federal payment was less than current AFDC benefits. Work incentives were provided on a sliding scale, and a $300 penalty applied for failure to accept suitable work or training. A limit was placed on what states would have to pay for AFDC benefits, with the federal government committed to picking up the remainder and all future costs. The bill passed the House, partly as an alternative to general revenue-sharing. But it was attacked and ultimately defeated in the Senate for provisions discouraging people from working their way off welfare, possible large additions in the welfare rolls, and general hostility to the idea of guaranteed income (conservatives) and the low level of benefits (liberals).

A second version of FAP met the same fate in 1971–1972. Despite a higher income floor, tougher work requirements and penalties, and greater financial assistance for the states, the program could not gain a majority in the Senate. The more attractive parts of the bill were detached and passed separately (federalization, expansion, and in effect a guaranteed income for the needy aged, blind, and disabled—SSI—and restrictive work requirements), in a manner similar to the passage of the greatly expanded food stamp program in the midst of bitter debates over the earlier version of FAP in 1970. Finally, President Nixon himself lost interest as the 1972 election neared, and the cause of welfare reform was simply abandoned.

The demise of the FAP is directly traceable to the dilemma between political feasibility and technical possibility set forth earlier. Concern over the two dimensions of the principle of work involved—i.e., that working families should not be worse off than welfare families (and particularly that fathers should not be tempted to desert their families), and that welfare families should have real incentives to find work—created pressure toward basic changes in the system. But this widely shared work-ethic principle could not be served unless either or both of the two other political imperatives were violated: current beneficiaries would have to be cut back in benefits and the criteria under which they were paid, and/or greatly increased costs (and the guaranteed-income principle) would have to be accepted. To include the nonwelfare working poor in the income support system *required* greater expenditures, *unless* the level of support was set quite low—in which case it would mean reduction in support levels for current recipients. There was just no way to fulfill all three principles— work ethic, no reduction in benefits, and tolerable increases in costs—in the same program.

One of the spillovers from this sustained debate, however, was acceptance in 1975 of the "earned income tax credit" urged by Senator Long and his Finance Committee. With childless people and the unemployed excluded, increasing tax credits up to $400 were made available as earnings rose to $4,000, and then reduced at a rate of 10 percent until earnings reached $8,000. People whose taxes were less than the credit would receive a (negative income tax) check for the difference, but nobody could receive any benefit unless employed. In these ways, aid was targeted at the families earning the very lowest incomes, but withdrawn as they approached the $8,000 threshold.

The Carter Program for Better Jobs and Income

The only Southern governor to have supported FAP, Carter at first and for a sustained period insisted that PBJI, his much-advertised and high-priority welfare reform program, would include no new costs. But he also said that there should be a decent level of support for all who needed it, access to a job for all were able to work, incentives to encourage employment—and that working families should have more net income than nonworking families. His advisers knew this combination was impossible, and finally prevailed upon him to allow significant cost increases.

The plan as finally proposed used this reluctant authorization to cover expansion of support to previously nonwelfare working poor, and to provide 1.4 million public service jobs, in which the government was the "employer of last resort" for those who could find no other jobs. Other provisions included the elimination of food stamps, several kinds of assistance to the states, and strong work inducements. The centerpiece of the program, however, was a guaranteed income built from a combination of cash assistance from the Department of Health, Education and Welfare and an expanded earned income tax credit administered by the Treasury Department. Families of four not expected to work would receive support of $4,200, with benefits at the rate of 50 percent beginning with the first dollar of earnings. Similar families with an employable head (all able-bodied people without children, heads of two-parent families, and mothers with no children under 14) would receive income supplementation of up to $2,300, with no reduction of benefits for the first $3,800 earned and a 50 percent rate thereafter.

Opposition focused on the idea of a negative income tax or guaranteed income itself, the elimination of food stamps, and preeminently on the probable costs of these changes. The HEW presentation had emphasized a number of offsetting savings and ignored some important costs, so that administration and congressional estimates of new costs ranged from $3 billion to more than $17 billion.[17] Some hostile estimates of the number of new beneficiaries, including many nonpoor working families, ranged as high as 22 million persons, or about a 50 percent increase in then-existing welfare rolls.

Efforts at compromise ran aground on the same rocks of validating work, avoiding reductions for current recipients, and limiting new costs that had wrecked FAP years before. The PBJI was quietly interred in 1978. As before, the Congress contented itself with minor increments— expansion of the public service jobs provided under the Comprehensive Employment and Training Act, and an increase in the earned income tax credit program. Major welfare reform simply could not gain a supportive constituency. Nor do the problems in the path of reform, expressed in our much-emphasized dilemma, show any signs of abating.

The Financial Future of Social Security: A Case Study

The financial difficulties of the Social Security System (now considered in its entirety, as OASDHI) are a classic case study in the interrelationship of population patterns, basic economic conditions and economy-managing policies, and particular political choices about how the System is to be conducted. We shall take up each category in turn, and then see what alternatives they leave for the future.

Population patterns are probably the most predictable of these factors. Birth rates, however, do fluctuate over time (e.g., from "population explosion" to "birth dearth" between 1960 and 1974, when the fertility rate fell from 3.6 to 1.9 per 100 married women of childbearing age). Long-range forecasting requires alternative estimates of birth rates in the future, but short-range forecasting based on existing populations can be fairly accurate. The ratio of workers to beneficiaries in 1980 was 3:1, but this will decline steadily to about 2:1 in forty to fifty years. By the year 2000, the total number of beneficiaries will jump from 1980's 35 million to about 47 million. And the ratio of working-age people to people over 65 will continue to drop. Thus, population patterns alone would generate financial pressure on the System.

More powerful and less predictable pressures are generated by *basic economic conditions and economy-managing policies*. As we noted earlier, the Board of Trustees of the OASDHI Trust Funds had begun in the mid-1970s to sound warnings about the implications of long-term population patterns, reduced growth, and inflation. They foresaw large payroll-tax increases and/or possible distant-future bankruptcy. In 1980, however, the Joint Economic Committee of the Congress published an alarming report about the cumulating effects of inflation, unemployment, low growth–recession, and low productivity for the System's *immediate* future.[18] Despite the recent increases in payroll taxes (to 6.65 percent of the first $29,700, or a maximum of $1,975 per covered worker), the report found the old age and survivors' trust fund (which covers nine out of ten Americans over 65) to be dangerously low. Years of stagflation and unemployment had reduced jobs and real wages, and hence contributions into the System, while benefits had been indexed to keep pace with rising inflation. For every 1 million workers unemployed for one month in 1980, for example, the Social Security Funds lost $100 million in contributions.

Finally, *political choices* of the recent past formed part of the System's problems. Indexing benefits to inflation was only the last in a series of expansions of beneficiaries and increases in benefit levels. Continuing refusal to tap general revenues and insistence on maintaining the insurance principle, however tenuous and eroded it might be in practice, forced the substantial payroll tax increases of 1977. This action cost the System public support and probably contributed to inflation. Some argue that the pattern of continued increases in benefits culminated by indexing has the effect of reducing the incentive to save, and thus the capacity of the economy to generate the capital necessary for investment and growth.[19]

The remedies for these problems are similarly intertwined, but seem to have as their core the basic health of the economy. Not much improvement can be expected in the ratio of beneficiaries to workers unless the availability of jobs increases dramatically. If the currently unemployed could be restored to jobs and/or the incidence of women in the labor force increased and immigration was encouraged, the ratio could be improved. But such changes presuppose growth in the economy, with accompanying growth in productivity and thus real wages. Unless wages increase in real terms (i.e., after inflation is taken into account), employer/employee payroll tax contributions cannot keep ahead of beneficiaries' entitlements.

The Joint Economic Committee report, therefore, heavily emphasized investment-focused macroeconomic policies. If new business tax cuts and newly increased depreciation allowances resulted in increased capital investment, the Committee argued, productivity, growth, jobs, and real increases in wages would follow. For the same reason, the Committee urged a larger role for private pension programs. These programs now represent a massive accumulation of capital available for investment ($330 billion in 1979, a sixfold increase from the $52 billion level of 1960). If they were more fully assumed as part of the premises of social insurance, further Social Security benefit increases could be resisted *and* more capital would be available for investment.

Table 11-3 shows the pattern of support that OASDHI recipients have from other sources. (The ratios are fairly constant over time, although private pensions have been rising.) It shows that private retirement systems make up a significant portion of total income. But so do continued earnings: in more than 40 percent of married couples over 65, one or both members was still working. Nor did the prospect of Social Security benefits appear to inhibit savings or other investment to provide for one's own old age: in every category of beneficiary, the largest proportion of income from other sources came from interest, rent, or dividends. This table should be read in conjunction with Table 10-2, in which the other public sources of Social Security beneficiaries' income are itemized in greater detail. But a cautionary note is in order. That people have income from other sources says nothing about how large that income is; repeated

Table 11-3   Percent of OASDHI Beneficiaries with Income from Other Sources, 1968

	Married couples	Unmarried men	Widows
Earnings	43	19	15
Retirement pension	30	22	12
Interest, rent, dividends	62	46	52
Public assistance	5	11	10
Relatives' contributions	2	—	5

Source: Derived from *Social Security Bulletin*, vol. 33, (April 1970), p. 12.

surveys show that the assets of Social Security recipients are very slight, a fact that is borne out by the high proportion of entitlement to public assistance of various kinds (Table 10-2).

More specific political choices were also recommended for consideration by the Committee. Delaying the age of eligibility for benefits was one of these: if more older people were encouraged to keep working, the total GNP would be larger and the benefit drain lower. Increasing the earned income allowance (before benefits were reduced) would also reduce pressure to increase benefits. Another possibility would be a change in the ratio of employer to employee contributions. In most European countries, employers pay more, sometimes much more, than workers; but in the United States, the shares have been equal since the System's inception in 1935. Because increased payroll taxes are a drag on the economy and a factor in inflation, some limits on benefits, or ("temporary") transfers from other social insurance funds or the general revenue pool itself, might have to be considered as well. But the report concluded that only a return to long-term growth with high employment and low inflation could really return the nation's primary retirement system to a sound basis.

III ALTERNATIVE POLICIES

However complex and demanding, the problems of the Social Security System seem at least to command policy makers' good will and public support for the best accommodation possible. The same is not true for the public assistance side of the income support system. Welfare is costly and lacks public support, but every nonpunitive alternative seems to add to costs and (if anything) to provoke public disapproval. Although almost everybody agrees that the welfare system is in need of basic overhaul, two major efforts at rather drastic reconstruction have failed in recent years because of an apparently intractable political-technical dilemma. With their failure, the only alternatives remaining are those at the poles of the political spectrum. One involves significant new federal government responsibilities and costs: expanded social insurance, provision of jobs in public employment, and acceptance of the principle of a "right" to high levels of public assistance when in need. The other is an attempt to turn the system back to a well-policed needs-only basis, thereby forcing people to find jobs and income in the private economy or suffer the consequences.

The first of these alternatives seems totally lacking in political feasibility. The failure of FAP and PBJI is only marginally the result of opposition from those who wanted higher benefits and greater entitlements in a federalized welfare support system. Both of these moderate reform proposals failed primarily because of opposition from people who wanted to do *less* in the way of support for the needy. There is neither a public nor a policy-maker constituency in the 1980s for an approach that would add significantly to the support levels of FAP or PBJI and supplant their stigmatizing work requirements and means tests with basic entitlement. Programs along European social welfare lines do not seem likely in the United States. If the political climate should change, of course, European models of social insurance and job provision, and American proposals for guaranteed income via the negative income tax, all stand ready and waiting for trial.

Instead, we must take seriously what is essentially a national version of the Reagan approach to welfare in California in the years after 1971. In his first announcement of his economic recovery program, President Reagan indicated the direction that his administration would take. First, certain basic "social safety net" programs assumed to serve the truly needy would be preserved intact. These include the retirement provisions of Social Security, Medicare, veterans' disability payments, Supplemental Security Income, and three lesser programs. Not listed, but clearly also to be preserved unchanged, were the retirement benefits provided for veterans and federal employees. Table 11-4 lists these programs, together with the number of people served by them and their projected costs in the 1982 fiscal year. Second, many other income support programs, nearly all of them forms of public assistance, were to be reduced or eliminated. The minimum monthly benefit of $122 paid to all retired workers regardless of their entitlement was to be eliminated, and disability payments and aid to

Table 11-4 The Social Safety Net Programs to Be Preserved from Budget Reductions in First Stage of Reagan Economic Program

Program	Millions of people served	$ billions in 1982 budget
1. Social Security, Old Age and Survivors (not including disability, minimum benefits, or student aid)	32.0	$140.0
2. Medicare	28.6	45.4
3. Veterans' disabilities	3.2	12.7
4. Supplemental Security Income	4.2	7.9
5. School lunches for low-income children	9.5	2.1
6. Head Start	0.4	1.0
7. Summer youth jobs	0.7	0.9

Note: Dollar amounts based on preliminary estimates for fiscal year 1982.
Source: New York Times, February 11, 1981, p. A1.

TABLE 11-5 The Big Losers: Income Support Programs Slated for Largest
Reductions, Fiscal Years 1982–1984 (in billions of current dollars)

Program	1982			1984		
	Current base*	Cuts	Reagan budget	Current base*	Cuts	Reagan budget
Food stamps	$ 12.5	$1.8	$ 10.7	$ 13.5	$2.5	$ 11.0
Social Security	157.8		156.1	191.1		188.5
minimum benefit		1.0			1.1	
student aid		0.7			1.5	
disability	19.2	0.6	18.6	21.9	1.7	20.2
AFDC	8.1	0.5	7.6	8.5	0.7	7.8
Medicaid	18.2	1.0	17.2	22.5	2.9	19.6
Unemployment insurance†	20.0	2.7	17.3	16.4	1.0	15.4
CETA jobs	3.8	3.6	0.2	4.4	4.4	—

*"Current base" is the figure used by the Reagan administration (which assumes its projected rates of growth, inflation, revenue, etc.) in its budget proposal of February 18, 1981.
†Combined figure, including long-term assistance, special assistance for high-unemployment states and military dischargees, and Trade Adjustment Act benefits.
Source: New York Times, February 20, 1981, pp. A11–A16.

college students whose parents are deceased were to be cut back substantially. CETA jobs, food stamps, AFDC, and extended unemployment insurance were similarly eliminated or cut back. Limits were proposed for the federal share of Medicaid. These actions and their projected savings are itemized in Table 11-5.

The underlying rationale for the nature of the income support approach suggested by these reductions may be that of Domestic Policy Adviser Martin Anderson in his lively *Welfare: The Political Economy of Welfare Reform in the United States*. His proposal is set forth in a basic thesis and seven supporting points. The thesis is:

> Practical welfare reform demands that we build on what we have. It requires that we reaffirm our commitment to the philosophical approach of giving aid only to those who cannot help themselves, while abandoning any thoughts of radical welfare reform plans that will guarantee incomes. The American people want welfare reform that ensures adequate help to those who need it, eliminates fraud, minimizes cost to the taxpayers, and requires people to support themselves if they can do so.[20]

The supporting points are intended to emphasize and enforce aspects of this thesis. The first calls for reaffirming as national policy that only the truly needy shall have access to welfare payments, and then seeing that those who write guidelines, regulations, and procedural manuals—and those who implement such rules—actually follow that basic principle. The second mandates intensive efforts to rid the welfare rolls of those who, whether by fraud or error, are ineligible for benefits and those who are receiving more than their entitlements. This is partly to save money and partly to restore public confidence and support for the system. The third requires able-bodied people to work or face denial of welfare benefits, rather than trying to induce work by means of financial incentives (which Anderson considers to be technically impossible and counterproductive in their present form).

These three points constitute the essence of this reform program, but the remaining four are not unimportant. One calls for the elimination of "inappropriate beneficiaries," such as striking workers or college students. Another seeks a determined program of pursuing deserting fathers or mothers and others with responsibility to support dependents and forcing them to contribute to the support of people otherwise likely to be welfare beneficiaries. The final two points urge improvement of the efficiency and effectiveness of welfare administration and shifting of greater responsibility to state and local levels.

The intent of the program as developed in California was to reduce the rate of the steadily increasing total costs of public assistance. By eliminating those not legally entitled to benefits and imposing strict criteria on new applicants, welfare rolls were in fact reduced and costs stabilized. Some beneficiaries actually received larger benefits than before. Liberal critics were much less generous in their assessments, contending that many deserving poor people were victimized in the process.

This approach is the only one of those reviewed that survives the dilemma that has prevented other types of reform. It vigorously fulfills the desire for reaffirmation of the work principle, at least in theory preserves the benefits of those now legally entitled to aid, and holds costs to the minimum level consistent with current entitlements (which might also be reduced as part of any legislative package mandating this program). But it would also make the United States, one of the world's most affluent nations, into the industrialized world's most penurious in providing income support to its needy citizens.

One possible direction for the income support system as a whole would be to implement such a cutback in welfare simultaneously with a major expansion of social insurance programs, perhaps including health insurance in a reconstructed Social Security System. This would allow a larger share of the costs to be borne by employed persons (and to some extent by employers) and shift administrative expenses to the private insurance companies (along with the profit-making opportunities). If the government undertook to promote jobs in various ways, or even supplemented contributions for social insurance, such investments might well be considerably lower than prospective costs under the present system.

Barring any of these changes, it seems likely that the income support system—Social Security and other social insurance programs as well as public assistance—will at best continue to limp along in fragmented and unsatisfactory fashion. At worst, it will crumble into increasingly marginal aid for mere fractions of a needy population, all of whom are targets of general suspicion and hostility.

NOTES

1 This account rests primarily on Roy Lubove, *The Struggle for Social Security, 1900–1935* (Cambridge, Mass.: Harvard, 1968), P. R. Kaim-Caudle, *Comparative Social Policy and Social Security* (London: Martin Robertson, 1973), and Arnold Heidenheimer et al., *Comparative Public Policy* (New York: St. Martins, 1975).

2 Hugh Heclo, "Income Maintenance: Patterns and Priorities," chap. 7 in Heidenheimer, op. cit., pp. 205–212.

3 Ibid., p. 205.

4 Ibid., p. 207. Germany was not included because of noncomparable data.

5 This analysis rests on Martin Carnoy and Derek Shearer, *Economic Democracy* (White Plains, N.Y.: Sharpe, 1980).

6 Heclo, op. cit., p. 195.

7 Bradley R. Schiller, *The Economics of Poverty and Discrimination*, 3d ed. (Englewood Cliffs, N.J.: Prentice-Hall, 1979), p. 21.

8 Martin Anderson, *Welfare: The Political Economy of Welfare Reform in the United States* (Palo Alto, Calif.: Hoover Institution, 1974), chaps. 1 and 2.

9 Data in regard to the makeup of the poverty population are drawn from Schiller, op. cit.; the work data are from p. 35.

10 Christopher Leman, *The Collapse of Welfare Reform* (Cambridge, Mass.: MIT Press, 1980), pp. 48 ff., is the source for all data in this paragraph.

11 Schiller, op. cit., p. 232.

12 Leman, op. cit., pp. 7–8.

13 Fay Lomax Cook, *Who Should Be Helped? Public Suport for Social Services* (Beverly Hills, Calif.: Sage, 1979). All data, findings, and interpretations in this paragraph are drawn from this source.

14 Presidents Nixon and Carter are cited in Leman, op. cit., p. 1.

15 Ibid., p. 56.

16 The story is told from one perspective by Anderson, op. cit., and from another by Daniel Patrick Moynihan, *The Politics of a Guaranteed Income* (New York: Random House, 1973).

17 Leman, op. cit., p. 105.

18 The Joint Committee Report is summarized in the *New York Times*, November 10, 1980, p. 1.

19 All issues surrounding Social Security's future are well aired in Alicia Munnell, *The Future of Social Security* (Washington, D.C.: Brooklings, 1976).

20 Anderson, op. cit., p. 153. The seven points follow immediately thereafter.

Part Three

Conclusions

Chapter 12

American Public Policy: Character, Causes, and Prospects

It is tempting to say that the factual record in each of the four policy areas speaks for itself, and that this chapter therefore embodies conclusions flowing inevitably from the data examined. But that would contradict everything said earlier about the inescapable role of values and preferences in reaching interpretations and making choices about public policy. Of course a final assessment and evaluation is a personal one with which equally informed observers may disagree. What follows is intended as a balanced and factually supported set of conclusions, but undoubtedly reflects my biases as well. I shall first review what I think the record shows about the causes of American public policies, and then look briefly at some implications in the alternative-choosing process. Finally, I focus on what all of the foregoing analyses mean for the capacity of the American social order to solve the policy problems we face, and on how some authoritative observers currently view this question.

EXPLAINING PUBLIC POLICIES

What explains the nature of current policies is an important issue because it bears on the question of whether and how such policies can be improved. There is only so much to be gained by upgrading the quality of information available to policy makers, or by changing institutional powers and procedures, if the real causes of the basic character of public policies lie at deeper levels of cultural values and fundamental economic and social structures. Throughout this book, we have seen effects on policy flowing *both* from characteristics of the structure and decision-making process of our political system *and* from shaping factors external to that system. The former, because the acts of individuals and groups are the dramatic daily fare of the mass media, often appear determinative. The latter, because they are less visible and/or taken for granted, are much less recognized. But certain recurring features of American public policies—nothing less than their basic assumptions, priorities, and distributive effects—are not only visible in each of our four areas but direct reflections of our cultural values and fundamental economic and social structures. It is these kinds of external factors that must be grasped to fully understand American public policies and our prospects for finding solutions to current problems.

This is not to say that political structure and process characteristics do not play significant roles, at times quite important ones, in shaping public policy. For example, the separated-powers system and the conflicts it encourages, together with the power of special-interest groups, made development of a coherent energy policy very difficult. Constituency concerns and the general vulnerability of Congress to special-interest pressures, together with the practice of legislating "entitlements" to take effect in the future, mean that Congress is likely to add several unanticipated billions to the federal budget each fiscal year—despite rhetoric about budget-cutting and budget-balancing. Special relationships between congressional committees or their chairpersons and key agency administrators may lead to a very small and isolated effective decision-making system for important policy areas, as was the case with Social Security for a period of several years. The constitutional powers of the states, together with widely differing implementing practices, mean that federal preferences and uniform national standards can be achieved only if the federal government appropriates vast sums of money to use as inducements; we saw such pressures at work in both health care and income support. We could identify many more consequences for policy substance that are brought about by characteristics of our policy-making system. All of them combined make for a distinctive political style of bargaining and compromising, and a rhythm in policy production in which delay occurs while pressures build, and then some triggering incident results in relatively drastic new policy departures that are followed by years of refinement and consolidation.

But all of them occur within a limited range of the possible that is set by cultural values and fundamental economic and social structures. From these sources comes the distinctive national character of our policies, at least in the four areas analyzed here and probably in most other areas as well. The emphasis we place on individualism, personal responsibility for one's circumstances, the work ethic, and property rights, for example, is profoundly revealed in each policy area. Because of such commitments, together with our firm belief in the effectiveness and desirability of the free economic market, our government is much less active in affecting the economy than those of other industrial democracies. The United States government owns less, intervenes less, and draws off lower shares of the GNP in tax revenues than is the case in such other countries. Policies are framed with market images in mind and with respect for individuals' (and corporations') property rights, even by those who assert some degree of social responsibility for the conditions of people's lives. The main opposition, of course, stems from that substantial number of Americans who believe that the government should do *less* in the way of managing the economy.

In the energy field, the property rights of the oil companies made unthinkable such alternatives as nationalization, detailed public controls, or public corporations for energy development. Instead, public money is used to underwrite development of future oil and gas and alternative fuel sources that will ultimately lead to massive private profits for many of those same oil companies. The basic American policy relied on the market (in this area, not a free one at all but one in which OPEC suppliers set world prices at ascending levels, thereby adding billions in income to domestic producers as well) to force conservation on the part of those who could not pay the rising prices. When shortages occurred, people were blamed for using too much energy; neither rationing nor detailed allocation in other ways was attempted.

But it is in the area of health care and income support that the impact of such cultural values is most powerful. It has simply not been possible to "interfere" in any significant way with the individual entrepreneurial behavior of the nation's doctors, for example, despite demonstrable health care needs and skyrocketing costs. The fee-for-service principle, defended by the concept of property rights, remains inviolate. Medical schools, hospitals, and the private insurance companies serve as independent, prestige- or profit-seeking barriers to effective social efforts to give health care needs first priority. Beyond them stands the solid opposition of the business community to increased efforts toward a healthier environment, such as by control of toxic waste disposal, greater work safety, or less polluted air and water. The only major government role permitted is provision of steadily increasing billions of tax dollars for individuals to make greater use of the existing system, a subsidy that deteriorating economic conditions alone may be able to contain.

Income support policies are designed and implemented with two major values in mind: personal responsibility and the work ethic. Only those with some personal contribution via a social insurance program are viewed as entitled to assistance. Others must repeatedly prove their destitution to qualify for assistance and suffer a variety of indignities and denigration as a result of their need for public assistance. Frequent efforts are made to force people to work, as a means of improving their character and perhaps as a lesson to others. The contrasts between the United States and the European democracies are sharpest in the last two areas, where American individualism, personal responsibility, and free rein for profit-seeking are most vividly displayed.

The effects of fundamental economic and social structures are equally powerful in the four policy fields. The private economy, meaning chiefly the great corporations and banks, is simply taken for granted and its needs accepted as part of the agenda and imperatives to which all policies must be adapted. The general level of prosperity within this economy is the single most important factor in shaping policy: if profitability and stability are threatened, all other policy projects must be adapted or abandoned and measures taken to restore the prosperity that alone sustains social services.

The social pyramid, with its sharply unequal distribution of wealth, income, status, and power, is equally accepted as a necessary component of the status quo. Government is staffed primarily from the upper-middle and higher levels, and programs that affect the distributions on which the pyramid is based do so almost entirely in terms of its lower levels. By providing a variety of services to the very lowest strata (e.g., job and training opportunities, affirmative action, desegregation, etc.), and thereby threatening and provoking the lower-middle and middle levels, the status quo of the whole social pyramid is actually enhanced.

The policy problem of managing the economy offers prominent examples of the effects of both sets of structures. The basic goal of such policies is to maintain profitability and stability for the great corporations and banks. Inflation must therefore receive first priority, and growth must be sought—and then employment opportunities can be spurred. The whole focus of reindustrialization is to provide tax inducements and investment opportunities adequate to cause businesses, bank and trust fund managers, and wealthy individuals to rebuild American productive capability. In the energy field, all policies revolve around the major units of the international oil industry. The political power that the oil industry can deploy is sufficient to withstand public resentment and assert its will in a variety of forms, from decontrol of prices to assistance with developing coal, synthetic fuels, and other sources of future profits.

The situation is much the same in health care and income support. The economic and social status of the doctor core of the medical cure system, enforced by the power and prestige of the AMA, is the fixed landmark from which policies take departure. The hospitals and private insurance companies complete the system, no part of which really can be controlled by government at any level. When conditions perceived as onerous are attached to the funds appropriated to pay for medical services, doctors have simply refused to provide such services. The social standing of the recipients of most public assistance programs is almost the opposite of that of the doctors: they are so low in public status and so powerless politically that they can be treated with little regard. With the exception of Social Security beneficiaries, most income support programs are designed to encourage people to make themselves available for the lowest-paid jobs in marginal industries.

The third set of external shaping factors, the nature and interrelationship of current problems, also has all too evident an impact in our policy areas. Sustained inflation and unemployment, for example, have completely disrupted policies and programs. Managing the economy becomes an insoluble dilemma in which efforts to solve one side of a problem (inflation) only worsen its other side (unemployment). The national government loses control of its own budget because revenues are unanticipatedly low and a variety of expenses (fuel costs, unemployment benefits, Social Security and federal civil service pensions indexed to inflation) are sharply higher. Energy costs spiral upwards in part because OPEC prices are set in relation to the dollar's value, and are increased as inflation (partially caused by higher energy prices) eats away at the real spending power represented by the dollar. Health care costs are pushed out of sight by doctors' and hospitals' uncontrollable efforts to acquire the newest high-priced technology and still stay ahead of inflation in real income. In turn, previously legislated entitlements force the government to pay its share of such costs and send its budget further into deficit. Social Security and other social insurance programs face bankruptcy as revenues fall and entitlements linked to the cost of living require higher payments. More and more people become entitled to public assistance and food stamp programs as lack of jobs reduces their incomes, with resulting higher costs to the government.

Other contemporary problems inhibit solutions and/or place additional strains on existing programs. The perceived need to substantially increase military expenditures, for example, contributes to inflationary pressures and requires new reductions in social services as well. Taxes cannot be raised to cover this new cost, because that would threaten economic recovery, reindustrialization, and growth. At any time, economic troubles abroad, small wars and threats of larger ones, social unrest at home, or other unforeseeable events may intervene to reshape the policy agenda and priorities. The interdependence and unpredictability of these problems and potential problems mean that public policy is now shaped almost as much by crisis conditions as by clear choices among desired goals and means for attaining them. Policy is increasingly reactive, seeking to preserve or enhance basic values and structures amidst deteriorating conditions.

The primacy of the external factors may thus be a time-specific one, the product of the world and United States economic crisis and the related social strains. But I would argue that such primacy is only more visible under these circumstances. In sustained hard times, we are more inclined to look beyond surface symptoms at underlying causes—although we may not be any readier to address cures to such fundamental causes.

ALTERNATIVES AND THE PROBLEM OF CHOICE

As we have seen throughout this book, no policy problem really exists in isolation from other major problems. Although we have analyzed alternatives in each area separately, actual choices between them can only be made in the context of the possible alternatives to be chosen in a variety of other important policy areas. Problems and policy choices are inextricably related to each other in many ways: the choice of one may foreclose dealing with another, it may lead in a direction that makes others more difficult, or it may simply consume so much time and money that others must wait.

The first issue is one of *priorities*. There is only so much time available to decision makers to study and act on problems, or to administrative personnel to implement policies that are established. Most important, there is almost always a scarcity of various other resources (sometimes physical things or human talent, but most often *money*), in the sense that perceived needs or opportunities for government action exceed the amount of such resources thought to be available to the government in practical political terms. The relative importance of each problem area and the severity of the issues in each must be determined. Areas and issues can then be ranked in some way, so that the most dangerous or compelling have first call on available resources.

But prioritization is not a technical-assessment question for policy makers to resolve in quiet solitude. It is an issue involving great controversy among many powerful groups and people, each of which insists that its rank-ordering is best. Nor are political participants free agents in this process. Unpredictable events thrust new problems with high priority into the process, or the cumulative development of old problems converts them into the most demanding question of all. The spreading consequences of continuing inflation and unemployment, for example, finally assuming crisis proportions in the 1980s, have both restructured priorities and forced substantive changes in every policy area. No other area, except military and foreign policy, can expect anything but contraction until stagflation has been cured and profitability/prosperity restored—and even then what can be done will be shaped by what was necessary to control inflation and restore growth.

Once priorities have been set, however uncertainly, the next question is one of *information*. The most important information is, of course, the costs involved in various alternatives, and their probable effects on the problems involved. Much is made of the ratio between costs incurred (calculated chiefly in terms of dollars spent, but sometimes also in terms of other things not done or political goodwill expended) and benefits realized. The estimation of benefits to be derived, either by the objects of policies or the policy makers themselves, is a highly uncertain task. Many factors intervene between policies and their results, and many of them are quite unpredictable. So is the behavior of the thinking human beings who are often the targets of policy "interventions."

Social scientists are often frustrated by the apparent lack of utilization of their research findings, but one major reason is simply inability to predict future human responses amidst unknowable future circumstances. Another is that research findings are too limited in scope or too long in being produced for policy makers to find them useful. Ironically, in the one major instance where social scientists had undertaken timely social experimentation on a scale adequate to produce policy recommendations (the negative income tax experiment in New Jersey, where the effect of a guaranteed income on work orientation was being tested), the results became embroiled in the political conflict over the Nixon proposals and were essentially negated anyhow.

Other analytical techniques have been developed by the social sciences in an effort to make the choice among alternatives more informed and "rational." Models of the process of choice making have been developed in which the costs of various decisions are clarified and the benefits calculated, again primarily in dollars in each case. The convenience and relative availability of dollars as the unit of measurement can lead to efforts to translate everything into dollar values or to ignore those intangible factors (such as moral and ethical questions) which cannot be so translated. The tendency in decision making and in the analysis of decision making is to focus on the tangible matters at stake, particularly the costs and benefits in dollars, on the grounds that these are at least relatively more identifiable.

As we have seen, however, cost estimates are themselves highly unreliable; they depend on estimates of future conditions that may be wholly wrong.

The problem with all such estimates and models, and with the utilization of social science research, is only partly that they cannot take into account the intangible dimensions that matter greatly (but differently) to people or the effects of unpredictable future events. It is also that political expediency and pressures flow through the entire policy-making and implementing process, often sweeping rationality and objectivity and factual data out when they are inconvenient.

Not that facts are irrelevant—sometimes they are so persuasive that they help to shape the way an issue is perceived and understood. Such was the case with the demonstrated nonuniformity of local draft board performance in the case study in Chapter 3. Unequal treatment of similarly situated men was so demonstrably pervasive and so clearly related to the structure of the Selective Service System that the President's Commission recommended and Congress enacted a means to take the selection of men for induction out of the hands of the local boards—the national lottery. But the point is that the facts must link up with strongly held values and powerful political forces before they become effective. In most circumstances, there are multiple versions of the facts and/or sufficient remaining doubts that their role is distinctly subordinate to that of values, ideology, special-interest pressures, and a variety of other factors.

The process of choosing among alternatives is thus anything but a neat and objective one. Instead, it is complex, contentious, uncertain, and in the technical sense, irrational. It rests heavily on values and preferences and political power. For all these reasons, it may be worth stressing again, citizens have every right and reason to try to see their preferences realized rather than those of technical experts or skilled lobbyists.

THE CAPACITY OF THE AMERICAN SOCIAL ORDER TO SOLVE TODAY'S PROBLEMS

With what we have seen about the shaping sources of our public policies, what can we say about the chances of solving the problems that face us? Do solutions depend on political will, availability of resources, technical creativity, new people in elective office, institutional changes, or more basic alterations in cultural values and economic and social structures? It may be tempting to answer simply, all of the above. More soberly, we should start by recognizing that there is no necessity, and maybe even no possibility, for any of the problems we have examined to be "solved" in the sense that they will then disappear. We can ask, however, that government try to see that conditions of life for people generally do not become worse than they are, either in material standard of living or in terms of economic, social, political, and cultural opportunities and satisfactions. And we can ask, consistently with out democratic commitments, that where possible in the context of available resources and capabilities, government policies seek to improve the quality of life for ordinary citizens. Such an assertion of what government *should* be doing, of course, is a controversial expression of values and preferences; others might prefer that the focus of concern be corporate profitability or preservation of the status quo or specific combinations of these three priorities.

But observers with quite different perspectives on the goals of government policy share a perhaps surprising degree of consensus about the American social order's capacity to cope with contemporary problems without basic changes of some kind. All across the political spectrum from far right to far left, there is agreement that the United States faces a profound economic crisis. The most moderate see the necessity of emergency measures, perhaps enduring for several years and resulting in austerity for people generally and some new ways of doing things, but essentially within the bounds of the present political system. The more drastic projections envision the crisis leading to fundamental changes in the social order: toward neofascism, toward constitutional reconstruction into a parliamentary system, or even toward a new decentralized form of democratic socialism.

Among those calling for emergency measures to deal with this crisis are several members of the Reagan administration and a respected member of the New York financial community who played the leading role in bringing New York City back from the brink of bankruptcy. Some free-market economists, like Friedrich Von Hayek, saw American inflation as controllable only after a major depression, but Reagan's Director of the Office of Management and the Budget, David Stockman, was the spokesman for a significant element in the adminstration that called for emergency measures to control inflation through strongly induced new economic growth. Drastic cuts in federal expenditures and regulatory efforts, and equally drastic tax cuts for businesses and investors, were the core of their program for restoration of prosperity.[1] They saw ahead a temporary period of austerity and unemployment, but then a relatively prompt and massive expansion of the economy that would provide new jobs and enable new government expenditures for military purposes and other support for new profit opportunities.

The arguments of Felix Rohatyn, architect of the new New York City financial governing system, are another version of the same perspective and purposes. Rohatyn foresees a national crisis equivalent to that of New York City, in which similarly stringent cutbacks in public services and the general standard of living will be necessary. He calls for a national program of targeted government tax incentives, reduced services, and general "belt-tightening" (by middle- and lower-class people) in order to reinvigorate the productive capabilities of American industry.[2] The means endorsed are new forms of corporate/banking-dominated national economic planning, on the order of the banker-dominated bodies created to oversee and control New York City's elected officials.

Other observers are less confident that the crisis can be controlled without significant and lasting change. Bertram Gross, a well-respected policy analyst ever since his efforts in drafting and implementing the Employment Act of 1946, envisions a drift toward a corporate-controlled system that he somewhat ironically calls "Friendly Fascism."[3] Lloyd Cutler, a moderate Carter White House counsel, calls for constitutional change to produce a more coherent and politically responsible type of government (i.e., freer from special-interest domination, more subject to popular control).[4] Two economists identified with the left have provided a detailed description of how the United States could move in a politically practical manner toward what they call "economic democracy," an undisguised American version of decentralized democratic socialism.[5]

It is hard to see how prosperity can be restored *and* energy shortages overcome *and* health care maintained or improved *and* income support continued under current conditions. At the very least, substantial change in some of the key sources and basic character of American public policy seems necessary. A form of economic prosperity for some might be assured at the cost of reduced services, such as health care and income support, for others. But this probably could not be justified for very long without some compelling reason for sacrifice, such as depression or war.

American public policy is thus locked on the horns of a grand dilemma. It can constantly seek to trim all other policies to fit with the imperative of restoring/maintaining economic profitability/prosperity (which provokes unrest and opposition from below). Or it can try to develop new priorities, values, and commitments that emphasize services to people and the quality of their lives (which will require intrusion upon profitability and private control and provoke opposition from the highest strata of the social pyramid). As the economic crisis deepens, fewer and fewer people seem confident that there is a middle way leading to social justice and harmony.

NOTES

1 These arguments are summarized in the *New York Times*, December 28, 1980.

2 For a full version of Felix Rohatyn's crisis analysis, see "The Coming Emergency and What Can be Done About It," *New York Review of Books*, December 4, 1980, pp. 20–26.

3 Bertram Gross, *Friendly Fascism: The New Face of Power in America* (New York: Evans, 1980).

4 Lloyd Cutler, "To Form a Government," *Foreign Affairs*, Fall 1980, pp. 126–143.

5 Martin Carnoy and Derek Shearer, *Economic Democracy* (White Plains, N.Y.: Sharpe, 1980).

Bibliography

MANAGING THE ECONOMY

Best, Michael, and William Connolly. *The Politicized Economy*. Lexington, Mass.: Heath, 1976. Challenges traditional interpretations of the political economy and public policy of the United States. The authors label market transactions, characteristic of capitalist economies, as the central cause of the socioeconomic ills now facing America. For them, market transactions which are carried out in the private sphere subordinate the worker to the owner, the consumer to the producer, the small producer to the large corporation, and the community interest to private interests. This unequal dynamic results in the problems that become issues in public policy debates—inflation, unemployment, inequality, environmental ills, the crisis of the cities, taxation, etc.

Bonello, Frank, and Thomas Swartz, eds. *Alternative Directions in Economic Policy*. South Bend, Ind.: University of Notre Dame Press, 1978. Collection of articles representing a solid teaching tool in the field of economic policy. Demonstrates that there are various explanations for economic problems and an equal number of policy options available for implementation.

Carson, Robert B., et al., eds. *Government in the American Economy*. Lexington, Mass.: Heath, 1973. Useful collection of essays which explore the ever-aggrandizing economic power of the United States government. Conventional and radical approaches to policy making in the economic sphere give the reader a sense of the pervasive controversy that surrounds both the understanding and explanation of current government economic directives.

Dowd, Douglas F. *The Twisted Dream*. Cambridge, Mass.: Winthrop Publications, 1974. A historical look at capitalist development in the United States since 1776.

Edwards, Richard, et al. *The Capitalist System*. Englewood Cliffs, N.J.: Prentice-Hall, 1972. Describes problems produced by a capitalist system of production and explains how government policies directed toward these trouble spots reflect the needs of a capitalist economy. More specifically, the anthology explicates the historical development of capitalism and its relation to inequality, alienation, racism, sexism, irrational production, and imperialism.

Galbraith, John K. *Economics and the Public Purpose*. Boston: Houghton Mifflin, 1973. Examines the functioning of a capitalist economy, demonstrates how it affects everyday living, lays bare its inequities.

Gilder, George *Wealth and Poverty*. New York: Basic Books, 1981. The most thoughtful presentation of "supply side" economic theory.

Heidenheimer, Arnold J., et al. *Comparative Public Policy*. New York: St. Martin's, 1975. Comparative study of differences in the health, education, housing, urban planning, transportation, and taxation policies of Britain, West Germany, Sweden, France, the Netherlands, Denmark, and the United States.

Mermelstein, David, ed. *Economics: Mainstream Readings and Radical Critiques*. New York: Random House, 1976. Presents conflicting approaches to the understanding and development of economic policy in the United States. Initially, the methodological and philosophical differences that sharply divide mainstream and radical economists are laid bare. Throughout the text it becomes obvious that these basic differences greatly affect how problems are interpreted and what solutions are offered. Materials on the corporation, defense spending, imperialism, the world economic crisis, the nature of work, poverty, sexism, ecological imbalance, and the urban crisis.

—, ed. *The Economic Crisis Reader*. New York: Vintage Books, 1975. One of the best collections on depression, inflation, unemployment, the energy crisis, soaring food costs, wage and price controls, militarism, and imperialism.

North, Douglas C. *Growth and Welfare in the American Past*. Englewood Cliffs, N.J.: Prentice-Hall, 1966. Useful economic history of the United States; begins at the colonial period and examines the economic growth of America. What makes his analysis so compelling is that he does not stop at simple descriptions of economic occurrences but also looks carefully at the effect of economic events on the everyday lives of people.

O'Connor, James. *The Fiscal Crisis of the State*. New York: St. Martin's, 1973. A Marxist analysis of the continuing growth of state economic power since

World War II. O'Connor examines the ever-increasing tendency of the state to spend in excess of revenue intake and contends that such a trend is a necessary response of the state in capitalist society as it attempts to fulfill its mutually contradictory functions of ensuring uninterrupted accumulation and maintaining legitimacy.

Thurow, Lester D. *The Zero-Sum Society*. New York: Basic Books, 1980. Argues that choices must be made, but emphasizes use of a standard of equity that leaves no group bearing the predominant amount of the burden.

Wilensky, Harold L. *The Welfare State and Equality*. Berkeley: University of California Press, 1975. A comparative study of the spending, organization, and administration of services and benefits in the more affluent welfare states of the world. The analysis gives useful insights into the differences that exist in the policies of France, West and East Germany, Italy, the Netherlands, Sweden, the United States, Britain, etc.

ENERGY

Barnet, Richard. *The Lean Years*. New York: Simon & Schuster, 1980. Analyzes the scarcity claim: Is there real scarcity? Who controls currently available resources? When these questions are probed, one sees the link between monopoly capitalism and scarcity.

Blair, John. *The Control of Oil*. New York: Pantheon, 1976. The classic study of the state of the world's petroleum supply and its effect on public policy, with detailed examination of the control of foreign and domestic oil and the changing balance of power that has affected world supply and demand.

Commoner, Barry. *The Politics of Energy*. New York: Knopf, 1970. A critical analysis of current energy policy in the United States.

Conant, Melvin A. *The Geopolitics of Energy*. Boulder, Colo.: Westview Press, 1979. Mainstream analysis of the current energy situation, incorporated into federal energy policy making.

Evans, Douglas. *The Politics of Energy*. New York: Macmillan, 1976. A comparative study of the energy policies of the United States, Europe, the Soviet Union, China, and Japan. Evans detects a centralization trend among these "superstates" that he believes threatens not only sound energy policies but also political freedom and individual liberty.

Lindberg, Leon N., ed. *The Energy Syndrome*. Lexington, Mass.: Lexington Books, 1977. A comparative study of the policy responses of the industrialized nations to the energy crisis. The central thesis is that developed nations share characteristics that lead to repeated and pathological failure to deal with the short- and long-term effects of the energy situation.

Lovins, Amory. *World Energy Strategies*. New York: Harper & Row, 1980. Scrutinizes fossil and nonfossil fuels, solar collection, and conservation. Pinpoints some ethical and economic conflicts that seem to continually surround energy discussions and offers options.

Reece, Ray. *The Sun Betrayed*. Boston: South End Press, 1979. A detailed study of solar energy policy in the United States. Argues that failure to develop a clear, coherent solar energy direction is the result of corporate control of solar energy policy decision making.

Stobaugh, Robert, and Daniel Yergin, eds. *Energy Future*. New York: Random House, 1979. Discusses the state of oil, coal, natural gas, nuclear, and solar power in the United States and considers the political choices that continue to surround future energy options.

HEALTH CARE

Anderson, Odin W. *Health Care: Can There Be Equity? The United States, Sweden and England*. New York: Wiley, 1972. A historical analysis of the development of the health care systems of the three nations, presented by time periods, trends, and problems rather than country-by-country. Valuable tables and source suggestions.

Battistella, Roger M., and Thomas G. Rundall, eds. *Health Care Policy in a Changing Environment*. Berkeley, Calif.: McCutchan, 1978. Focuses on pressures making for change and possible future issues in United States health policy. Not a comprehensive description, but includes some helpful essays.

Braverman, Jordan. *Crisis in Health Care*. Washington, D.C.: Acropolis, 1978. Poses the costs problem versus the recent policy initiatives and National Health Insurance. Informally written and informative. Includes a useful glossary and explanation of abbreviations and acronyms used in the field.

Ehrenreich, Barbara, and John Ehrenreich. *The American Health Empire: Power, Profits and Politics*. New York: Vintage Books, 1970. This is the product of group research on the New York City medical/hospital establishment and its practices by the Health Policy Advisory Committee, a body of health care workers and activists. Many good insights from a case study perspective, from the perspective suggested by the title.

Enos, Darryl D., and Paul Sultan. *The Sociology of Health Care: Social, Economic and Political Perspectives*. New York: Praeger, 1977. A thorough, data-based survey of the health care system and its problems. The system, delivery and reception of services, and directions of change are the foci of an extensive and comprehensive analysis.

Fuchs, Victor R. *Who Shall Live? Health, Economics, and Social Choice*. New York: Basic Books, 1974. A short, incisive study that poses all the basic issues in terms of choices to be made between competing uses of available resources. Good data, lively presentation.

Jonas, Steven, ed. *Health Care Delivery in the United States*. New York: Springer, 1977. A collection of essays by health professionals focusing on the intersection of public policy with the operations of all the major units of the health care system. Very comprehensive, with helpful suggestions on finding and using data sources.

Rayack, Elton. *Professional Power and American Medicine: The Economics of the American Medical Association*. New York: World Publishing, 1972. One of several studies of the AMA, particularly good on economic and political impact over time. Not intended as an overall analysis of the organization.

Sidel, Victor W., and Ruth Sidel. *A Healthy State: An International Perspective on the Crisis in United States Medical Care*. New York: Pantheon, 1977. Perhaps the best source of data and provocative ideas for reconstruction of the system, from a perspective similar to the Ehrenreichs'. Less incisive but richer than Fuchs.

Sobel, Lester A., ed. *Health Care: An American Crisis*. New York: Facts on File, 1976). Good bare-bones factual material on conditions and United States policies.

Wilson, Florence A., and Duncan Neuhauser. *Health Services in the United States*. Cambridge, Mass.: Ballinger, 1976. Good data and other factual material on all aspects of the health system—institutions, personnel, policies—with definitions, explanation of acronyms, and details of Social Security law.

INCOME SUPPORT

Anderson, Martin. *Welfare: The Political Economy of Welfare Reform in the United States*. Palo Alto, Calif.: Hoover Institution, 1978. The best statement of the conservative view.

Bell, Winifred. *Aid to Dependent Children*. New York: Columbia, 1965. A thorough analysis of the welfare assistance program (Aid to Dependent Children), necessary reading for those who wish to understand the social and cultural context that surrounds the development and administration of the program that has been the core of aid to poor families in the United States.

Derthick, Martha. *Policymaking for Social Security*. Washington, D.C.: Brookings, 1979. The best background book on the process of Social Security policy making.

Gough, Ian. *The Political Economy of the Welfare State*. New York: Macmillan, 1979. This book is a holistic critique of the welfare state from a Marxist perspective. Gough argues that the development of the welfare state reflects a change in the nature of advanced capitalist society and looks at the expanded state role in income maintenance, health, welfare, education, housing, etc., to see these programs as attempts to sustain capitalist growth. While his account seems concentrated on British welfare, Gough makes it clear that such an analysis applies equally well to most advanced capitalist nations, including the United States.

Heidenheimer, Arnold J., Hugh Heclo, and Carolyn Teich Adams. *Comparative Public Policy*. New York: St. Martin's, 1975. The best comparative study.

Kamerman, Sheila B., and Alfred J. Kahn. *Social Services in the United States*. Philadelphia: Temple, 1976, Perhaps the most comprehensive descriptive text on social services in the United States. The authors present an analysis of the more traditional service sectors—education, health, income maintenance, housing, and employment—and then pinpoint growing activity in the personal service arena which is providing benefits to a larger number of persons not categorized as poor.

Komisar, Lucy. *Down and Out in the USA*. New York: Franklin Watts, 1973. Another comprehensive history of public welfare in the United States; more condensed than Trattner's book, it links poverty with industrialism and capitalism in a way that he does not. Komisar's thesis is that the ideas and beliefs engendered by the Protestant Reformation, capitalism, and the industrial revolution have affected and continue to affect the manner in which Americans approach the problem of poverty.

Leiby, James. *A History of Social Welfare and Social Work in the United Sates*. New York: Columbia, 1979. A history that emphasizes the part played by the growing professionalism of public assistance personnel.

Leman, Christopher. *The Collapse of Welfare Reform*. Cambridge, Mass.: MIT Press, 1980. An excellent comparison of the United States and Canada with respect to public assistance policy and reform.

Levitan, Sar. *Programs in Aid of the Poor*. 3d ed. Baltimore: Johns Hopkins, 1976. While the book lacks substantive analysis, it presents useful descriptions of the four types of programs at the center of American aid to the needy: cash support programs, goods and services provision, education and daycare, and programs for the employable poor.

Lubove, Roy. *The Struggle for Social Security, 1900–1935*. Cambridge, Mass.: Harvard, 1968. Very useful comparative history.

Mandell, Betty Reid, ed. *Welfare in America: Controlling the Dangerous Classes*. Englewood Cliffs, N.J.: Prentice-Hall, 1975. This anthology is a collection of radical critiques of welfare in America. The central argument of the book is that welfare as it exists in the United States is geared to the needs of a capitalist economy and not the needs of society's victims. Mandell and her coauthors scrutinize and critique federal workforce programs, social service spending, Social Security, health care, and the criminal justice system, and point to the dominant values that have been the foundation of such programs.

Piven, Frances Fox, and Richard A. Cloward. *Regulating the Poor*. New York: Pantheon, 1971. Argues that throughout history relief programs have served to legitimate and preserve existing society in two ways: by maintaining social and political stability, and by reinforcing work norms, ethics, and practices.

Schiller, Bradley R. *The Economics of Poverty and Discrimination*, 3d ed. Englewood Cliffs, N.J.: Prentice-Hall, 1979. The best background book on poverty.

Sheehan, Susan, *A Welfare Mother*. New York: Mentor Books, 1976. Presents a day-by-day look at the life of one welfare mother in New York City and in doing so eradicates many myths and reveals hard truths largely ignored by policy makers.

Trattner, Walter I. *From Poor Law to Welfare State*. 2d ed. New York: Free Press, 1979. A comprehensive history of social welfare in America from colonial times to the present. Trattner lays bare some of the political, social, and cultural factors that have shaped and defined how Americans historically have dealt with poverty.

Index

Index